Pruno, Ramen and a
Side of Hope

and a side of

Stories of Surviving Wrongful Conviction

Written and Edited by
Courtney B. Lance and Nikki D. Pope

Stories and Poems by Exonerees and Their Loved Ones

A POST HILL PRESS BOOK
ISBN: 978-1-61868-925-2
ISBN (eBook): 978-1-61868-926-9

PRUNO, RAMEN, AND A SIDE OF HOPE
Stories of Surviving Wrongful Conviction
© 2015 Courtney B. Lance and Nikki D. Pope
All Rights Reserved

Cover design and interior layout by Ken Maynard (www.themaynidea.com).

Post Hill
PRESS

Post Hill Press
109 International Drive, Suite 300
Franklin, TN 37067
www.posthillpress.com

Dedication

This book is dedicated to our mothers, Joyce Lance and Lena Pope, for nurturing our curiosity, encouraging our artistry, and channeling our activism. Meet you in the Rookery!

TABLE OF CONTENTS

List of Contributors

Anonymous
Denise Anthony
Obie Anthony
Carissa Bermudez
Fernando Bermudez
Deborah Caldwell
Maurice Caldwell
Antoine Goff
Tabitha Hershberger
Paige Kaneb
Gloria Killian
Larry Lamb
Courtney Lance
Alex LeFever
Virginia LeFever
Michael McGee
Suenjae Ostrowski
Patricia Pemberton
Nikki Pope
Joe Porter
Sabrina Butler Porter
Maurice Possley
Della Reyes
Joyce Ride
Cookie Ridolfi
Ronnie Sandoval

Foreword

Pruno, Ramen, and a Side of Hope: Stories of Surviving Wrongful Conviction is not like other books on wrongful conviction. It's not just about prison and politics, legal philosophy, or jurisprudence or about how the system went wrong or ways to fix it. It's a book that documents the everyday experiences of ordinary people pulled from their lives, from everyone and everything they know, accused of unspeakable crimes and sent to prison for longer than they can comprehend. It is also a book about the stories of the people who do not first come to mind when you think about wrongful conviction—those left behind. It describes the experiences of the sister, the mother, the daughter, the cousin, and the friend who are left holding the lifeline. It shares the fears of people saddled with the stigma of a wrongfully convicted loved one, left without their parent or their child, left with the feelings of helplessness in their search for justice and it tells us where they found the strength to get them through this incomprehensible ordeal and the resilience to carry on.

This is an important book. It addresses what went wrong in the justice system that got the wrongfully convicted there in the first place—what we have to understand if we are ever going to turn the system around and stop the conviction of innocent people. In the book exonerees share intimate accounts of how they survived years in prison without giving up hope and how they came through to the other side spiritually intact and without anger.

Maurice Caldwell served twenty years, six months, and four days in prison. When he first got there, he was deeply depressed and afraid. "I seriously feared I would not make it back home . . . it was almost impossible to keep my mind right . . . all I was able to think about was my family and friends and the life that was taken away from me." He struggled with how to survive, to cope, how to manage his situation. So he tried to be positive, he counted his blessings, his ability to read and write and his sister on the outside who never gave up on him.

Deborah Caldwell couldn't believe her brother had been convicted on such a paucity of evidence—a weak identification by a witness rewarded for her testimony. She describes her anguish. "I was so sad for him. I had no doubts that he would come home. I just didn't know when. I prayed on it every day . . . Our brother and mother died when 'Twone [Maurice's nickname] was in prison. That was the hardest thing to deal with." Deborah never left Maurice's side. She was there twenty years later on the day that he finally went home.

Wrongful conviction can happen to anyone, even a child. This book includes the story of a sixteen-year-old boy wrongfully convicted and sent to prison. Seven days after his sixteenth birthday, Arthur Carmona was stopped by police while he was riding his bicycle. He had a plan to meet up with neighborhood friends in Costa Mesa, California. Forty-five minutes before, a juice bar in the nearby town of Irvine had been robbed. The robbery suspect, was described by witnesses as "a Latino person, about 5'6" or 5'7" and skinny," about "seventeen or twenty years old," clean shaven, wearing a black L.A. Lakers baseball cap, and carrying a backpack. Although the description did not fit him, Arthur was detained.

Arthur had a thin mustache. He was five foot eight and one-hundred and sixty-five pounds, not "skinny." He was not carrying a backpack or wearing a baseball cap. While Arthur was being held by police, other officers brought eyewitnesses to him for identification. Four of the witnesses could not identify Arthur the person who committed the robbery. One witness identified him but only after police put the Lakers cap on Arthur's head. That witness would later testify that he identified the Lakers cap, not Arthur's face. He said he explained that to the police. The officer had not bothered to mention to the witness that the hat was not found on Arthur. Later in the investigation, a second witness pointed to Arthur's picture in a six-pack of photos saying Arthur looked most like the man who committed the robbery but that Arthur was younger than the person he had seen.

Although he was just sixteen and without a criminal record, prosecutors tried Arthur as an adult. The only alibi witnesses were the friends he was on the phone with at the time the juice bar was robbed. At trial his lawyer did not call them to testify, a fact the prosecutor pointed out to the jury in his closing argument noting that if Arthur had been on the phone with friends, they would have been in court to testify on his behalf. Despite all that was happening, Ronnie Sandoval, Arthur's mother, held onto her faith in the system, sure the truth would come out and Arthur would come home. But that didn't happen. Arthur was convicted and sentenced to twelve years in prison. Their lives would never be the same.

Ronnie spent every day after that trying to help her son. With a ferocious determination to get at the truth, she pounded on doors until a law firm agreed to take his case pro bono. His new lawyers began their investigation and, when the eyewitnesses recanted their testimony, they filed a motion for a new trial. Hours before the hearing on the motion, prosecutors offered a deal. They would dismiss the charges if Arthur agreed to sign away his right to sue the Irvine Police Department. Arthur did not want to sign it, but his mother insisted. She wanted him out of the clutches of the system. At that point, she feared for his life. So Arthur did what his mother asked and signed the plea agreement.

To this day, prosecutors insist that Arthur is guilty. They say it because there is no power or authority to stop them. After an exoneration, it is common for prosecutors to mischaracterize what happened, to refuse to admit the system got it wrong, to cover up their own mistakes. Ronnie began her crusade to free Arthur the moment he was found guilty. When you're innocent and in prison, it's important to have someone on the outside fighting for you, remembering that you're locked up inside, and trying anything and everything to win your release.

Aleka Pantazis would not rest until her brother, George, was released from prison. George Souliotes, whose shocking story is detailed in this book, spent sixteen years in prison, wrongfully convicted of arson and murder. The exhaustive work of his defense team led to dramatic new scientific evidence that directly contradicted the prosecution's case. Without solid evidence left to support their conviction, prosecutors stipulated to the lack of evidence of arson and the irrefutable evidence that chemicals found at the fire scene did not match chemicals found on George's shoes—the linchpin they used to convict him. Based on the prosecutor's agreement that these were the facts, the court dismissed the charges. But instead of acknowledging their error, when George was released, the District Attorney issued a statement claiming that George was guilty and blaming the court for discharging his case.

These stories, shocking as they may seem, are commonplace. During my twelve years as executive director of the Northern California Innocence Project, our office fought in case after case as police and prosecutors defended their convictions. It did not seem to matter how compelling the evidence of innocence was. Almost every case was an uphill battle.

Years before that, through most of the 1980s I was a public defender in Philadelphia. I represented countless people prosecuted in our judicial system and saw first-hand what can go wrong in a criminal case. I had clients who confessed to crimes they had not committed and cases built on the testimony of jailhouse informants lying to gain favor in their own cases. I questioned witnesses, including forensic and police witnesses, who perjured themselves to help prosecutors. I tried cases against prosecutors who failed to turn over evidence, met drunken attorneys in court, saw defense attorneys taking cases to trial they hadn't bothered to investigate. But what was most disturbing was how little any of this seemed to matter. The general atmosphere seemed to be that if police and prosecutors go to the trouble of bringing someone to trial, that person must be guilty. We believe our justice system starts with a presumption of innocence, when in fact the opposite is true—for the defendant, there appears to be a presumption of guilt.

For the general public in the 1980s and 1990s, when civic education about the justice system came from television shows like *Columbo* and *Law and Order*, it was impossible to convince people outside of the system to appreciate what really happened on the inside. How could any of this be true in a system that we understand to be based on principles of due process, reasonable doubt, and the presumption of innocence? But it was true and to a large extent still is true today.

What is different now is that we have DNA. Testing DNA evidence collected at a crime scene has finally put to rest the question of whether innocent people are being convicted in the courts of this country. According to Maurice Possley, a senior researcher at the

National Registry of Exonerations and the author of the first chapter of this book, as of October 2014, there are a documented 1,480 cases of wrongful convictions in the United States.

DNA has completely changed the landscape. When DNA exoneration stories started showing up in the news, attitudes started to change. DNA exonerations accomplished two very important things. They established that innocent people were, and are, being convicted. They also allowed us to pinpoint the sources of the problems in the justice system.

By the time of the first DNA exoneration in 1989, I had left the public defender's office and moved on to teaching law. But I can still remember reading about the first DNA exoneration. Gary Dotson was convicted of aggravated rape and kidnapping and was serving a sentence of twenty-five to fifty years in prison. There was plenty of evidence against him: a composite drawing by a police artist based on the victim's description, the victim's identification of Dotson in a police mug book and later at a lineup, a forensic analyst who testified that he found Dotson's blood type on the victim's underwear and a pubic hair that appeared to come from Dotson. This was damning evidence for sure. But Dotson's case had gone to trial before the advent of DNA testing and before we knew about the inherent fallibility of forensic expert testimony about blood type evidence and the guesswork that goes into relying on pubic hair as identifying evidence. It was ten years before the victim would recant her testimony and admit to fabricating the rape as a cover story to hide a consensual sexual encounter with her boyfriend. The then newly developed DNA testing established that the biological material attributed to the sexual encounter was not that of Dotson. And so it went in Gary Dotson's case and how it goes with so many wrongful convictions. There is a mountain of damning evidence that falls apart, piece by piece to reveal yet another wrongful conviction and one more American tragedy.

The DNA exoneration cases are just the tip of the iceberg—over ninety percent of them involve sexual assaults where there is biological evidence to test. Most wrongfully convicted people do not have the benefit of DNA testing and, without DNA, proving innocence is so much harder. Harder because of the high burden of proof and the many obstacles in the way of uncovering evidence in cases that are decades old in a judicial system that resists efforts to challenge convictions at every turn.

Despite the magnitude of the problem, inroads are being made, not yet at an acceptable rate but its happening. Innocent people are being returned to their lives and to their families. Many of those being released are dedicating themselves to helping others who are left behind and there are many. With two million two hundred thousand prisoners in the United States, even a one percent error rate means thousands of wrongfully convicted people remain imprisoned.

There are many victims here. The wrongfully convicted, their families and the victims of the crimes they are convicted of. In Maurice Caldwell's case, while he was in prison, the real killer went on to kill a cab driver in Nevada. The cab driver is a victim too.

While there is no denying that lives are devastated by these miscarriages of justice, we can all learn from them. *Pruno, Ramen, and a Side of Hope* is a teacher. From the experiences of the people whose lives are reflected in this book, we are learning. Not just about how important it is to improve the system and what it might take to do it, but about human compassion and the exquisite resilience of the human spirit to deal with adversity despite all odds and rise above it.

Cookie Ridolfi
San Jose, CA
December 6, 2014

Preface

One of the most surprising common characteristics shared by many men and women who have been wrongfully convicted of a crime and subsequently exonerated and released is their lack of animosity at what happened to them. This is not to say that they are not angry at the injustices inherent in our legal system. It also is not meant to suggest that they do not continue to fight for compensation for the disruption to their lives and the lives of their families. Some of them become advocates in the fight to correct the systemic problems that lead to wrongful convictions. Others choose to stay out of the spotlight, focusing instead on recovering their lost lives and building a new place for themselves in their communities.

In our many conversations with each exoneree who told a story for this book, they spoke of their time in prison not only as a wrong that was done to them, but also as a time for reflection. One man said going to prison changed the trajectory of his life. Another, while acknowledging that prison was an awful place, also spoke of prison as giving him time to reflect on the path his life had been taking until that point. One man, having spent decades in prison, said what happened to him affects the choices he makes now that he has regained his freedom. Before prison he would not have given a second thought to writing bad checks or driving without a license or making any number of bad choices. Now, he thinks about the consequences of his actions. He is law abiding in ways that many of us take for granted. Spending time in prison has made him mindful of how his choices can affect his life. Most exonerees learned this lesson early in their incarceration and their good behavior was rewarded with special privileges like family visits, small plots of land to grow vegetables, aquariums to breed tropical fish, and other activities not normally identified with prison life.

Each man and woman asked of themselves, "How did I get here? How am I going to get through this?" Their methods for surviving prison are as varied as the men and women themselves. They were so focused on proving their innocence and getting out of prison, they didn't really think about what happened next—after their release.

In most states, exonerees get no post-exoneration support services. When we first heard this, we thought it could not be true. Both of us believed that, exonerees would get housing support, psychological counseling, and other services that are provided to parolees. That's not the case in most states, where laws are written to cover people who are paroled, not people who are exonerated. As illogical as it sounds, being exonerated in a post-conviction proceeding means that the former prisoner did not commit a crime and therefore is not eligible to receive support. Not only did our justice system fail the innocent and wrongfully convicted person, it also failed to correct the problem it created. Exonerees who spend decades in prison are returning to a world that is much different from the one they left. Imagine you were locked up in 1993 and exonerated in 2013. You would have to navigate a world moving at a much faster pace, with an overload of information, and seemingly endless choices—from methods of communication to transportation to entertainment. During that time you probably lost friends and family members. Add to that the memories of what you experienced during your twenty years behind bars. Would you need help to readjust to life in the twenty-first century after such a shocking re-entry?

Listening to stories of cell block chefs, jailhouse lawyers, and prison yard gardeners sparked the germ of an idea. If we could collect recipes from exonerees, we could create a prison food cookbook and share the proceeds from the sale of the books with the exonerees who submitted recipes. Brilliant idea, right? Absolutely. So brilliant that there are at least eight such books already available on Amazon. com. The more time we spent talking with exonerees, the more we realized that their answers to the question "how do I get through this" could offer all of us so much more. How does an innocent person go through hell and come out the other side with their humanity still intact? At what point does a person stop bemoaning the fact that the justice system failed them and begin to focus on surviving prison? What effect does their wrongful conviction have on the other people in their lives? Many books have been written about cases of wrongful conviction. Each of them tells one person's story of how that person came to be convicted of and sentenced for a crime they did not commit and how they proved their innocence and were released.

Each chapter of this book focuses on a single exoneree. We hope you will be as moved as we were by their stories. Some exonerees wrote their own stories and others told us their stories over the course of a series of interviews. Each exoneree asked a close relative or close friend to provide a companion story that shares the person's perspective either by writing a story or being interviewed. Most of the companion stories were from family members. We also describe the circumstances that led to each wrongful conviction and what each exoneree has been doing since his or her release. Our hope is that these stories will show all of us how to find within ourselves that strength of character that helped these men and women survive prison, retain their humanity, and regain their lives.

We are sharing the proceeds from the sale of this book with the exonerees who participated in this project and with some of the legal defense and post-exoneration support programs that assist the wrongfully convicted in winning their freedom and returning successfully to society. We hope that there are a lot of you out there so the share for each exoneree is enough to make a difference in their lives and the share for the organizations is enough to help at least some innocent people still remaining in prison and provide re-entry services for some of the lucky few who have proven their innocence and been released from prison.

We thank you.

CHAPTER 1
Wrongful Conviction—The Basics
By Maurice Possley

"Our procedure has always been haunted by the ghost of the innocent man convicted. It is an unreal dream."
—Judge Learned Hand (1923)

The unreal dream that Judge Hand wrote about nearly a century ago is a proven nightmare. Sadly and tragically, his unreal dream has been shattered by the truth of more than 1,480 known wrongful convictions in the United States since just 1989—the era of criminal justice that is defined by the emergence of DNA testing.

DNA testing first emerged in the United States criminal justice system in the late 1980s, but the defense community quickly realized the exactitude of the testing process could work to prove innocence just as definitively. The first conviction bolstered by DNA testing occurred in Florida in 1987. The first DNA exoneration occurred two years later, in 1989.

Since then, DNA testing has been established as the greatest truth serum the court system has ever known. By demonstrating innocence where juries and judges found guilt, DNA testing has shown that although the criminal justice system has a number of safeguards designed to ensure that wrongful convictions are avoided, the innocent are still convicted and sentenced to prison. In fact, during the twenty-five years from 1989 to 2014, on average a defendant has been exonerated of a crime they did not commit in the United States every single week. In recent years, the rate of exonerations has been accelerating with sixty-nine, ninety, and ninety-one exonerations in 2011, 2012, and 2013, respectively, and eighty-eight exonerations in 2014 as of October.

More importantly, DNA testing has opened a window into the engine room of the criminal justice system to reveal how the various parts of the justice machine have broken down. This book represents just a small cross-section of the 1,480 exonerations and each is a vivid example of how the criminal justice system gets it wrong.

Each of the 1,480 exonerations is uniquely different. The defendants are different and the facts and circumstances are different. The charges are as serious as murder and as innocuous as shoplifting. The penalties range from death to probation. Despite these differences, there are common threads that the truth serum we know as DNA testing has revealed as the most frequent causes of wrongful conviction.

Based on an analysis of the 1,480 exonerations in the National Registry of Exonerations, the most common cause of wrongful conviction is perjury or false accusation by victims and witnesses. The most common example of victim-generated false accusation occurs in sexual molestation or rape cases. About twenty percent of known exonerations involve cases where no crime occurred. While some of these are accidents that are mischaracterized as crimes because of shoddy forensics, most of these no-crime cases involve allegations of rape or sexual abuse based on false accusations by accusers. The especially sad instances of these types of wrongful convictions occur where young children falsely accuse a relative or a parent of sexually abusing them as part of a fractious divorce or custody battle. Years later, plagued by guilt, the now adult accusers recant and tell the truth. Tragically, not all of these cases become exonerations even when the defendants are innocent because historically recantations have been viewed with great skepticism by the courts.

The second most frequent cause of wrongful conviction is official misconduct by police and prosecutors. Official misconduct is documented in nearly half of the 1,480 exonerations in the United States. There are many ways that prosecutors or police can skew a case to the point where an innocent person is convicted. The most serious is the failure to disclose evidence of a defendant's innocence—a receipt that shows a defendant was thousands of miles away when the crime occurred or a statement from a witness who said the criminal was white when the defendant was black. The failure to reveal this evidence is a violation of court rules and a violation that the US Supreme Court at one time said should be punished at a minimum with disbarment of the prosecutor and perhaps criminal prosecution. Such punishment virtually never occurs and this evidence—described as exculpatory evidence—is hidden time and time again. Because it is an act of secrecy, there is no way to know how often this deception actually occurs. This category includes police officers who testify falsely and who intimidate witnesses to testify falsely as well as officers who destroy or hide evidence favorable to a defendant and never inform prosecutors. Another form of official misconduct occurs when prosecutors make deals to reduce charges against co-defendants in return for their testimony—a virtual prescription for perjury. This is compounded by the failure of prosecutors to disclose to the defense these deals with the witness. This, too, is a violation of the law. Repeatedly, prosecutors who take an oath to uphold justice have been found to have abandoned that oath and crossed the line of injustice in and out of courtrooms in pursuit of a conviction at any cost.

Mistaken witness identification is a well-identified cause of wrongful conviction. Numerous studies have exposed the precarious nature of witness identification and all the factors that can cause a witness to mistakenly identify a defendant as the perpetrator of a crime. Most significantly, research has shown that the human mind is not like a video camera which records what it sees and then replays the images later. Research also has shown that police, through suggestive lineup procedures, have influenced witnesses to make incorrect identifications. In some cases, witnesses were threatened, directly or implicitly, with criminal charges unless they agreed to identify defendants. Powerful reforms, such as conducting sequential lineups where witnesses are shown photographs one at a time and must make a judgment on each rather than seeing several photographs and making a comparative decision, have been proposed to reduce the chance of wrongful witness identifications. In police precincts where the reforms are being adopted, the incidence of mistaken eyewitness identification is declining. While many police departments have adopted the changes, many more still resist such reforms.

The idea that someone who is not insane or subjected to torture or physical abuse would falsely confess to a crime, particularly a crime as serious as murder, is counterintuitive to most citizens. But false confessions have been documented repeatedly in wrongful convictions. Nearly three-hundred wrongful convictions have involved false confessions or false confessions by co-defendants who implicated an innocent person.

There are three basic types of false confessions—voluntary, internalized, and compliant. A voluntary confession usually is given by someone who is mentally ill, is seeking publicity, or is trying to cover up for the true guilty party. There also are confessions made where individuals come to actually believe that they committed the crime. These are known as internalized confessions. These are not the norm, however. The most common form of false confession occurs when a suspect, even though they are innocent, simply breaks down and tells interrogators what the suspect believes the interrogators want to hear. Why do they do this? Most simply want to end the interrogation ordeal. This may occur in as little as a few hours or after as long as two or three days of relentless interrogation. Sometimes suspects say they were physically abused, but most frequently the pressure is exerted psychologically, through threats, cajoling, and promises. Innocent defendants who falsely confess frequently are mentally challenged or have a serious mental illness, such as schizophrenia. Confessions from torture fall in the compliant category. In Chicago, a police lieutenant and his detectives tortured murder confessions out of dozens of men. Defendants were shocked with alligator clips attached to a hand-cranked generator, had guns stuffed in their mouths, plastic bags pulled over their heads, and were subjected to other forms of physical torture.

The power of a confession in the criminal justice system cannot be underestimated. Such is their sway on juries that confessions become the bedrock of convictions despite evidence that points to other suspects or that should eliminate the defendants who have falsely confessed. Another tragedy of false confessions is once a defendant is convicted, legal opportunities to overturn the convictions are lessened significantly. It took over thirteen years to exonerate five young black men, known as The Central Park Five, because of the coerced confessions that were used to convict the teens of brutally raping a young woman jogging in New York's Central Park late one night in 1989. Even the existence of an alternate suspect,

4

who had committed a similar crime in Central Park, was not enough to cause the police and prosecutors to entertain the thought that the five teens might be innocent. Only after this same suspect later confessed to the crime and his DNA matched evidence taken from the crime scene did the authorities begin to believe the young men's confessions might be false. Even then it took years for the men to be released from prison.

Misleading or false forensic evidence—whether described as bad forensics or good forensics practiced badly—have contributed to hundreds of wrongful convictions. This spans an array of disciplines, including blood analysis, hair analysis, bite mark analysis, even fingerprint analysis. For years, the Federal Bureau of Investigation (FBI) and scores of forensic analysts trained by the FBI testified improperly about the reliability of hair comparison—and numerous convictions based on that testimony have been overturned. Analysts have been found to have overstated other similar inexact forensic procedures such as blood analysis and bite mark comparisons. DNA testing has exposed the inherent flaws of these types of pseudo-scientific evidence in hundreds of cases. In some bite mark cases, the saliva from the bite mark was tested by DNA and excluded the convicted defendants.

In some cases, the science—not the scientist—was at fault. For years, the criminal justice system embraced the science that said, if a dead or badly injured baby was found to have certain symptoms, the only possible explanation was that the mother, father, or caretaker had violently shaken the child in a fit of anger. Known as Shaken Baby Syndrome, the physical findings have been proven to be caused by accidental falls. Arson science is undergoing dramatic changes. Until recently, fire investigators relied upon a set of physical findings to determine that a fire was caused by arson and was not accidental, resulting in the wrongful conviction of numerous defendants. Scientific testing has debunked virtually all of these so-called arson indicators. Undoubtedly there have been executions of innocent people. The Cameron Todd Willingham case in Texas has raised serious questions about the faulty arson science used to convict Todd and sentence him to death. He was executed on February 17, 2004.

In hundreds of cases, forensic analysts misstated their findings both intentionally and by mistake. They concealed test results that showed defendants were innocent. They testified they had performed tests that proved defendants were guilty when in fact the tests were never conducted.

The failure of criminal defense attorneys to provide a constitutionally adequate defense to their clients also has contributed to hundreds of wrongful convictions. Most frequently, the problem is that defense attorneys fail to investigate the case on behalf of their client. No investigator is hired, or if one is hired, the pay is so meager it ensures that little work is performed on the case. The public popularly blames public defenders, but in fact much of the poor defense work is performed by private lawyers who are retained by families who must mortgage their homes or borrow from friends to make the initial payment. Defense lawyers have been found to ignore credible alibi evidence, to refuse to hire experts to counter prosecution experts, and to not even bother to challenge forensic evidence presented by the prosecution.

And finally, there are cases where defendants have been wrongly convicted due to judicial error—a judge makes a decision to bar evidence proffered by the defense or prevents the defense from effectively cross-examining prosecution witnesses—rulings that are later deemed erroneous by an appellate court and overturned.

Perhaps one of the greatest benefits of the introduction of DNA testing has been not only to systematically document causes of wrongful conviction, but to demonstrate that wrongful convictions don't just occur in cases that have biological evidence that can be tested. In the past decade, the number of exonerations resulting from DNA testing has dropped while the number of exonerations in cases without biological evidence has grown substantially. In 2013, there were at least seventy-three non-DNA exonerations—more than has been recorded in any previous year.

Wrongful convictions wreak an enormous cost on society. While innocent defendants were imprisoned and their families shattered, the true criminals went free and many went on to murder and rape and rob time and again. The cost to taxpayers is in the hundreds of millions just in the judgments obtained by defendants who are wrongfully convicted. There is no calculus that can tell us the emotional toll on the wrongfully convicted, victims, and families of both victims and defendants.

These 1,480 wrongfully convicted men and women spent a combined total of more than 13,873 years in prison—on average nine years per person. A few of them had their convictions undone before they were sentenced and they never went to prison. Almost all were imprisoned for years, with forty-one percent spending ten or more years and sixty-two percent spending at least five years in prison. Many spent decades and a few defendants spent more than thirty years in prison. Some were exonerated from death row and, in one infamous case, within days of being executed.

All of this time was lost for something they did not do and in more than three hundred sixty instances, for a crime that never occurred.

More than 100 of these exonerated defendants had been sentenced to death. Fourteen innocent defendants were exonerated posthumously. Many more left prison with disabling physical or psychological injuries or diseases. Some died within a year or two of release, sometimes at their own hands. Others returned to prison for new crimes that they did commit. Almost all of them irretrievably lost large portions of their lives—their youth, the childhood of their children, the last years of their parents' lives, their careers, their marriages.

Each and every one of these cases is a tragedy for the wrongfully convicted, their families, the victims and their families, and the subsequent victims of the real criminals who went free and committed more crimes. In most cases these innocent defendants were convicted of vicious crimes in which other innocent victims were killed or brutalized. Many of the victims who survived were traumatized all over again, years later, when they learned that the criminal who had attacked them had not been caught and punished after all, and that they themselves may have played a role in condemning an innocent person.

The lessons that have emerged from these cases are not being ignored. Innocence projects and lawyers across the nation, including prosecutors such as Craig Watkins in Dallas, Texas and Jeff Rosen in Santa Clara, California, have stepped forward to fight for the wrongly convicted and just as significantly, to propose and implement reforms designed to reduce or eliminate the possibility of the nightmare of a wrongful conviction. The most powerful voices are those of the exonerated defendants themselves—those whose writings and stories you find here.

They have survived.

Their words must be honored and remembered.

Maurice Possley is a Pulitzer Prize-winning journalist who has helped free innocence defendants from prison and is senior researcher at the National Registry of Exonerations, an online database of wrongful convictions in the US.

CHAPTER 2

Defending the Innocent—A Lawyer's Perspective

By Paige Kaneb

When I first started working as an attorney at the Northern California Innocence Project, I thought that once the evidence of innocence was uncovered, the doors to the prison cell would open—simply and quickly. I had no concept of how hard it is to uncover that evidence. I had even less understanding of all the twists, delays, roadblocks, and impediments to presenting the evidence to courts and winning an innocent person's freedom.

You've all heard that people convicted of crimes lose rights. Well, it might not have occurred to you that once you have been convicted, you no longer have any right to the physical evidence that police collected from the crime scene. Shocking, right? If you want access to that evidence for DNA testing, you need to obtain the court's permission by meeting whatever statutory requirements are in place in your state. If you want it to get an expert to review fingerprints or other forensic evidence because your defense attorney failed to do so, best of luck to you. You have no right to that evidence. In the vast majority of cases, neither the district attorney, nor the police have any obligation to provide post-conviction discovery—at least until a court rules that you have presented facts that, if true, would entitle you to post-conviction relief, but there's no way to do that without the evidence.

In California, where I practice, police reports are exempt from public records and you don't even have a right to get a copy of the police reports after you have been convicted. Are medical records relevant to the crime? Good luck getting them. Phone records from twenty years ago might have key information? We don't even have the power to subpoena people or records. Want to know if the evidence even exists before litigating a motion for DNA testing? It's worth asking, but chances are you will have to go to court just to find out if there's any evidence to DNA test because your particular district attorney refuses to answer the question without a court order. Still not shocked? Well, best of luck to you when you ask your attorney to find a man named John Smith who was in his twenties when the crime happened, but for whom you have no date of birth or former address.

Uncovering the evidence of innocence in most post-conviction settings is a herculean task. Fifteen to twenty years after conviction, physical evidence has often been lost or destroyed, witnesses' memories have faded and details are fuzzy or even inaccurate, alibis are nearly impossible to establish, and we often find ourselves trying to do or doing what the police could not—identifying the real perpetrator and uncovering reliable evidence of guilt.

Uncovering the evidence of innocence, however, is just the first step. Once someone has been convicted of a crime, the presumption of innocence disappears. Reasonable doubt is no longer enough. You have to show more. For instance, in California, newly discovered evidence must "undermine the prosecution's entire case and point unerringly to innocence...with evidence no reasonable jury could reject." The conviction is presumed to be correct, and the facts must be construed in the light most favorable to the prosecution. Pre-conviction, the burden of proof is on the prosecution— they have to prove, beyond a reasonable doubt, you committed the crime. Post-conviction, the burden is on you to prove that you did not commit the crime, and we all know how difficult it is to prove a negative.

Many convictions are reversed on grounds other than innocence—because affirmatively proving innocence is incredibly difficult no matter how innocent the person. Many exonerations begin with a reversal based on a constitutional violation, meaning you have to prove that you did not receive a fair trial and that you likely would have been acquitted had your trial been fair. That means you cannot simply show that your attorney did not do what a reasonable attorney would have done (such as investigate, have experts examine the forensic evidence, show the witness who testified against you was lying); you also have to do what your lawyer failed to do and show how it would have made a difference. Your attorney slept through the trial? So what! You also have to prove that an attorney who was awake would have done something that probably would have resulted in the jury acquitting you.

10

Your attorney failed to investigate and talk to witnesses? The only way to show that would have made a difference is to conduct that investigation and obtain from witnesses declarations or affidavits showing what those witnesses would have said. Good luck getting that done while you're in prison. If you had any money before you went to trial, which is unlikely, you don't have any left by the time you get to prison. Your prison job, if you've waited in line long enough to get one, pays between eleven and thirty-three cents per hour, and saving up enough to hire an investigator and an attorney will take decades (especially since nearly half of your salary will be going to restitution funds for that pesky wrongful conviction). So how exactly are you supposed to do what your attorney didn't do in order to prove it would have made a difference? And beware: if you're lucky enough to have family or friends who are able to find witnesses and get the declarations, the authorities assume they coerced or influenced the witnesses.

There's a saying, "crimes that happen in hell don't have angels as witnesses." This is yet another problem facing the wrongfully convicted. The witnesses who can exonerate them often come with their own credibility problems. That's assuming they're willing to sign statements, testify in open court, and put themselves at risk of becoming a target (of law enforcement, gangs, or even other civilians) for something that happened years ago involving someone they haven't seen or spoken to in decades.

Even assuming you're able to obtain compelling evidence of innocence, post-conviction court proceedings move slowly, even once the evidence of innocence has been presented to the courts. Speedy trial rights no longer apply. The case is generally not treated as a priority by crime labs, police departments, or the district attorney's office because officially, the case already has been solved. Open cases have priority, especially those with upcoming trial dates.

Further, there are procedural barriers to presenting new evidence after your conviction. For instance, in some states, if you've already asked the court for post-conviction relief, you may not be permitted to do so again or you may have to litigate whether you've met the showing required to bypass the procedural barrier (generally a showing of innocence) before the court will even consider your claim for relief. Of course if you've already presented evidence of innocence and the court or the jury found it wasn't enough, you can't rely on that evidence again.

You're probably starting to get the picture of what an enormous victory it is when a court reverses a wrongful conviction. Yet remarkably, the reversal still isn't the end. The State then has sixty days to appeal the reversal, retry you, or dismiss the charges. There is an awfully good chance that you'll remain in prison during this time, but if you're lucky, you may have bail set or even be released on your own recognizance. Appeals can take years and can be taken up through each of the various levels of review, extending the time further and further. Most likely you're staying in prison during those years of appeals. If the state elects retrial, the district attorney might offer you a time-served deal before you go to trial, meaning that if you plead guilty to something (often a lesser charge than the original conviction), you can walk out of jail that day without risking a jury trial and with no possible future threats of re-prosecution for that offense. Even if you decide to turn down the offer, risk another life sentence, keep fighting, and you convince the court or the district attorney to dismiss the charges or the jury acquits you in the retrial, you might still have to prove your innocence yet again in order to be compensated for your time in prison.

This is what makes those who make it through this process all the more remarkable. They don't just survive time in prison for a crime they didn't commit. They survive a system that is almost hopelessly stacked against them. They overcome every obstacle with almost no resources, endure every delay with model patience, face impossible choices with admirable strength, and celebrate with utter joy even when it takes twenty years for the truth to set them free and for justice to finally prevail. These men and women are a testament to the human spirit. To each of you who have been exonerated, I'm just sorry it took so long.

I went to law school unsure of whether I really wanted to be a lawyer. I knew I wanted to help people, but I was not sure how. In law school, I learned about wrongful convictions and innocence projects and decided to volunteer at the Northern California Innocence Project during the three months while I waited to see if I'd passed the bar (I had to convince my future colleagues at NCIP that this was a good idea) and thought if they hired me, I might stay for a few years. Seven years, four exonerations, and an acquittal later, it's hard to imagine leaving, even when I receive job offers that would more than double my salary.

I search for truth. I fight for justice. I only represent people I truly believe are innocent. Every time I work with a lawyer from a law firm or private practice or a public defender's office, someone inevitably describes our work together as the case of a lifetime or the most meaningful thing they have ever done. I feel so lucky because that's all I do. Each one of my innocence cases is the case of a lifetime. I love being right (doesn't everyone?) and in my job, I'm always right. Truth and justice are on my side. That's a pretty great place to be.

As one insightful exoneree wrote, "I know I've said my thanks but it just doesn't seem enough. From the first time I met you, I didn't know what to expect. I took it as it came. It felt good knowing people like you guys help people like me. You didn't know me, never met me before, I was a convicted murderer with a past not to be proud of. My good fortune was you guys believe in truth. And forever I'll be grateful."

My job is also really fun. I love building the perfect case that proves my client should be released. I equally love knocking on doors and finding and talking to the people who know what actually happened. What's more, I find myself in the most unlikely situations. I cannot imagine other circumstances outside of this job that would have led me to be sitting on a pimp's porch in Watts in South Central Los Angeles learning the details of a murder. It's equally unlikely that, after hearing something resembling gunshots, I would have to convince another lawyer to turn the car around and go back for my boss who we left behind on a street corner in Lynwood, California. We were reenacting a drive by shooting for a judge to show that witnesses were telling the truth when they testified that they hadn't been able to see the shooter's face and instead had made their identifications based on influence from law enforcement and other witnesses. Twenty years earlier they had pointed to an innocent seventeen-year-old at trial and now wished to recant.

I love my work and I love being on the side of truth and justice. Still, that's not what keeps me fighting day after day; spending absurd amounts of time struggling just to get evidence, then to get a court to hear the evidence...it's the people. I meet these men and women behind bars: Maurice Caldwell, who went to prison when I was nine years old for a murder he didn't commit and who is now one of my dearest friends and easily the most honest and loyal person I know; Franky Carrillo, who reminds me so much of my college friends who went into finance and politics, defying the odds to turn himself into the person he is today after becoming a man in prison; Obie Anthony, who would have been a lawyer by now had he had the good fortune to be born into my life instead of his; Armando Ortiz, who feels like my younger brother, making it that much harder to know that he's in a place filled with lethal dangers from which I could never protect him and yet in his letters, he always tries to make me laugh and enlightens me by focusing on the bright side of everything. Slowly but surely as I believed more and more firmly in their innocence while also admiring them for the remarkable human beings they are, I realized I would never leave this job until each was exonerated. Of course, now that they have been exonerated, there are others I need to get out of prison before I can even consider doing anything else with my life.

I don't have the words to convey how appreciative and wonderful my clients have been, how their letters have kept me going when I start to feel like I'm treading water no matter how hard I try to move forward. Instead, I'm going to share some of their words and acts of kindness.

Just a few weeks ago, I received a letter from one of my favorite clients who is still in prison—there was an index card inside and on the back of it was a drawing of a beautiful butterfly flying around my name. The postscript to the letter explained: "I watch this show called *Believe*. This little girl is special and could move matter with her mind. She's always helping people and bringing balance. In every episode there is a butterfly that lands on her. The butterfly is a symbol of hope, a symbol of what's right. Every time I see the butterfly it reminds me of you. I thought you should have your own."

When Obie was still in prison, I told him that we were changing office buildings and that I was hoping to get my own office and, ideally, one with a window. After we moved, he asked if I had a window. I did not so he commissioned another prisoner to paint me a picture of window that looked out on a peaceful landscape. The letter that accompanied the painting explained that he'd been wondering, "how can I show a miniscule of my appreciation? And it hit me, a window—because one, you wanted an office with a window and two, you are opening up a window of opportunities for a brighter future for me." I do have a small window now, but that painting remains on the wall next to my computer.

Every time I told Maurice that the prosecution had received another extension of time and further delayed his case, he would respond with a joke about his life sentence: "Don't worry, Miss P, I got nothing but time." He always made me feel like he was carrying me through the process rather than the other way around. Once he got out, Maurice made it his personal mission to inform the world that I was his lawyer, that he was exonerated because of me, and that he thinks I'm the best lawyer out there. In the statement he wrote for the press as he waited for days while the prisons and jails finished their paperwork to process his release, Maurice called me "the #1 lawyer," and wrote "she gave me hope and helped to restore my faith." During a radio interview, he told listeners that he had gone from "the dump-est truck lawyer to the one who should be in the dictionary under the definition of lawyer." He has written on Facebook that I'm "The best lawyer in the world," and "Paige is my super hero and best friend... Oh not to mention, everybody already know[s] that she is truly one of the best, most dedicated lawyer[s] any client can wish/hope for...plus she really cares about fighting against injustice." When I thanked the universe for my wonderful life in a Facebook post, Maurice commented, "You are the best part of other people's universe, and hav[ing] you in our lives really makes a good meaningful difference always." Is there any wonder that I adore this man? He is the gift that keeps on giving.

Watching justice happen—and knowing I helped make it happen—for these amazing people is a privilege. I've cried every time a judge has reversed one of my clients' convictions. Watching them walk out of jail and experience freedom? Easily the best days of my life.

The days leading up to the release of an innocent person are filled with tension and impatience, and, at least for me, fears of something going wrong. Another shocking fact about innocence work: even after the court orders your release or all charges are dismissed, it usually takes days before you're released because the prisons and jails have to do their paperwork and run warrants checks and who knows what else. Some prisons will isolate you to lessen the risk of you being attacked or injured in the final days before your release. You might think that risk would speed up the process, but you would be wrong. I've had California prison officials tell me they have five to ten business days to process release paperwork. Once I tried to hurry the process by telling an official that my client was innocent and had already spent nearly two decades in prison. The official responded, "Then what's another few days?" He was not joking and had no appreciation of the irony of the situation.

After all of the hurdles of proving my client's innocence, the moment of release is easily worth the years of frustration and setbacks. It is a moment of pure joy. Giddy are those first moments of freedom, of unrestricted hugs with loved ones, of choosing anything you want to eat, of knowing you'll be able to take a bath and lay in a real bed with a real pillow, and even be truly alone in a room that's truly dark for the first time since you were locked up.

I'll never forget Franky Carrillo diving into the world with wide eyes and an even wider smile as he picked and inhaled flowers, bit into an orange straight from a tree and let the juices drip everywhere, soaked up time with his son who had been born shortly after Franky was arrested, and tasted—with great appreciation—his first avocado in more than two decades. I've never met anyone as ready to embrace and conquer the world as Franky. It has been such a pleasure to experience the world along with him, accepting everything as it comes with remarkable grace, enjoying the ocean air, and seeing him touch the hearts and minds of even the most unlikely people.

Spending time with any exoneree is a gift. It's amazing how much an exoneree can make you appreciate everything anew. They walk out of prison with literally nothing more than the clothes on their backs and yet for them everything is wonderful, astonishing, thrilling, or as Maurice used to say, "Tony the Tiger, grrrreeeeeaaaaat!" Seeing trees with someone who spent years in yards that have no trees, no grass, and in some cases no green in sight, brings trees into a whole new perspective. Imagine seeing someone getting overwhelmed by all the choices on a menu and remembering not only did they not choose their meals, but worse still, they were given a peanut butter and jelly sandwich and a green apple for lunch every single day for the past 6,387 days. I don't even like peanut butter and jelly, and if I eat the same thing for more than three days in a row, I want nothing to do with that food for weeks if not months. Yet I've only heard one person mention this once. I think prison is such an unimaginable experience for me that the only piece I can comprehend is eating the same thing every day and that sounds terrible, but of course for inmates, it's surely the least of their concerns.

The fortunate exonerees with a lot of family and outside support are better able than most to get on their feet and sustain the happiness of those first moments of freedom. For many, however, their frustration grows as the system continues to fail them and the opportunities to be a productive member of society, which were minimal at best, continue to shrink. Still, my exonerees manage to maintain an enviable optimism about life. I thought getting someone out of prison was a happy ending, but I was wrong. It's not an ending. It's another beginning and lives started anew come with struggles and setbacks and heartbreak, but also happiness and opportunities and love and family.

It's a privilege to do this work, to represent the innocent, to fight for justice; and it comes with obligations and responsibilities. I worry about my clients—the ones who are in and the ones who are out. I spend nights and weekends thinking about how to free my innocent clients and how to make the lives of my exonerees better. I also have fun at work, I feel good about what I do, and my coworkers and exonerees have become wonderful friends. I get letters calling me an angel, I have people telling me I've saved their lives, and friends who I know would do anything for me. I search for truth and I fight for justice for clients I believe in. I'm an extremely lucky person.

Paige Kaneb is an Assistant Clinical Professor at the Northern California Innocence Project at Santa Clara University School of Law. She has served as lead attorney in two exoneration cases and was a member of the legal team in two additional exoneration cases.

The Case of George Souliotes

The case of George Souliotes provides a heartbreaking example of the countless hurdles faced by lawyers who defend the innocent and what happens when a prosecutor is more concerned with preserving a win than reaching a just decision.

Very late on a misty January night in 1997 a fire destroyed a house on Ronald Street in Modesto, California and killed a mother and her two children. The Modesto Fire Department arrived at the scene early on the morning of January 15. Two fire department veterans investigated the cause of the fire and both determined that the fire had been set intentionally. The intensity of the fire was indicated by the melted garage door, charred trees near the garage, and the collapsed ceilings of the garage and part of the house. According to the fire investigators, the house did not have enough fuel sources to have burned as hot as was necessary to do the type of damage they found. Furthermore, they believed that the burn patterns found on the floors and the curled floor tiles indicated that an accelerant or ignitable liquid had been poured and that made the fire burn hotter than it otherwise would have. Since the investigators determined the cause of the fire was arson, they began to look for witnesses to support their theory.

By the time the sun was up the police were looking at George as a suspect in starting the fire. George owned the house that caught fire and they knew he had been trying to sell it. The police theorized that he set the fire to claim the insurance money, ignoring the fact that a buyer was willing to purchase the home for its fair market value. The prosecution would continue to put forth the insurance claim theory even after learning the insurance payout on the property would have been less than the balance due on the mortgage and that George did not even need the insurance money.

In the early morning hours of January 15, Monica Sandoval, had been standing on her balcony in a nearby apartment building waiting for her boyfriend to come home. By 2:30 a.m. she was shivering on the balcony smoking a cigarette and becoming angrier with each passing moment that her boyfriend still had not come home.

She went inside to put on some warmer clothes and turn off some lights. According to Monica, while she waited she noticed a white or off-white RV driving back and forth along Ronald Street. At one point, the vehicle stopped across the street from the house and Monica saw the driver get out carrying a white sack. She couldn't see his face clearly, but thought he was in his thirties. He crossed the street and returned a few moments later without the sack. After the driver got back into the vehicle, he drove back and forth a few more times, eventually slowing down and turning his head to look toward the house. Monica caught a brief glimpse of the lower part of the driver's face through the windshield. She could tell he wore glasses and was wearing a blue and white checkered Pendleton-type shirt, but she still had not seen the driver clearly. Not long after that the driver drove away and Monica noticed that the house he had been looking at was on fire.

George Souliotes and his girlfriend were avid ballroom dancers. They often took extended trips in George's RV, a Winnebago adorned with lights around the top, to ballroom dancing competitions across the State of California. On the evening of January 14, 1997, the night before the fire, George parked his RV in his driveway. He and his girlfriend were leaving the next day to take a trip down the California coast, and planned to camp in the RV along the way before attending a swing dancing convention in Monterey on January 23. George had gone to bed early so they could get an early start.

Later on the morning of January 15, police officers investigating the possibility of arson interviewed Monica. A police officer drove Monica to George's home to see if she would identify his RV as the one she had seen driving back and forth on Ronald Street. She told the officer it was not the RV she had seen. The officer then took her to an RV dealer to see if she could find one that looked like the RV she had seen. While they were looking at RVs, the officer received a call telling him to bring her back to George's house to look at his RV again, which was now parked on the street at police request. One of the detectives at George's house checked the RV's engine to see if it was still warm to the touch, which it would have been if it had been driven that morning. It was cold. By the time the officer returned with Monica, there were a number of police cars in the area. Monica, seeing the police cars, told the officer the vehicle was the one that she had seen. That afternoon, Monica was unable to identify George in a six-pack that included his picture along with five fillers. She did not identify anyone as the alleged arsonist. With so little evidence against George, why did the police continue to focus on him as their sole suspect?

Over the next few months the newspapers and local television news heavily covered the story of the house fire and the deaths of the mother and two children who lived there. The fire investigators had determined that the fire was intentionally set and the press identified George Souliotes as the primary arson suspect. Like almost everyone in Modesto, Monica saw the newspaper articles and news stories that included a picture of George.

George's preliminary hearing was held six months after the fire. At the hearing, Monica still had not identified George as the RV driver. She did, however, add descriptive details such as the driver had a narrow face and a long pointy nose, which conveniently described some of George's facial characteristics. The prosecutor concluded Monica's questioning and the court went into recess. When court reconvened after the recess, the prosecutor, in an unusual move, asked the judge to allow him to bring Monica back to the stand for additional questioning. It was during the follow-up questioning that Monica pointed to George sitting at the defense table wearing the red jumpsuit of a prisoner. She identified him there in court for the first time. What happened during the recess that caused Monica to suddenly be able to identify George, when she had not been able to identify him before the recess? By the time of the trial she was unable to provide an explanation.

At the time of the fire, the tenants in the house were under an eviction notice that required them to move in December. The tenants had made arrangements to move into a mobile home park in the area, but a flooding incident at the mobile home park delayed their ability to move in at the scheduled time. George graciously extended the time they had to move so they would not have to find a place to live during the holiday season. The manager of the mobile home park testified at trial that she witnessed an argument between

George and the tenant and that another man had witnessed the same argument. When questioned, the other man confirmed that he was at the mobile home park at the time the manager said the argument took place, but he contradicted her testimony. He testified that he had not seen an argument and added that the manager called him before the trial and threatened to report him for unlicensed business activities if he did not "get his story straight."

Two different juries tried George for arson and three counts of murder. At the conclusion of the first trial, the jury could not reach a verdict and the judge declared a mistrial. Before the beginning of the second trial, George rejected a plea deal for a fifteen-year sentence, declaring once again that he was innocent.

At the second trial, George's defense team inexplicably did not present a defense, although they did illustrate the many inconsistencies between Monica's initial statements to fire investigators and her testimonies at trial during cross-examination. In his closing statement, the prosecutor discounted those inconsistencies by arguing that the scientific evidence was the most important evidence. He reminded the jury that the substance that started the fire also was found on George's shoes. He said, "...you're thinking Monica's not completely certain, but the person she said it was, is the person who has the stuff on his shoes..." In true Law & Order fashion, he hammered home his point declaring "...the finger of guilt points to the defendant. Doesn't point to the one-armed man, it points to George Souliotes because he's the one. The shoes tell the tale."

Although the prosecutor requested the death penalty, the jury rejected his request and recommended instead life without parole. On October 20, 2000, George Souliotes was sentenced to three consecutive terms of life without the possibility of parole. He was fifty-six years old and would die in prison.

By 2003, George's case had been brought to the attention of the Northern California Innocence Project (NCIP). NCIP, along with attorneys from the law firm of Orrick Herrington & Sutcliffe (Orrick), filed a habeas petition on George's behalf on December 10 of that year. The Stanislaus County Superior Court, without holding a hearing to discuss the disputed facts, denied the petition on January 6, 2004. On March 1, 2004, NCIP and Orrick filed a habeas petition with the Court of Appeal, which was summarily denied on August 26, 2004. They filed a third petition with the California Supreme Court on October 12, 2004. This petition also was summarily denied on April 19, 2006.

During this period, George's sister, Aleka Pantazis, refused to accept her brother's conviction. She vowed that she "would leave no stone unturned" in her efforts to prove her brother's innocence and secure his release. John Lentini had been hired by George's defense team in 1997 to analyze chemical samples from the fire scene. At the time of the first two trials, national standards were not sophisticated enough to differentiate between substances that were in the same general chemical compound group. In this case, the group was medium petroleum distillates, or MPDs. All of the forensic experts agreed that MPDs were present on the samples from the fire scene and on George's shoes.

In 2005, Aleka went back to Lentini and asked him if there was anything he could do to help her prove her brother's innocence through chemical analysis of the samples from the fire scene. Lentini reviewed his results from 1997 and realized there might be a way to differentiate between types of MPDs. For the first time, in November 2005, Lentini figured out a way to distinguish unequivocally the MPDs found at the fire scene from the MPDs found on George's shoes. Lentini reported his findings to George's attorneys in December 2005.

While Aleka pursued evidence of her brother's innocence with Lentini, the defense team hired investigators to challenge Monica's eyewitness identification testimony. In addition to the inconsistencies between her statements to investigators and her trial testimony, the defense team investigators also knew that Monica's boyfriend had stayed out late on a previous occasion and she had stabbed him with a switchblade knife when he finally came home in the middle of the night. She admitted to the investigators that the night of the fire she had been preoccupied with where her boyfriend might be and was not really paying close attention to the RV most of that night. The defense team staged a reenactment of what Monica testified she saw the night of the fire. A videotape of the reenactment showed that Monica could not have seen the face of the RV's driver, even the lower portion of it, while he was driving or when he walked from the RV to the house. When she was first interviewed by the fire investigators, Monica told them that she did not get a good enough look at the RV's driver to be able to identify him. During the reenactment, the woman standing in Monica's place was unable to see the face of the RV's driver.

Monica's inconsistencies did not stop with the RV's driver. She also did not consistently describe the RV itself. She changed the RV's color, its shape, and the accessories on it. George's RV had a string of lights around the top, making it particularly festive. Monica did not recall seeing any lights on the top of the RV she saw driving around the night of the fire. The vehicle she saw the night of the fire had a curtain in the rear window. George's RV did not have a curtain in the rear window. Monica initially did not describe the RV as a Winnebago, but as a Dodge Caravan. She did not recall that there was a large "W" on the side of the RV when she gave her statement to the fire investigators.

The defense investigators were able to discredit or create doubt about other circumstantial evidence as well. Surprisingly, they learned that there were other witnesses that night who had not been interviewed by the police. One witness saw a car resembling a Ford Taurus parked across the street with a driver inside watching the burning house. The witness described the driver as a white male in his late twenties to early thirties, longish light hair, a moustache, and glasses. The witness thought the driver was "watching his work" as he looked at the fire. As the witness approached the car, the driver sped away, his tires squealing as he fled the scene. Another witness saw a beige or off-white, older model Winnebago with a brownish-green stripe and a "W" on the side driving around the parking lot of an unopened shopping center at around seven o'clock that morning. She was certain the Winnebago she saw was not George's Winnebago. She called the police later that evening when she returned home from work, but the police never followed up on the lead.

Since George's conviction, advancements in fire science have discredited the findings of both fire department investigators in his case. What the investigators originally pointed to as evidence of accelerants is now known not to demonstrate their use, or that a fire was intentionally set at all. In fact, the same type of evidence also has been found to exist in accidental fires. Reviewing the evidence also indicated that there actually had been a sufficient fuel source to stoke the fire to temperatures that would melt the metal garage door, collapse the roof, and char the tree.

On May 20, 2006, the defense team filed a petition in federal district court, but the California Attorney General's office challenged the petition as being filed too late. The district court agreed and dismissed the petition for being filed five days too late. Even multiple direct appeals to California Attorney General Kamala Harris to intercede were rejected. It did not matter that the forensic evidence used to convict George, namely the MPDs on his shoes and the supposed indicators of arson, had been discredited by more advanced scientific analysis. Based on improved science, the burn patterns observed at the scene of the fire were inconclusive about whether arson had been committed, but that also did not matter to the prosecution, the Attorney General tasked with defending the conviction, or the court. Shocking though it was, the defense team was time barred from making an argument of actual innocence.

The defense team spent the next six years arguing that the petition should be heard, despite being late, because George had a claim of actual innocence. Fortunately, there were cases being heard in higher courts that would bear directly on this issue of whether evidence of actual innocence could be considered even if the petition requesting review was filed late. The reversal of a decision in the Ninth Circuit Court of Appeals and the opinion in another decision by the United States Supreme Court laid the groundwork that allowed the district court to consider the evidence of George's actual innocence. Had these two cases been resolved differently than they had been, the evidence of George's innocence never would have been heard and he would have lived his life out in prison.

In George's evidentiary hearing the Attorney General's expert admitted, and the Attorney General therefore stipulated in court, that there was no longer any scientifically valid evidence to suggest that the fire had been set intentionally. The expert also admitted and the Attorney General stipulated that the MPDs found on George's shoes were not consistent with the MPDs found in the samples taken from the fire scene. The court then considered the remaining evidence that consisted of Monica's questionable and unreliable identification and testimony at George's preliminary hearing. The court largely adopted the testimony of an eye-witness identification expert who suggested that Monica's identification of George was likely influenced by having been exposed to his face in multiple photographs during the initial photo lineup and in the press afterwards, and by him sitting at the defense table at the preliminary hearing. The court further noted that "A reasonable juror might well wonder whether the dismissal of criminal charges for assault with a deadly weapon influenced her testimony, despite her assertions that there was no "deal" with the prosecutor." It seems too much of a coincidence, not to be connected.

On April 26, 2012, Judge Michael Seng, a US magistrate judge, determined that George successfully presented a sufficient showing of actual innocence and recommended that the district court consider the merits of George's writ of habeas corpus. Seven years had gone by between the time Lentini told the defense team about the MPDs and Judge Seng's recommendation. It took another fourteen months before George would finally have his day in court and prove that he had not committed arson and had not killed his tenants. Most of the delay was due to stalling tactics by the Attorney General who continually requested extensions to file their responses—ironic considering the Attorney General wanted to deny George his day in court because of a five-day filing delay.

Despite the lack of conclusive evidence that a crime had even been committed, the prosecutors would not drop the charges against George and decided to try him again for triple murder. They intended to rely on Monica's discredited testimony even though in closing arguments the prosecutor had told the jury that the scientific evidence was the most important evidence. George's defense team began to prepare for trial, but before the trial could begin the prosecution offered George a deal. He eventually agreed to plead no contest to three counts of involuntary manslaughter for failing to maintain smoke detectors in the rental home, in return for the arson charge and all allegations that he was responsible for the fire being dropped. With this plea George did not admit responsibility for the death of his tenants, but he accepted the sentence of six years. Having already served sixteen years, the court ordered George's immediate release, which occurred two days later.

On July 3, 2013, George Souliotes, now seventy-two years old and in poor health, was released from prison. He was met by his family, his friends, and his defense team. He was grateful to see the sun. Despite the long ordeal they endured to prove his innocence, George and his family did not appear bitter. The prosecutor, however, was not as gracious. District Attorney Birgit Fladager issued a statement that she continued to believe George is guilty of murder but that the prosecution opted for a plea agreement because the court rulings "gutted" the prosecution's case. Apparently Ms. Fladager was under the delusion that we don't understand the meaning of "stipulating to the facts." We were not fooled by her attempt to blame the court for her inability to prosecute a case of murder by arson when it was the prosecution's stipulation that gutted their case. The prosecution stipulated to the lack of evidence of arson and the irrefutable evidence that the chemical compounds found in samples taken from the fire scene did not match the chemical compounds found in George's shoes. If there had been any solid evidence of a crime that George had committed, the prosecution would have tried their case. Why not, when the prosecution had already tried him without any solid evidence? Apparently the shoes had no tale to tell after all.

PRUNO, RAMEN, and a side of HOPE

Their Stories

CHAPTER 3
Obie Steven Anthony III

In the fall of 1993, Obie Anthony was living in Ventura County, California and holding down two jobs. He worked in Camarillo, a small suburban community northwest of Los Angeles, for the California Conservation Corps (3Cs) in the Department of Forestry's Fire Division. He also worked at the Hilton for a janitorial service owned by his girlfriend's aunt.

Obie had been spending time driving back and forth between home and Los Angeles visiting his sick mother. One night on the way to visit his mother in Los Angeles, he ran into his older sister, Yolanda, and discovered that she, too, was sick. When Obie returned to work he asked for and was granted a transfer from the 3Cs office in Camarillo to its office in Los Angeles, but when the San Bernardino wildfires erupted, he was called to join that crew. This conflicted with Obie's plans to live in Los Angeles so, as soon as the fires were put out, he left the 3Cs. Obie kept the job with the janitorial service and decided to go to college. He got an apartment and began looking into schools. Unfortunately, when Obie moved back to Los Angeles he also found himself thrust back into that "street" lifestyle he thought he had left behind.

Obie's young life had not been easy. He was six years old and living with his family in St. Louis, when his stepfather passed away and his mother moved him and his two older half-sisters to South Central, a Los Angeles neighborhood with a reputation for violence. His mother, strongly affected by her husband's death and the family's subsequent move, succumbed to serious drug use, making it difficult for her to care for her children. Obie kept his family fed by stealing food and doing whatever else it took to support them. Finding himself in a neighborhood beset with gang activity and violence made it difficult for Obie to separate being a resident in his neighborhood from participating in some of the neighborhood's more questionable activities. Obie grew into his caretaker role. This would be a theme throughout his life. He forged allegiances, occasionally sold drugs, and got mixed up in some petty activities in the effort to support his family. Obie says, he was "in the mix." As a teenager raising himself, what else could he to do? With no father and a drug addicted mother, the only direction Obie got was his own. Obie was no angel when it came to the law. He needed to make choices that would ensure his family's survival; they were not always the easiest choices nor were they always legal, but they were not based in violence.

Obie's mother died in January 1994, the same month that the Northridge Earthquake leveled his apartment building. Soon afterwards he moved into his mother's house and became more responsible for his family, especially the young children of his eldest sister, Darlene. California Social Services had given Obie's mother full custody of Darlene's children and, with the death of his mother, that custody passed to Obie. He was only nineteen years old, but family was the most important thing to him. Obie continued to work for the janitorial service and manage the house. He also continued to take advantage of the occasional neighborhood opportunities to keep his family fed.

Obie's sister, Yolanda, did not live at the house with him and the children, but she often visited. It seems as though she felt her territory had been infringed upon when Obie moved into the house after their mother's death. In late March 1994, everything came to a head one evening when Obie was attempting to put the children down to sleep. Yolanda was watching television and the volume was extremely high. Obie asked her to turn it down.

"You cain't tell me what to do!" Yolanda shouted. "This ain't yo' house!"

Obie tried to remain calm but his voice betrayed his anger. "What do you mean, girl?" he snapped back at her. "*I* pay the rent! *I* pay the gas bill *and* the light bill!" He sighed in resignation. "Just turn it down. The kids wanna sleep."

Obie and Yolanda continued to yell back and forth at each other. Anyone who saw them would think they were watching a scene from a John Carpenter film. Yolanda had grabbed a butcher knife and threatened to cut him. Obie grabbed the knife from her, but when she pulled the knife back from him, she cut Obie's hand. He managed to knock her down and thought that was the end of the fight. Obie turned and walked back to the kids' room to check on them. He heard his sister's labored breathing and her crazed scream-ing behind him. Obie turned just in time to see the knife slashing through the air at him. This time he grabbed the knife carefully. He was able to break the knife, but not before his sister stabbed him in the head. Despite his injury, Obie was able to subdue Yolanda. He was fighting mad at her, but he still loved her. She was his mother's child and therefore a part of his family; someone he'd always love, no matter what.

* * *

When Obie thinks about his mother, he remembers a conversa-tion they had the day before she died. "Obie," she whispered weak-ly, "when I pass away, you should go home." She wanted him to go back to Ventura County and get away from the bad influenc-es in South Central. Obie shrugged off his mother's warning say-ing, "Momma, look, you're getting better. My family is right here. You crazy; I'm not goin' nowhere." Obie's mother passed away the following night. Her warning proved prophetic when only a few months later Obie was arrested for murder. If Obie had listened to his mother, he might have been at home in Camarillo the night Fe-lipe Gonzalez Angeles was killed.

* * *

On a rainy Sunday night in March 1994, a young man was gunned down on a street in South Central. Earlier that evening, Fe-lipe Gonzalez Angeles had been enjoying some after-dinner beers with his friends and roommates, Victor Trejo and Luis Jimenez. The men were varying degrees of intoxicated. Even though Felipe was flat out drunk, he still wanted to go to South Central to hook up with one of his girlfriends. Victor, having drunk only two beers, was in better shape to drive than either of his roommates. The three friends climbed into Victor's car and drove to the corner of Forty-Ninth and Figueroa, a street that was a mixture of run-down residential and commercial buildings.

Sometime after 11:00 p.m., the car pulled to the curb in front of an apartment building. Felipe hopped out and staggered up the steps to the front door. Someone inside the building told Felipe his girlfriend was not home. Victor started the car and, as Felipe walked back toward it, three young black men approached. One of the men ran to the passenger side of the car yelling "Stop the fuckin' car!" He opened the passenger door and tried to pull Luis out, but Luis was wearing his seatbelt. The robber shouted, "All right, muthafucka, gimme your money, asshole." He pulled his gun out of the waistband of his pants and held it sideways like gangbangers did in movies.

Luis was too slow to react and the robber hit him in the face with the gun. Victor tried to defuse the situation and assured the robber they did not want any trouble, but the robber thought they were stalling.

He yelled, "Too slow," before shooting Victor three times and Luis five times.

Victor's foot slammed down on the accelerator and the car sped off, leaving Felipe alone with the other assailants. Through his rearview mirror, Victor saw Felipe break free from the men who had attacked him. He heard the man who had shot them shout out to his friends, "Kill him! Kill him!"

As Felipe tried to run away, they shot him in the back and he went down. The three attackers started running away when more shots rang out, hitting one of the robbers in the leg, but not stopping him.

In the apartment building, two young girls, seven and nine years old, were watching the action. Through their window they saw everything that happened on the street. They excitedly recounted to their father everything they had seen.

Victor and Luis ended up at County Hospital in critical condition. Felipe died at the scene from the gunshot wound that entered his back and exited his chest. Later that night, one of the robbers entered the emergency room of Martin Luther King Jr. Hospital seeking treatment for a gunshot wound in his leg. Two security guards on duty at the hospital that night saw the injured man waiting to be treated but he left before hospital staff could get any information about him.

That same night, Obie was at home recovering from a hangover. On Saturday night, the night before the murder, Obie attended a birthday party where he overindulged and got really drunk. He was supposed to pick up his girlfriend from work, but he was too drunk to drive. A friend drove Obie home in his girlfriend's car and on the way there, Obie threw up in the car. By the time they made it to the house, Obie was so drunk his friend had to help him inside. The next day, Sunday, Obie's girlfriend discovered what he had done. It was bad enough that he vomited in her car, but he had been too hung over to clean it up. She made him clean it up.

Sometime just before midnight on Sunday night, Detective Marcella Winn, still in training, was assigned Felipe's murder as her first investigation. She met her partner at the scene of the crime and the two detectives worked the crime scene to find any evidence that would help them identify the shooters. They found empty shell casings and latent fingerprints. These are the type of fingerprints that are not visible to the naked eye, but can be revealed with magnesium powder and photographed or lifted. They found shoe prints that looked to be from more than one person fleeing the scene. They found a car with a bullet hole in the windshield that was at the wrong angle to have come from the locations of the shooters. Detective Winn and her partner thought that shot might have come from higher up, perhaps from the rooftop of a building. The crime scene investigators lifted the latent prints and took casts of the footprints.

The two detectives split up to go over the crime scene. While her partner checked out the car and the alley, Detective Winn checked out the building on the corner and there she found an eyewitness to the crime—John Jones, initially described as the manager of the apartment building that overlooked the crime scene. In reality, Jones was a well-known pimp and the "apartment building" was his brothel, but this information would not come to light to the defense until much later. Jones also was the father of the two young girls who had witnessed the crime as it occurred. Detective Winn hit the jackpot. The building had a security camera and the videotape showed Felipe ringing the doorbell and being told that his girlfriend was not home. Shortly after Felipe left, the tape's audio track caught snippets of voices shouting at Victor and Luis and yelling for the other guys to kill Felipe. The shouts were followed by multiple gunshots. The detectives heard three distinctly different guns because of the three unique sounds each gun made, reinforcing the evidence of a third shooter. Who fired the third gun?

Following Jones's lead on the injured shooter, the detectives checked area hospitals for anyone seeking treatment for a gunshot wound. They found the two MLK Hospital security guards who described a man who came in with a gunshot wound in his leg. The man had left the hospital before his identity could be logged and authorities contacted.

About one month later, in mid-April, Obie and his friends, Reggie Cole and Michael Miller, were arrested on unrelated robbery and carjacking charges that ultimately were dismissed after the victim admitted he had lied about the incident. A week after their arrest, Detective Winn received an anonymous telephone tip. The tipster said one of the shooters was a member of the Five Deuce Avalon Crips with the street name "Baby Day." The tipster said, "Baby Day from Five Deuce Avalon Crips made a move on Forty Ninth Street with two guys and it went wrong."

Detective Winn eventually concluded that Michael Miller was "Baby Day" even though he was a member of a different gang, but at the time, she was uncertain whether any of the three men arrested on the robbery-carjacking were "Baby Day."

Detective Winn generated three six-pack photo line-ups, one each for Michael Miller, Reggie Cole, and Obie Anthony. Between Victor, Luis, and Jones, the police had three eyewitnesses to Felipe's murder. Detective Winn brought Jones in to look at the six-packs. After the detective administering the photo line-up tapped on Obie's picture, Jones identified Obie as the shooter. He also identified Reggie Cole, but he did not identify Michael Miller. After Jones made his identifications, the police called Victor and Luis to the station and told them they had "caught the guys" who did the shooting. Victor identified Obie as someone who "looked like" one of the shooters, but he did not identify Obie as one of the shooters. Luis did not recognize Obie or Reggie in either six-pack. In fact, Luis described the shooters as being between twenty-five and thirty years old," while Jones had described them as teenagers. The detectives also had a live line-up that included both Obie and Reggie. Neither Victor nor Luis identified Obie or Reggie at the live line-up.

Based on Jones's identification, the detectives brought in Obie and Reggie for questioning and to see if either of them had a gunshot wound in his leg. The male detective had Obie strip down to his shorts to check for bullet wounds. He didn't find any. Reggie, on the other hand, did have a bullet wound in his leg, but the wound predated Felipe's murder. That did not prevent the detectives from arresting Obie and Reggie for Felipe's murder and the attempted murder of Victor and Luis. After Obie and Reggie were arrested, Detective Winn learned that Michael Miller's nickname was "Baby Day Day" and that Obie's nickname was "Day Day" or "Lil Day," but this information was not shared with Obie's attorney.

Over the course of the next few months, Jones changed his story multiple times. First he claimed to have been an eyewitness, but it actually was his two daughters who were the eyewitnesses. Jones convinced the prosecution to keep his daughters off the witness list and the girls did not testify at trial. Early in the investigation, Jones denied being the third shooter, but asked questions of the detectives that suggested he might have been the third shooter. He said he saw the crime from his bathroom window as it was being committed. Then he said he did not witness the actual crime. Instead, he claimed to have seen the shooters running away and that the shooters shot at him when they realized he might be a witness. He claimed to have seen their faces when they shot at him. The detectives found no bullet casings in the area where Jones claimed the shooters were standing. Furthermore, evidence suggested that Jones was on the roof at the time of the shooting, a location that was the correct angle for the car with the errant bullet hole in the windshield and the shot that struck one of the suspects in the leg. Jones denied being on the roof but took the detectives up to the roof when they came to talk with him the day after the shooting to show them where the third shooter might have been positioned. When describing the scene, Jones initially said he saw a car, and then denied there was a car. He claimed he saw four men attempting to rob Victor, Luis, and Felipe, and then claimed there were only three men and a dog. He claimed he saw one of these men get shot, but then changed that to the man falling and spraining his ankle and then changed that story back to seeing the man get shot, stating he was "absolutely sure" of this version of events.

In exchange for Jones's cooperation, the LAPD wrote two letters in the fall of 1994 requesting leniency and probation on a pimping and pandering charge against him. The mandatory minimum for the offense was six years and the Probation Department recommended twelve years. Although neither letter was signed by the detectives investigating Felipe's murder, Detective Winn wrote the letter that identified her as the contact person for more information. This letter was dated September 8, 1994, prior to Jones's appearance to testify at the preliminary hearing for Obie and Reggie. Jones insisted there was no promise of leniency on any outstanding charges against him and the prosecution did not challenge that assertion despite knowing that both letters had been sent and that Detective Winn had made phone calls urging a sentence of probation only. At trial, Jones identified Obie Anthony and Reggie Cole as the shooters. Jones received a sentence of probation on the pimping and pandering charge. He subsequently recanted this identification, and then recanted his recantation.

Aside from people who were present at the time of the shooting, there were four other witnesses, but only two testified at trial. Arthur Jones (not related to John Jones) and Ronald Brock were the security guards on duty at MLK Hospital when the suspect who had been shot by the "unknown" third shooter entered the emergency room with an injured leg. Initially, Arthur Jones identified Obie's photo in one six-pack as "...looks like subject who was carring [sic] the other subject in to [sic] the MLK Hospital and the [sic] both left together in a white Toyota." He did not identify Reggie in the other six-pack. Instead, he identified a filler photo as one of the shooters. He subsequently changed his mind at trial to say that he possibly saw Obie and Reggie at the hospital, but this is unlikely since neither had a recent leg injury. Ronald Brock also failed to identify Obie and Reggie after viewing the six-packs. Isaac Gaston knew Obie as "Day Day" not "Baby Day" and knew that John Jones carried a 357-Magnum and that he would go up on the roof of his building "all the time." Gaston was never contacted as a potential witness. Mike Corwin was a reporter for the Los Angeles Times at the time of the murder. He was shadowing Detective Winn to observe the investigation first hand. Corwin wrote an article about the investigation and ultimately a book titled *The Killing Season*. The article was published before Obie's trial and the book was published after the trial. Corwin did not testify at trial and destroyed his notes after the book's publication. Facts in the article and the book contradict the testimonies of Detective Winn and John Jones.

Detective Winn grew up in South Central and took a personal interest in this case, perhaps because it was her first homicide, but also because it was her neighborhood. She was reported to have said that night at the scene, "Maybe nobody else cares about this killing, but I do. I want the predators who did this off the street. I don't want them walking around this community jacking people I care about." Perhaps it was this personal interest that caused her to exclude some potentially exculpatory information from her reports and withhold key facts from prosecutors. She did not include Brock's failure to identify Obie or Reggie or Arthur Jones's identification of a filler in her report. She also did not include her second conversation with John Jones on the roof of his brothel in her initial report and she did not tell prosecutors that she thought John Jones might be the third shooter. She did not share her belief that Michael Miller was the subject of the tipster's call. She did not share her involvement in the request for leniency for John Jones. Detective Winn was aware that Jones had a seventeen-year criminal history, including a homicide, and she did not include that in her report. Detective Winn's determination to solve the crime probably caused her to ignore the inconsistencies between the various eyewitness identifications.

In the end, Detective Winn's misconduct and the misconduct of the prosecutors along with the perjured testimony of the prosecution's key witness, the pimp John Jones, led to the 1995 wrongful conviction of Obie Anthony and Reggie Cole for the murder of Felipe Gonzalez and the attempted robbery and attempted murder of Victor Trejo and Luis Jimenez. It would be seventeen years before Obie Anthony would prove his innocence and regain his freedom. He had to keep his wits about him and stay focused to survive long enough to do that.

An Innocent Kiss

As Told By Obie Anthony

Obie has a lot to say about his stay in prison. He wouldn't wish the experience on anyone and recalls being completely terrified as he got off of that bus and took his first step onto the grounds of the prison that would become his home. That fear helped Obie set himself apart. As harrowing an experience as prison would turn out to be, and even though he was in a prison uniform, Obie knew he was still a man. For the entire time he was locked up, Obie would respect others but also would require respect in return from prisoners and guards alike. He used common sense and a bit of humor in his efforts to remain human in such an inhuman place; lighting up his life in that very dark world.

It was common for guards to search all prisoners going into and coming out of the chow hall to ensure no contraband went in or came out, but the search of inmates leaving was the most critical. In addition to ensuring that no life threatening utensils would be removed, guards also were concerned about food, such as chicken breasts and burgers, sugar and condiments; foods and supplies that could be fashioned into saleable contraband.

One night, on the way out of the chow hall, prisoners were being searched after a disgusting meal of chicken a la king, which Obie notes was nothing like the chicken a la king he or anyone else had eaten. He described it as something "that wouldn't satisfy a third grader, covered with a cloudy, thin gravy with maybe a dash of carrots and celery, and with a horrendous odor that reminded me of a public toilet. If there was any chicken, it was scrawny strands of what was once a shredded piece of chicken. In a word—nasty!" When it was his time to be searched he couldn't believe it. Obie was outdone by the audacity of a pat down for chicken a la king. The meal didn't require the use of knives, and there was nothing in the meal tangible enough to sneak out. Rather than be searched, Obie started taking off his uniform, all the way down to his skivvies. Obie already had a reputation for being rather informal and light-hearted with many of the guards and they knew his antics. On this particular night there was a new guard trainee so the tenured guards let Obie perform. The new guard didn't know what to do; he worried about the rules and protocol while the other guards let him worry. Everyone got a good laugh that night. It was moments like this that helped Obie get through his time in prison. This was partly how he retained his confidence and self-respect.

Obie also stayed far away from prison politics and drama. Taking sides was a dangerous proposition and the consequences of getting involved in what he called "that mess" could be detrimental to his health if not his life. "Mess leads to arguments, maybe fights," he explained, "fatal fights in fact, and as an innocent man, why would I get into a fight with a man who could be in for murder? Who knows what the other guy might do?" Obie separated himself from that mess by spending his time reading, studying, and writing poetry. These were solitary activities and it was their solitude that kept him from fraternizing with the prison inmates who engaged in the kind of behavior and influences that Obie wanted to stay away from; those folks that were always in fights—racially motivated or territorial altercations mostly—or about the kinds of things that turned your mind into "prison putty," like drinking pruno or taking drugs. These were the guys who would most likely be the ones to return to prison after their release or parole. They were the ones institutionalized into depending on prison life; the only life they knew and of which they had no fear. Obie wanted no part of prison life.

Obie knew that staying away from these "conditioned" inmates was smart. "I made sure it was clear to my fellow inmates that bothering me with mess that wasn't about protecting my *own* life was a no-no." The isolation of reading and writing poetry kept Obie safe, sane, and hopeful.

Love is a Powerful Emotion

A Poem By Obie Anthony

Love is a powerful emotion

The flames of which burn with the intensity of that of a phoenix

Undying and unquenchable constantly rebirthing itself

With greater intensity and a stronger passion and desire.

I've been burned by the wings of its flames

And my loneliness has turned to ash

But, the flame has kindled inside me and refined my soul.

I am emboldened by the power of your love and the emotion is
so strong

So take my heart and decorate it with those things that sustain

Our passion, strength, courage, devotion, loyalty, and faithfulness.

Love is a powerful emotion

And I've been shaken by the way you let it flow

Through me.

Whole

A Poem By Obie Anthony

Enlarge my heart.

Take advantage of my desire.

Take my love and counsel.

Give consideration of the devotion that makes itself inside my soul.

Take courage in the foundation of our union

And reject any fears.

Take solace in my love to love you

And if you'll come a little further we can rest our love indefinitely

And share companion of passion and intimacy.

Take advantage of my desire and take my love and counsel.

There is another reason for Obie's endurance, and probably the most important one; the one that consistently kept his hopes high, his confidence strong, and made prison life bearable. That reason was his cellmate's sister, Denise.

It was either a great coincidence or a sign that the universe was looking out for Obie that Denise Merchant's brother, Curtis Merchant, would be in the same prison as Obie. The men knew of each other from the neighborhood, but they didn't hang with each other on the outside. When Curtis got to prison, he recognized Obie. Somehow they ended up as cellmates, "cellies," and eventually their conversation turned to Denise.

When he was only twelve years old, Obie had been enthralled with an older girl named Denise. She was sixteen. Because Denise was four years older, they didn't run in the same circles, but they lived in the same neighborhood. Obie sometimes saw Denise when he was riding around on his scooter. Denise was friends with Obie's sister, Yolanda. When Denise came to Obie's house or when they ran into each other in the neighborhood, they would speak to each other, but mostly Obie watched her. At one point, he got tired of just watching and asked his sister to hook them up. What twelve year old asks to be hooked up with a sixteen year old? Obie, a twelve year old with moxie; a twelve year old with a little confidence, a little conviction, a lot of charm, and somewhere deep down working its way to the surface, endless tenacity. These were characteristics that apparently got the girl and characteristics that provided the necessary tools to navigate a prison world in which he did not belong.

As the story goes, the hook-up was one kiss; not a deep one. Actually, it was more of a lip-peck, but for Obie, a memorable lip-peck. They had no way of knowing there would be only a few more times that they would run into each other and maybe a few more times when Obie could watch Denise from afar. It was seven years after that first tentative kiss that Obie would be wrongfully convicted and sent to prison, and another fourteen years after that before Denise would re-enter Obie's world.

After The Kiss

As Told By Denise Anthony

I don't remember how the kiss happened. I don't remember how we started kissing, but we were on Colden Avenue at the back of the apartment. There we kissed. It wasn't a deep kiss or anything. It was like a test kiss, just to see, I guess, if we would do it and what it would be like. It's funny because, when I asked Obie if he remembers how we got to that kiss, he doesn't remember either. But we both remember the kiss.

I was sixteen years old, and Obie was twelve when we first met. The first time I saw Obie he was riding a scooter outside. I also used to see him at his mother's house when I was visiting his sister, Yolanda. She and I were friends. And that's how I would see Obie, either at his mother's house or riding his scooter in the neighborhood. That's about it. We didn't talk much, but I knew when he would ride on his scooter near the house he was always looking at me. We were never boyfriend and girlfriend. I found out somehow that Obie wanted his sister to hook us up. We didn't hook up though, we just had that kiss.

We continued to see each other around the neighborhood after that kiss, for about six or eight months. But then after that, I didn't see Obie. It seemed like he just disappeared. I thought maybe he was at camp or something. But I didn't know.

My brother Curtis, who had been in a fight, was sent to the same prison where Obie would eventually end up. Curtis surprised me in one of our regular phone calls telling me that he found somebody from the neighborhood there. It was Obie. He had been transferred to Calipatria and strangely ended up being my brother's cellie. We all grew up near each other, in the same neighborhood, on the same street. My brother Mark knew Obie because they were about the same age and kind of hung out with the same folks, but Curtis really didn't know Obie that well. They would just see each other around the neighborhood, and that was it.

Being cellies, in one of their conversations my name had come up. Curtis called me and said, "Guess who's here?" and I said

"Who?" Curtis said "Obie." I was surprised. I asked him, "Does he get any visits? Who's taking care of him?" But Curtis didn't know. About two weeks later, Curtis called again. We talked a little bit and then I asked him to put Obie on the phone.

Obie got on the phone and I was able to get all the answers to my questions, like who was taking care of him, if he had any visitors. I was really making sure that there was no girlfriend or anybody like that. I wasn't trying to be his girlfriend. I was trying to find him a girlfriend; someone to take care of him.

I was married, but I had fallen out of love with my husband. There was nothing that you could pinpoint as to why. I just fell out of love, and the feeling was mutual with my husband at the time. He fell out of love too. At this point I was secretly kind of excited to just talk with Obie. I kind of liked him back then when we were young, even though he was twelve. There was just something about him. But I was married, and I really at this point wanted to be his friend. Especially since there was no one visiting him or sending him stuff he needed.

I was a little nervous at first to talk with Obie. I hadn't talked to or seen him in a long time. I think it was about twenty-two years since the last time we saw each other. I knew that I wanted to talk with him, though. I wanted to see how he was doing.

I decided to go see Obie. I took my niece so that we could call out both Obie and Curtis. I was extremely nervous. When I got to the prison, and they called Obie out, he was behind the glass. I wasn't expecting this because I thought I would see him like I would see Curtis, sitting at a table in the visiting room. But he was behind that glass. I was really nervous, my heart felt like it could come out of my chest it was beating so hard, and I think my hands were trembling. I went to sit and talk with Obie, and when I started talking my nervousness went away. But I could see that Obie was a bit nervous himself. When he talked, I could see that he was trembling too.

We talked about his sentencing, and we talked about that kiss. Then Obie said, "Tell me something that you've never told anyone else before." I replied, "I have not been happy in my relationship." Then I asked him to tell me something that he never told anyone. He said "My daughter, Latoya, is not my biological daughter." It felt good to share with each other things that no one else knew. We continued to talk and reminisce about our lives; what was going on back then, and about my life now. We had a really nice time.

Honestly I was trying to find out if he had a girlfriend. When he said "no," I was happy and disappointed at the same time. Disappointed that no one was taking care of him, but really happy that no one was because then I could. I told him that I would come and visit, he just needed to send me the visitor papers. I would fill them out and send them back right away. I also told him that I was going to send him a little something in the package I would be sending to my brother. I told him to ask Curtis to give him what I put in the box for him.

I had asked a friend of mine to fill out a visitation form to see Obie, and had hoped that they would like each other. I thought she could be Obie's girlfriend. But that was then, and here it was now. After talking with Obie and seeing him and remembering that kiss, I started to change my mind about my friend coming to visit Obie. In fact, when I returned home, my intention was to tell her never mind.

Before reconnecting with Obie, I used to visit my brother about once every other month, maybe sometimes every three months. But when Obie reappeared I would talk with him all the time. I began to go to the prison every weekend. It was difficult for me at first, just because I was at the prison visiting Obie instead of visiting my brother. That was kind of hard. They won't let you visit more than one person at a time. So I didn't see my brother that often, at least in the beginning. Eventually I began taking my nieces with me. In this way we could call out both of them. My niece would visit with Curtis while I would visit with Obie. Eventually we would be able to sit closer together and then I could talk to both. It was also kind of hard because I had learned to drive not too long before I knew Obie was in prison. I was not going to drive the highway. So I asked that same friend who I wanted to meet Obie, to come with me to the prison. She always drove, but soon she would have conflicts and I wanted to see Obie, so I learned how to manage the highway.

My first visit with Obie was behind the window. I don't know why, there seemed to be some kind of mix-up or something. I don't really know what happened, but after that first visit we were able to sit together at a table. This made it much easier for us of course. As the guards got to know me better they would often put my brother and Obie at tables near each other so we could all talk.

From that first visit I felt close to Obie. I wanted to take care of him. I felt like he needed to be taken care of and I wanted to be the person to do that. From that first visit I was at the prison every weekend. The only time I didn't go was when the prison was on lockdown. I didn't know this at first. I loved going to visit him every weekend and sometimes I wanted to surprise him. He told me not to do that, though, because I might get there when they were on lockdown. I learned this the hard way. I did go there one weekend to surprise him and the prison was on lockdown. I wasted my whole weekend, but it didn't matter because, the closer I was to him, the better I felt.

Since I had my own business, it wasn't hard to visit Obie every weekend. It was costly though. Gas wasn't cheap and we stayed in a hotel for two nights which cost eighty-seven dollars a night. I was able to manage. It's funny how we can always manage the things we want to do no matter how difficult or demanding it may seem. On some visits I would make the trips to Calipatria by myself and the other times with my nieces. It was a long drive but it didn't bother me at all. Some visits I was there for three nights when there was a holiday. I would usually take my nieces on these visits and we would sleep in the car on the first night and then stay in the hotel for the next two nights. I had a lot of nieces and they all got a chance to go with me. I think they liked it. It was an adventure.

The more I visited Obie, the stronger my feelings for him became. We talked about everything and he taught me some things. I was never bored and always, always looked forward to seeing him. I never got tired of driving all that way. I looked forward to each and every weekend as if it was what got me through the five days that I wasn't able to see him. And I like my work. We played cards and checkers and we just had a lot of fun together. During the week we might talk at least a couple of times. I think Obie was a little worried about the money I was spending to see him, but I knew it made him happy to see me, and to talk to me. It was never a problem for me. I always hoped that I was bringing a little joy into his life. I wanted him to be secure in knowing that I was going to be there for him no matter what. I would send him packages whenever he asked me, stocked with clothes and shoes and music and whatever else he needed. Didn't matter what, I just made sure he would have what he needed. I made sure he was cared for.

Because I knew it was the right thing to do, it was time to have a conversation with my husband. It was at the right time to talk to my husband about our relationship, because I was beginning to have deeper feelings for Obie. My husband and I talked and we decided it was time to end it. It was easier than I thought because he wasn't happy with our relationship either. So we separated in 2008. Our divorce was final in 2012.

The separation, and later the divorce, made it easier to be freer with Obie. We began dedicating songs to each other on the radio. It was Art Leboe who helped us share our love through music when we could not see each other or talk with each other. He was an old school DJ for Hot 92.3 Los Angeles radio. He was a really good DJ. He opened the dedication lines to both call-ins and write-ins. It allowed Obie to write in dedications to me that I would get to hear about two weeks later. He was really good about that for anybody who couldn't call in. Obie and I dedicated love songs and slow jams to each other as often as we could. We both listened to the radio all the time waiting for our dedications. We also wrote letters to each other, and after a while the weird thing was we would answer each other's questions long before we got the questions in the letters we sent to each other. It was as if we could read each other's minds, the connection to each other was so strong.

When I think back on those days, I believe there always has been a place in my heart for Obie. During the time that we talked to each other while he was in prison, my feelings for him grew. As we spent more time together I never doubted that we would be together. That was never a question, and I was never worried that he wouldn't get out of prison. Obie wasn't a murderer and I knew he was innocent. I was sure he would get out, and I was sure we would be together.

I was saddened to learn that no-one was visiting Obie. He cared deeply for his family, and I was surprised that they never went to see him. I worked on them to come with me to visit Obie. It didn't happen right away, but I did get them to come with me. It made Obie happy and that was good.

Obie is a good man. Very loyal and loving and appreciative of everything that I ever did for him. It's hard to find good men like that. I'd like to believe that my care helped him make it through prison. We got married a year after Obie was released. It was a flash wedding at the courthouse. I am extremely happy and so is Obie. We are tremendously happy.

Obie is trying hard to find a job. He wants to be able to support us and we want to start a family. It's difficult for him because of the length of time he has been without a job; all of those years in prison. But I know he'll find something just as strongly as I knew he would get out of prison. I stuck by him then, and I will continue to stick by him. It's my way.

* * *

On September 30, 2011, Judge Kelvin Filer vacated Obie Anthony's conviction after hearing evidence of John Jones's false testimony. Judge Filer also found that the prosecution had intentionally withheld important and potentially exculpatory evidence from the defense. Testimony by Detective Winn and Arthur Jones contained incorrect information, the prosecution did not correct at trial. While no defendant is entitled to a perfect trial, Judge Filer found there were so many "instances of prosecutorial misconduct and other legal errors" that the total effect was to preclude Obie from having a fair trial. He walked out of Twin Towers jail in Los Angeles on October 4, 2011.

Reflecting back, and as unbelievable as it may sound, Obie is grateful for his time in prison, if only because he learned so much about himself and about the mistakes he made as a young man. His attitude may seem bizarre to someone who has never been imprisoned, but it is not that unusual for an exoneree.

* * *

Obie was very disappointed that his family didn't visit him or communicate with him very often while he was in prison. Initially,

Denise was his only visitor and it was Denise who got Obie's sisters to finally come visit him.

Obie found out that Yolanda lied about having a tumor and seizures. She didn't have a tumor and she'd been faking the seizures since she was a little girl to keep from getting whippings. If not for her lies, Obie would not have moved back to Los Angeles. He would not have fallen back into old bad habits. He would not have been in a position to be accused, sentenced, and imprisoned for a crime he never committed. Yet, Obie sees the benefit in his prison experience. He feels that he is a better person for all of it. He's even reconciled himself with Yolanda's behavior. Although he thinks his sister is a little whacky, as he says, he still loves her to death.

His sister's lying, his life in prison, and his mother's wisdom were his downfall and his uplifting. "It tore me up," he says pensively, "but at the same time it sewed me up. An amazing process."

Obie is in college now working towards a degree in psychology. The most difficult thing for him has been getting a job. It's tough to explain to potential employers the lengthy gap and his lack of employment history. He wants terribly to a have a job to support his family and to get health benefits. That is Obie, ever the caretaker. The other hard thing is the realization that he has no reserves set aside. Not working means no payments into the social security fund. This weighed heavily on Obie's mind as his fortieth birthday approached.

Since his exoneration, Obie has become an advocate with the Innocence Network by speaking and volunteering or in an administrative capacity. He really enjoys the investigative work he has been doing on cases and plans to continue helping when and where he can. As long as he can speak to and educate the public on wrongful conviction and be a part of the Innocence Network, Obie will be happy.

When asked what he wanted to do the minute he was free, the only thing Obie wanted was to see and be with Denise. He wanted nothing more than this in that very moment and every other moment since, except he also wanted to take Denise to a Lakers game, which he did!

Obie and Denise were married in a civil ceremony in Los Angeles in September 2012.

In his order of September 30, 2011, Judge Filer stated that Obie had not met his burden of establishing his actual innocence under the standard applicable to innocence claims at that time, which required that he undermine the prosecution's entire case and point unerringly to his innocence with evidence no reasonable jury could reject. Until Obie could establish his actual innocence, he would not be eligible for compensation by the State of California for his wrongful conviction. On February 4, 2014, Obie's attorneys petitioned the court to find Obie actually innocent under a new process the legislature had adopted recently. Subsequent to his exoneration in 2011, the California legislature passed a law that would allow the court to find actual innocence if a preponderance of the evidence shows innocence. The petition reiterated the evidence of innocence presented during his 2011 hearing, including the lack of any physical evidence against Obie; descriptions of the shooters that did not match Obie's description at the time; the inconsistencies in testimony of the prosecution's primary witness, John Jones; and misconduct by the prosecutors and police, including withholding exculpatory evidence.

On May 30, 2014, Judge Filer found that, by a preponderance of the evidence, Obie was not involved in the murder of Felipe Gonzales Angeles or the shooting and beating of Victor Trejo and Luis Jimenez. The order stated "...the Court hereby finds that Obie Steven Anthony III is innocent of the charges for which he was erroneously convicted on August 1, 1995..." Obie and his lawyers have filed for compensation from the State of California. They are hopeful that the State will do right by Obie, but they also know it may take years before the State decides to do the right thing.

Obie and Denise Anthony live in Southern California. When he is not studying, Obie advocates for the rights of the wrongfully convicted and against the death penalty. In 2013, he testified before the California Legislature in support of new laws to protect innocent people from wrongful conviction and make it easier for the innocent to receive compensation from the State. Governor Brown signed SB 618 in October 2013.

CHAPTER 4

Fernando Bermudez

Little Mouse

A Poem by Fernando Bermudez

Little mouse,
Where are you tonight?
You sneak into my cell,
Explore, relax and bite.

Little mouse, I hate you.
You're fast, elusive, free.
Please skip my cell. Go elsewhere.
I have enough misery.

Honestly, I'm frustrated
At all the things you do.
One day I'll getcha, if not with a
Trap or my hands, with a shoe.

Recently, you entered my cell,
An intruder better off dead.
Last week you ate my cookies,
Yesterday, my bread.

Things would be easier
If you could tell me what you want
Rather than visiting my cell
As if it were a restaurant.

What makes me mad,
What makes me sick,
Is the time you and your friends
Peed, ate and left me shit.

You must've thought it funny to add
Insult to injury with such a nasty exchange
But I forgave you not once, but twice.
Now I'm full of rage.

Little mouse, I'm telling you,
You won't last long.
You'll scream when you least expect it.
Then you'll be gone.

That's how I feel and
I can't be hushed.
Your existence will soon end.
It will end with a flush.

* * *

The scene at the Marc Ballroom in Lower Manhattan on the night of August 3, 1991 was no different than any other Saturday night at the club. A mostly young crowd jammed onto the dance floor, gyrating to the thrumming bass line the dancers could feel pulsing through their bodies. Men and women congregated by the bar, some hooking up for the night. The club goers had no idea their party scene would end with one young man, Raymond Blount, dead and another young man, Fernando Bermudez, wrongfully convicted of killing him.

Sixteen-year-old Efraim Lopez was enjoying the five-day work release furlough he had earned just that morning. Lopez was serving time for stealing cars, but was one of the fortunate inmates who could work outside of prison, so long as he stuck to the rules. One rule was a 10:00 p.m. curfew every night while he was home. Since it was almost midnight, Lopez was violating that curfew. He hit the club earlier that evening to celebrate his five days of freedom and was having so much fun dancing and hanging with his friends he didn't even think about the time.

On the other end of Manhattan, over ten miles away in a neighborhood called Inwood, twenty-two year old Fernando Bermudez, nicknamed "Most," was hanging out at home with his friends, to-

[handwritten margin notes: "what Happend?", "how can you do that?"]

tally unaware of what was happening at the club. Fernando had a lot of close friends in the neighborhood. They did what most young people did—hang out together, go to parties, and have fun. Fernando was a self-described "dater." He loved going out on dates. "Yes, I had a nice close knit circle of friends," he said, "and we had a lot of fun together and did a lot of dating. My favorite pastime was dating. I really enjoyed dating. I really enjoyed that."

[handwritten margin note: Sounds Like A Rep of it rentoreller]

Back in Lower Manhattan, Raymond Blount, another sixteen-year-old young man, was standing on the other side of the club talking with some friends and taking in the scene on the dance floor. Like many of the young people out that night, Blount was there to see and be seen. As the evening wore on, Blount made his way around the club, stopping occasionally to talk to friends or dance with a pretty girl. Sometime around midnight, Blount saw Lopez dancing with a girl. Blount said something to the guy standing next to him and pointed at Lopez. The two men approached Lopez and his dancing partner. Lopez stopped dancing.

"Do you know me?" Lopez asked.

Before anyone knew what was happening, Blount punched Lopez in the face. Some of the people nearby jumped in to stop the fight. The club's bouncers took both young men outside, but let them back into the club a few moments later after they had both cooled off a bit. Lopez had a bruise on his cheek and the beginnings of a black eye.

[handwritten margin note: Storted It]

"Shorty," one of Lopez's buddies chuckled, "bru' jacked you up, man."

[handwritten margin note: Instigation]

"You awright, Pito," asked another of Lopez's friends. "C'mon, let's go to the john and get you straight. You cain't go home lookin' like dat."

Lopez stopped to use the payphone in the club to call his grandmother and tell her he'd been in a fight. Blount went back to his friends on the other side of the dance floor. Instead of getting cleaned up and going home, Lopez stayed at the club with his friends. About thirty minutes after calling his grandmother, Lopez saw fellow Puerto Rican Luis Muñoz in the club for the first time that evening. Lopez knew Muñoz from the neighborhood, for nearly two years, by his nicknames "Lou" and "Wool Lou." The twenty-one-year-old

Muñoz sold crack in the park near Lopez's grandmother's house on West Ninety-First Street, where Lopez had seen him earlier that evening. The crack cocaine Muñoz sold was rolled up in tobacco called "wool" on the street. Crackheads would twitch their way up to Muñoz and whisper, "you got that wool, Lou?" Sometimes they'd just ask, "Wool, Lou?" and the name stuck—Wool Lou.

At nearly six feet, Wool Lou was tall for a Puerto Rican and slim at a hundred and sixty-five pounds. That night Wool Lou wore beige shorts and a white t-shirt with black designs on the front. He had a large gold Gucci gold rope chain around his neck with a big medallion hanging from it. His hair was styled in a fade with the sides cut close and the top high and full and he had acne.

"Damn, man!" Muñoz exclaimed when he saw Lopez's face. "What the hell happened to yo' face?"

"I was in a fight, man."

"Bru', you just got outta juvie today and you already in a fight? Who with?"

Pointing at Blount and tilting his head, Lopez replied, "That dude over there, the one in the brown hat, clocked me when I wasn't lookin'."

Last call at the club was at around 3:00 a.m. Folks started leaving but hung around out front. Lopez and Wool Lou were among them. A few minutes later, Blount walked outside with some friends. "That mofo still here," Lopez muttered. Wool Lou asked Lopez again which guy punched him. Lopez cocked his chin in the direction where Blount was talking with a group of friends, and said "like I told you, that mofo in the brown hat."

"I got a lil' somethin' for him," Wool Lou said. He walked over to a black Nissan Pathfinder and spoke to someone sitting inside. The Pathfinder moved slowly to block in Blount and his friends. As soon as the Pathfinder was in place, Wool Lou jogged over to where Blount stood. When Wool Lou pulled a gun from behind his back, Blount's friends scattered. Wool Lou held the gun sideways like he'd seen gangbangers do in movies, and shot Blount in the stomach. The scene was chaotic. Clubbers were scattering as Blount tried to run down the street. Not long after he collapsed, an ambulance came to take Blount to St. Vincent's Hospital, where he later died. Lopez and

Wool Lou immediately went their separate ways. The police arrived and identified seven people who witnessed some part of the events related to the shooting.

Over the next two days the police began to put together what happened at the Marc Ballroom early that Sunday morning. Some of the witnesses knew Lopez as "Shorty," and identified him as the guy who got into a fight with the dead man. On the day after the fatal shooting, the police brought Lopez in for questioning. They held him for more than a day without sleep until he made a videotaped statement, a statement that contradicted in many respects the written statements he'd made earlier during his interrogation. Lopez described what Muñoz had been wearing the night of the fatal shooting. He noted that the shooter had acne but did not recall any facial hair. When questioned on videotape by Assistant District Attorney (ADA) James Rodriguez and Detective Daniel Massanova, Lopez initially insisted he didn't know Wool Lou.

> *ADA Rodriguez*: And what kind of relationship did you have with him? Were you friends with him? Were you friends with him, did you talk with him?
>
> *Lopez*: There was no relationship, but I knew his name. He name was Lou and...
>
> *ADA Rodriguez*: Lou?
>
> *Lopez*: Yeah. They used to call him "Wool" Lou.
>
> *Det. Massanova*: Woo...Wool Lou?
>
> *Lopez*: Wool.
>
> *Det. Massanova*: Like, "wool?" Like, "wool?"
>
> *Lopez*: Yeah, be...
>
> *Det. Massanova*: "Wool," "Lou?"
>
> *Lopez*: Yeah, becau...yeah, because crack, they call it wools. So that's what he was selling.

Det. Massanova: What, the little vials of crack are called wools?

Lopez: Wools. So that's why they named him "Wool" Lou. You understand. That's why...

When asked to spell the name, Lopez answered "w-o-o-l-l-u." When asked if "lu" stood for anything, Lopez replied "It's probably his nickname. I don't know." During this exchange Detective Massanova also asked Lopez if he knew of anyone named "Most." Lopez shook his head and replied "no."

The police issued material witness warrants for seven teenagers who were at the club the night of the murder. The teens described "Shorty" and the shooter. As a group, they described the shooter as wearing a t-shirt (described as "white" and also as "black and white"), holding a gun in his hand, and wearing a gold medallion. The police should have questioned each eyewitness separately and not allowed them to influence each other as a group reaching consensus on the shooter's description. Nevertheless, that's what they did. The eyewitnesses agreed that the shooter was a good-looking Puerto Rican man with a light goatee (one said a mustache that grew into a goatee), approximately five foot eleven and weighed about one-hundred and sixty-five pounds. Fernando Bermudez is Dominican and at the time of the shooting he was six foot two and weighed two hundred and twenty pounds. He had a thick, bushy mustache, no beard or goatee, and no acne.

"I want you to look at these photos here in front of you," the detective told the eyewitnesses, "and decide which one you think is responsible."

This instruction is exactly what the eyewitness administrator is *not* supposed to say. What the detective should have said is: "The person who committed the crime may or may not be present. Do not assume I know who the perpetrator is. I want you to focus on the photo array and not ask me or anyone else in the room for guidance during the procedure." The only other people in the room while an eyewitness is viewing the photos should be police personnel, *not* other eyewitnesses.

[handwritten margin notes:] False → descriptions

should've been key →

This whole thing is a problem with the witnesses are false descriptions *who are they are they the witnesses?*

Terrence Hall, Nkosi Boyce, and Lawrence Darden were given drawers of photos and told to look through them to see if anyone looked like Shorty. The three teens were close friends of Blount and had been standing right next to him just before Wool Lou shot him. *Arrow* Jaime Velasquez, Okpa Iyesi, Frank Kent, and Michael Thompson were given drawers of photos and told to look through them to see if anyone looked like the shooter. The eyewitnesses began looking through the photos. After a while, Darden picked up a photo and looked at it. "I found Shorty!" he shouted, waving the photo in the air.

Iyesi, looking over Darden's shoulder, also recognized Lopez. "That's him! That's him!" Iyesi exclaimed.

"I know that's him," said Darden. "That's him. That's the one that got beat up."

The detective told Darden not to show the others the photo and warned the eyewitnesses not to talk to each other, but it was already too late. Iyesi had seen the photo and everyone had heard the two of them talking about what they saw.

Not long after that, Velasquez, the only female witness, found two photos. "Who is the cutie?" she asked, holding up a photo of Fernando Bermudez. The rest of the witnesses began looking at and discussing Fernando's photo with her. The detective took Velasquez out of the room to another office where she identified Fernando as the shooter or someone who looked like him. She told the detective "this is the guy who shot the guy." While Velasquez was out of the room, the police generated a photo six-pack that included a photo of Fernando and showed it to all of the remaining witnesses. Not surprisingly, the three who had been with Velasquez identified Fernando as the shooter. The three who had not been with Velasquez, however, did not identify Fernando. Despite the inconsistency, those identifications were enough for the police. They ended the identification procedure and issued a warrant for the arrest of Fernando Bermudez.

The next day, Fernando was included in a seated lineup. Again, the eyewitnesses were left together prior to the lineup although each entered the room alone to view the seated lineup. No one commented on Fernando's full mustache and lack of a goatee or acne. Again,

57

the witnesses identified Fernando as the shooter. Because he and the other lineup participants were seated, the eyewitnesses had no way of knowing that Fernando was taller and heavier than the man they had described as the shooter.

After the line-up, Fernando was charged with the murder of Raymond Blount. Towards the end of his trial, Fernando's lawyer learned of the existence of Luis Muñoz when the prosecution turned over interrogation transcripts and videotapes they had been withholding, but the lawyer's private detective could not locate Muñoz. The prosecution team suspected that Muñoz had something to do with the shooting, but by the start of the trial they had not tried to connect Muñoz to Wool Lou. The prosecution's evidence at trial consisted of Lopez's testimony and eyewitness identification and the testimony of the other eyewitnesses, that Fernando was the shooter. When questioned on the stand, Lopez pointed to Fernando, seated at the defense table, and identified him as Wool Lou, the shooter. The defense called witnesses, including Fernando, to testify that Fernando was nowhere near the Marc Ballroom at the time of the murder. The jury discounted this as the testimony of friends who did not want to see Fernando go to jail. On February 6, 1992, after eleven days of testimony and closing arguments, the jury found Fernando guilty of Blount's murder.

After the jury rendered its verdict and before the judge sentenced Fernando, a private detective hired by the Fernando's lawyer, contacted Detective Massanova to report he had information that Luis Muñoz was the real Wool Lou. By then, Fernando's lawyer had reviewed the interrogation transcripts and videotapes that the prosecution had held back until the last minute. The private detective knew Muñoz's address on West Ninety-First Street, which he gave to Detective Massanova. The police detective promised to follow up on the information saying, "I'd be negligent if I didn't follow up on this lead." The private detective believed Muñoz had fled New York after the shooting.

True to his word, Detective Massanova relayed the defense detective's information to ADA Rodriguez prior to Fernando's sentencing. ADA Rodriguez already had an inkling that Lopez had lied on the stand and that he actually did know Wool Lou's identity. It is possible the ADA suspected that Fernando was not Wool Lou. The timing is critical because the ADA could have contacted the judge to delay sentencing until the police detectives had time to investigate this new information. Had ADA Rodriguez done that, not only would Fernando have been released from jail, he also would not have a record because the judge would have vacated the jury verdict and the charges against Fernando would have been dropped. Instead, ADA Rodriguez opposed the defense team's claim that Muñoz was the shooter.

ADA Rodriguez bears much of the responsibility for the interruption of Fernando's life plans, but he also shirked his professional duty. As an officer of the court, a prosecutor has a duty to the court to correct testimony known to be false. ADA Rodriguez had cut a deal with Lopez protecting Lopez from prosecution in connection with the shooting if he testified against Fernando. Telling the judge that he thought Lopez had lied about Fernando being Wool Lou would have put the conviction—a "win" for the prosecution—at risk. Without Lopez's identification of Fernando, ADA Rodriguez might not have been able to prosecute anyone for the crime. Instead of choosing to meet his duty as a prosecutor, ADA Rodriguez chose to keep the truth from the court and on September 18, 1992, the judge gave Fernando a sentence of twenty-three years to life. Fernando was sent to prison and almost immediately the prosecution's case started to unravel. Within a year of Fernando's sentencing, the eyewitnesses began recanting their testimony, but it was too late. The judge didn't believe the recantations and ADA Rodriguez was still insisting that Fernando Bermudez and Wool Lou were the same person. Courts are reluctant to accept an eyewitness recantation, suspecting instead that the witness might have been coerced or felt guilty about being instrumental in sending someone to prison.

Born to Fernando (Frank) and Daniela Bermudez, immigrants from the Dominican Republic, Fernando grew up in the predominantly Dominican Upper Manhattan neighborhood of Inwood, not far from the Bronx. Fernando was the oldest of five children in a close knit and loving family. His father worked in the parking garage business, and his mother was a stay at home mom until she began cleaning houses after Fernando was incarcerated. They were a de-

what?

voted Catholic family living a healthy and loving life. Their devastation when Fernando was convicted was the start of the unraveling of their tight-knit family unit.

Fernando may have described himself as a "dater" and he may have loved dating, but there was more to him than that. Fernando also had dreams. He had enrolled in Bronx Community College to study medicine, "I was on the verge of entering the medical profession with hopes and dreams of making my family proud and contributing to society when I was arrested and I was no longer able to pursue that goal."

It would take Fernando more than eighteen years and eleven hearings to convince a judge of his innocence. During that time, Fernando never gave up hope that he would prove his innocence and regain his freedom. During those years, Fernando was sent to seven different prisons, spending the most time and his last years in the infamous Sing Sing. The challenges facing innocent people in prison are often insurmountable. In most cases, like Fernando's, there is no DNA evidence. These are the most difficult cases of innocence to prove. In the face of this impossible challenge, how did Fernando continue to believe he would convince a judge of his innocence and be released from prison? What sustained him through more than eighteen years behind bars?

Although it is hard to imagine in this horrific situation, there can be some light in the darkest of days. Not long after his conviction, Fernando met and married his wife, Crystal, while in prison. Because of his good behavior, Fernando and Crystal were given family time every few weeks, when they were allowed time together alone in a mobile home on the prison grounds. Fernando and Crystal had three children during those incarcerated years—an unusual occurrence, but salvation for Fernando. His wife and children, along with his parents, are the joys of his life. They are the main reasons he remained hopeful during his years in prison, even in the face of repeated losses in hearing after hearing.

Through the Eyes of My Children

By Fernando Bermudez

Is this his as he is in Prison

Poets and philosophers alike have marveled over experiencing the world through the eyes of children, as if food for one's soul. Whenever I saw my three children, while in prison, they nourished me beyond what prison deprived me of. They offered pure joy and innocence in a world torn by contradictions. Their love and hope consoled me. They inspired purpose and meaning in our struggle to repair our family's broken unity, until, after completing over eighteen years of a life sentence in prison, my actual innocence was proven.

The first nudge towards that repair, thanks to my wife, Crystal, came with our oldest daughter, Chayla. Early in my incarceration the idea of "Daddy's Little Girl" developed by exchanging letters, drawings and books with Chayla. Excited about being a father, I attended parenting classes inside New York State prisons through the Osborne Association, which offered parenting strategies to help incarcerated men and women become better parents. I learned how teenage peer pressure can trump parental influence. This echoed my own rebel yell many moons ago; it also drew me closer to Chayla, close enough to ask her for Usher and Chris Brown-style dance lessons to supplement my somewhat outdated robot moves.

Chayla was a good big sister to my second daughter, Carissa. During their visits, she helped keep Carissa calm while Crystal handled the stressful processing correctional officers would put visitors through. This eased the prison-visit registration process for my wife and me, which in turn, allowed us to take early advantage of the prison vending machines before pushy crowds devoured all the best selections. We were able to share vending machine food as a family, which gave me a break from the less than appetizing food served in the prison mess halls. Who would not want to skip hockey puck Salisbury steak or Hungarian goulash that left you hungry because it was nasty and no one wanted to eat it? I sure didn't miss the chicken cacciatore that required a dessert course of Pepto-Bismol!

Our second daughter, Carissa, was born in 2001. Many considered Carissa's birth a symbol of new hope. I agreed, for Carissa's birth juxtaposed loss and grief with renewal, love with hate, and justice with injustice. Carissa was born right after the September 11 terrorist attacks and at a time when a promising appeal of my wrongful conviction was underway. Consequently, I baptized Carissa with tears of joy and appreciation and with hope that my wrongful conviction would be overturned and set me free.

There is a Portuguese proverb that says, "Provide a nest and your woman will lay an egg." Even with two children, our growing family felt incomplete without a boy. Crystal and I kept the stork flying, so to speak, until my son Fernando was born in 2005. Together our greatest family happiness in prison came from New York State's Family Reunion Program, or FRP, visits.

FRP visit privileges are granted to New York state prisoners who have exhibited good behavior and completed certain prison programs. Well behaved inmates are rewarded with greater freedom, privacy, and quality time with family members inside a trailer that replicates a home-like setting on prison grounds. There, released from the grip of prison realties—violence, deprivation, stress, and bad attitudes—we were able to create priceless good memories. My children participated in FRP visits every fifty to one-hundred days or so, thanks again to Crystal who, as our family CEO, fought poverty and near homelessness to ensure their arrival for the FRP visits.

A typical visit involved Carissa pushing Fernando in his stroller with Chayla carting groceries and Crystal and me pulling heavy suitcases that I'd haul into the FRP trailer. Amid palpable excitement, I'd watch Fernando, wearing his "Proud to be Loud" T-shirt, wobble as he carried vegetables to the refrigerator, and Carissa as she climbed onto the counter to shelve items passed to her by Chayla. Crystal, meanwhile, railed at the prison system about the unsanitary conditions of the trailer. Not unlike at home, I imagined, Crystal made sure that everything in the trailer was hospital clean, requiring that we all abide by her "hot water" rule; no exceptions, no escape! All chores completed, Crystal would prepare the most delicious food I had ever tasted within prison walls. I was able to eat as much as I wanted without being embarrassed.

One thing about FRP benefits was that I was able eat Crystal's wonderful food. Her FRP recipes ranged from tender garlic and pineapple chicken with buttered asparagus on soft pillows of brown rice to fried okra and ox tails marinated in her secret sauce, or her delicious fried chicken and fried fish. These gastronomical delights contrasted with the bad prison food I ate whenever I was unable to cook in my cell with the higher quality food I purchased in the prison store. Canned roast beef and beans cooked into a seasoned stew using my prison hot pot was just one of my recipes for me and other prisoners. Hot pot cooking allowed me to make a little money. Prisoners provided the canned food I needed to prepare the dish. Selling this food allowed me to send money home to Crystal and my kids. I was also able to save money and purchase books and clothing wholesale that I'd in turn sell at retail in prison to help me remain self-sufficient.

Some of my other prison recipes were ramen noodles and canned salmon with beans, fresh garlic and onions, or cheesy spaghetti mixed with oysters, garbanzo beans and cashews. I also made canned mackerel, a prison favorite when fried with battered corn flakes and cheese crackers. I typically used the top of a metal can to cut vegetables. I'd get the can from the prison kitchen where I worked to advance my cooking contracts and where I found peaceful solitude; that is, until correctional guards staged their regular raids of my prison cell. In a cell shakeup anything the guards deemed dangerous would disappear, like my can opener which, as a rather useful and valuable utensil, was an unfortunate loss. However difficult it might have been, prison cooking helped me. Through the wondrous smells from my hot pot and listening to music on my Walkman and the almost hypnotic rhythm of slicing and dicing of the food, I was able to meditate.

FRP visits brought me even greater peace, than cooking. Bonding with my children and cooking on the prison barbecue pit, despite guard towers and barbed wire fences surrounding us, brought a needed calm. We would chase stray cats, play hide and seek, and use tented bed sheets for makeshift shelters. I loved playing make-believe with my children. Sometimes they tied me up as if I were Lemuel Gulliver in Jonathan Swift's imaginary land of Lilliput. Other times we'd wrestle from room to room, Chayla pounding me with the strength of a lightweight boxer until I shot baby powder as a smoke screen to aid in my escape. There'd also be time to practice my new dance moves until sourpusses and confused faces pleading "Dad please quit," would stop me in my tracks.

I usually helped my children with their homework, drilling them on their vocabulary words. I also talked with my children about their misbehavior, explaining why some behavior was wrong. No approach guarantees success, I've found, but discussing concerns with children can help them feel loved enough to make less selfish choices.

During FRP visits, I especially appreciated my children's wake up calls full of bedside hugs and kisses. At times my son in his irresistible nature would be missing a sock or endearingly rubbing sleep out of his eyes. These flashbacks are reminiscent of other cherished moments—when Chayla first reunited with me and shyly said hi; when Carissa pointed to the sky saying, "burr-burr!" as a bird flew by; and when I gave Fernando his very imperfect first haircut. I even cherished my children's burning questions on when I would be coming home; questions that only my freedom would truly answer. I despaired at not being able to give them the answers that we all wanted to hear. Their questions choked me up with anxiety and anger, burdening me with impatience.

Fortunately, in addition to parenting classes, the Osborne Association's Children Center at Sing Sing offered consolation for incarcerated parents by providing an enclosed area in the prison visiting room in which to spend time with their children. At this center, Fernando was able to cut paths with toy trucks, ramming my feet when not punching toy cash register buttons like a disgruntled cashier. Carissa drew and colored, and prepared rubber food while Chayla, if in an "I'm-too-cool-for-this" mood to play waitress, ventured to the computer and arts and crafts departments.

My family grew stronger this way, reinforcing that an involved father, even one behind bars, beats ten deadbeat dads any day. As a behavioral science major, I was greatly encouraged by scientific research indicating that fathers could reduce the risk of early sexual activity in their daughters by helping them raise their self-esteem. The research also showed that parents can be important role models by maintaining a healthy relationship with their children and each other, thereby reducing the risk of increased sexual activity in their teenage daughters. This is why I strove to communicate with my children, especially Chayla, who on the cusp of womanhood while I was incarcerated, deserved the best wisdom and care a father could provide.

All told, it was my honor and privilege to experience the world through the eyes of my children while in prison because I am my children and my children are me. I may never learn the best dance moves, but my children's energy and love still enhance parenthood for me. The injustice of being wrongfully convicted strengthened my resolve to leave prison not broken, but better. This resolution still nourishes me as an exonerated man in his fourth year of freedom who keeps a vigil in his heart. I share my hard-won story through the eyes of my children to encourage factually innocent prisoners to remain vigilant in their pursuit of freedom, to encourage society to demand a more just system for all of us, but mostly so that my social justice work will continue to be a legacy for my children.

* * *

In October 2009, Judge John Cataldo of the Supreme Court of New York County presided over Fernando's eleventh and final hearing. One objective of this hearing was to determine whether there was new evidence which, if it had been available at the time of the trial, would have resulted in a not guilty verdict. The defense team also believed at least one prosecutor knew that Lopez had lied on the stand and that this was known before Fernando had been sentenced. The defense team believed the police had not followed proper procedures for eyewitness identification and that the failure to do so violated Fernando's rights under the New York and United States Constitutions. Finally, the defense team believed Fernando was actually innocent. They did not want his conviction to be overturned only on technical errors, however significant those errors might be. The defense team wanted Judge Cataldo to find that Fernando was actually innocent on the basis of clear and convincing evidence.

This claim of new evidence illustrates the lengths to which some prosecutors will go to preserve a "win" and avoid admitting they convicted an innocent man. During the trial, the prosecution's theory was that Fernando Bermudez was the shooter, a theory based solely upon Lopez's perjured testimony. Before sentencing and on appeal the defense team repeatedly sought to enter evidence that Fernando was not Wool Lou and that Luis Muñoz was Wool Lou. Each time, the prosecution argued against this claim—until the 2009 hearing. The prosecution finally interviewed Luis Muñoz in 2007 and Muñoz admitted to being Wool Lou. At the 2009 hearing, the prosecution conceded that Fernando was not Wool Lou and that Luis Muñoz was Wool Lou. Amazingly, the prosecution argued that this was not new evidence because the defense had been making this claim all along and that it was too late to make the claim in any event. Judge Cataldo refused to accept the prosecution's argument calling it "unreasonable." Not willing to concede the point without a fight, the prosecution argued, after the hearing, that ADA Rodriguez acknowledged in his 2002 testimony that Luis Muñoz was Wool Lou. The question that elicited this information and the answer itself had been stricken from the record at the prosecution's insistence. Fortunately, Judge Cataldo saw through this subterfuge and refused to consider this testimony precisely because it had been stricken from the record. Judge Cataldo found that this was new evidence that probably would have resulted in a not guilty verdict.

Judge Cataldo did not stop there. He found that ADA Rodriguez knew, prior to Fernando's sentencing, that Lopez had lied on the stand. ADA Rodriguez knew that the shooter's name was Lou or Luis, not Fernando—evidence Judge Cataldo found to be material. "The failure to correct false or mistaken material testimony of a prosecution witness is a violation of a defendant's right to due process of the law," he wrote. On this second point, Judge Cataldo found that "the prosecutor knew, or should have known, that Efraim Lopez gave materially false evidence at trial, prior to the entry of judgment."

Judge Cataldo continued to review evidence and testimony, not content to leave the third and fourth questions unanswered. Considering Fernando had spent more than eighteen years in prison for a crime he did not commit, perhaps Judge Cataldo thought he deserved to have all four of the defense team's questions considered and answered. Given the epic failure of the NYPD to follow proper procedure in eyewitness identification, Judge Cataldo found the eyewitness identification procedures were unduly suggestive and that they "violated [Fernando's] rights under the New York Constitution." At trial, the witnesses were not positive of their identifications, using phrases like "fleeting glimpse," "I only glanced at him," and "saw him out of the corner of my eye," when describing what they saw the night of the shooting. Even if the identification procedures had not been unduly suggestive, the eyewitnesses recanted their testimony and Judge Cataldo found the recantations to be reliable. Judge Cataldo vacated Fernando's conviction, noting that under rules of criminal procedure, a new trial is the appropriate remedy. Judge Cataldo also noted that Fernando demonstrated his actual innocence and dismissed the indictment with prejudice, foreclosing the ability of the prosecution to re-try Fernando.

On the claim of actual innocence, Judge Cataldo reviewed all of the evidence in great detail to reach a finding of actual innocence and that evidence was plentiful. Efraim Lopez lied on the stand and the prosecution knew of it and conceded that Lopez lied. The eyewitness identifications were not reliable because of the improper identification procedures, the inconsistencies in physical characteristics of Fernando and Luis Muñoz, and the recantations of the eyewitnesses. The evidence that Muñoz was the actual shooter was credible and abundant. Judge Cataldo was unequivocal in his finding, stating "I find, by clear and convincing evidence that the defendant has demonstrated his actual innocence."

The final nail in the prosecution's case was the judge's conclusion: "Accordingly, the defendant's motion to vacate his conviction is granted and the indictment is dismissed with prejudice." Perhaps Judge Cataldo's thorough review and discussion of the facts is the reason the prosecution chose not to re-indict and re-try Fernando.

For Fernando, being exonerated and released from prison was the end of a nearly two-decade battle. Now that he is a free man, his struggle continues—the struggle to reclaim himself and his life. As when he was in prison, his family stands beside him, giving him strength. His youngest daughter, Carissa, understands that the struggle is not done.

The Fight for My Father

By Carissa Bermudez

has to have a traumatic effect on her ?

I was a few days old before I visited my first jail. I was there not to see one of my parent's friends but to see one of my parents. My mom, my big sister Chayla, and my little brother Fernando and I would visit my incarcerated father almost two times a month. Most kids are free to see their father almost every day; I didn't have that liberty. Your father is supposed to be your first love, but instead my first love was a man in a plain green shirt and pants—the "normal" clothes prisoners get to wear when they have family visits. Yeah, he was still my father, but he felt like a man I kept visiting who only built prison memories with me instead of playing with me in the park or taking me to eat ice cream in freedom.

I remember one time when I was in first grade visiting my dad on Father's Day. During that visit I drew a Father's Day card for him. I had used all my crayons to make my card special for my dad. I was so excited to give my dad the brightly colored card. When I handed it to him he looked at it, smiled, and kissed me, but said he could not keep it. I was only six years old, so I didn't understand why my dad couldn't keep the card. I realize now that he couldn't leave our temporary trailer home with anything from our prison visit or he'd get in trouble.

The prison rules were really strict and some of the guards were not very pleasant. Sometimes I would watch the prison guards be so rude to my mom. Some of the rules were about the clothes visitors could wear. A female visitor could not wear an underwire bra. If my mom was wearing the wrong bra she would have to walk almost a mile to the nearest store to get a new one, all while pushing my crying brother in his stroller joined by my teenage sister who had to be like my second mother because times were so tough. My family had to go through this ritual to see my father every two weeks this until one day just before recess in second grade I got called to leave school earlier than usual.

Now being an eight-year-old about to play with my friends at school I was upset. As I slowly walked down the hallway into the

68

main office I saw my sister's big smile. Her smile got bigger as we walked to my brother's preschool. I asked why she was picking me up so early. She smiled and replied, "Someone is coming home today!"

When I realized who that "someone" could be I gasped in excitement, twirled and squealed "Really?!" We rushed into my little brother's classroom where I jumped on him and laughed, "Someone's coming home!" He snatched his backpack up like we were headed for a free shopping spree in a toy store. After that we rushed home, laughing all the way. My mom called. She had gotten into trouble for leaving work early that day to go visit my dad. She told us to get the house cleaned up for our surprise visitor. Mom's parents had come all the way from Oklahoma and all of us cleaned and cleaned and cleaned, getting the house perfect for her, just the way she liked it. I don't know how long we cleaned, but after a few hours we heard a knock at the door. We ran to open the door, us kids stumbling over each other to get there first. What we saw wasn't exactly what I expected.

There stood my dad with TV cameras behind him, and he looked just as surprised as the shock we were feeling. We ran down the front stairs together and all three of us jumped in his arms and cried and kissed and hugged him with my mom like never before. A week earlier I had celebrated my eighth birthday. When I closed my eyes, I wished that my dad would come home, then I blew out the candles. My birthday wish had come true. My dad was free. I felt so happy that the kids at school would stop teasing me about having a fairytale dad. I also hoped that my dad coming home meant that my family would have a happy ending.

The truth is, some part of my dad remains in prison even though he is now free after his eighteen-year incarceration ended. As thrilled as I am to have him home, when he came home he didn't come home as the father I had hoped, prayed, and wished for. He returned with post-traumatic stress. I don't think he means to act strange, like when he spends hours alone in my little brother's small bedroom, or when I find him crying in our living room on days when I get up early for school. I am happy that I still have my dad to help me and my little brother and I enjoy his company during school field trips.

He often takes us with him when he goes on speaking engagements. I enjoy traveling to schools with him so I can learn how to lecture.

What jail does to the innocent is terrible. I hope this never has to happen to another innocent person again, even though I know it will because the system is imperfect. I believe that until authorities make much needed changes in our criminal justice system, there is no real freedom in America and our society is in danger. This is why I want to become a lawyer, to help others like my dad prove their innocence and regain their freedom. This is why I want to become a lawyer, to protect society from the crime of wrongful convictions.

* * *

Nearly five years after his release from prison, Fernando and his family were in the midst of moving. They had been moving for the last couple of weeks. Their new home was close to where they had been living, so Fernando had been slowly carting all of his family's belongings, either to the new house or to the Salvation Army or Goodwill. Getting this new home was a milestone for Fernando. He had been in prison since age twenty-two and had never lived on his own. Once he was released from prison he moved into the house his wife had leased. Imagine having a home that is yours—in your name—finally—at the age of forty-five. Fernando is understandably proud of this accomplishment. His next step is to own his own home and he is really looking forward to the day they sign a mortgage.

Where would Fernando be today if he had not been wrongfully convicted in 1992? Fernando is an intelligent man with a quiet confidence. He is confident about his abilities and talent and truly believes in himself. He is filled with a certain empowerment that must come from adversity and, in this case, being wrongfully convicted. How does a person endure a lengthy incarceration that is based on false evidence, misidentification, and prosecutorial misconduct? Fernando continued to remain hopeful as the years passed. He tenaciously and prolifically appealed to any and all who might help him in his legal battle to regain his freedom. Fernando did not waste time while he was in prison. Instead, he educated himself on the law and in other disciplines. He protected himself from the chaos and violence that plagued each of his prison communities. After fighting for more than eighteen years and then being exonerated how does Fernando not believe in himself? To be found innocent and released after such an arduous and dreadful experience you would have to believe that this confidence comes from an inner strength and determination born out of what may seem like insurmountable circumstances. Empowerment fueled by such an ordeal may be rare or it may be typical. Whatever the case, Fernando had this.

Conversely, there also is an inner sadness in Fernando—perhaps for goals and dreams unrealized; for those opportunities missed during the eighteen-plus years of his incarceration; for the stress of wanting so much to care for and support his wife and family in the best way possible, but hardly be able to due to his circumstances; or the stress of prison life and the anxiety and fear and scars that would beset him and become his life. You can hear the sadness in his voice. You can feel it in his words. It is stirring.

Finally, after so many years of imprisonment, Fernando was released and found actually innocent. His transition hasn't been an easy one, though, even with the benefit of his family's support. "I never knew I would be conditioned to the prison environment," he said. "There were certain things that I accustomed myself to while in prison which now required un-accustoming [sic]."

"I am not comfortable with disorder. I try to have order in the house in terms of everything being compartmentalized, really, the naïve sense that things should be perfect from this point on, that there should be an order in life. It seems like after what I have been through, nothing should go wrong. But I realize this is not the case. In this life there is chaos too.

"Before my arrest in 1991, I was really a happy, sociable person, and I never experienced anxiety. I was never really an unhappy person and I just lived a happy life that was sociable with my friends in a close knit community with my family. My prison experience changed me. It left scars in ways that I would never have imagined. I dealt with a great deal stress while in prison; feelings of anxiety and fear and resentment, anger and bitterness and humiliation, but which I really thought would leave upon my exoneration."

SIGNS that this is not the place b/c?

Fernando was diagnosed after his release with Post-traumatic Stress Disorder (PTSD), an anxiety disorder that can occur after someone goes through an extreme emotional trauma where threats of injury or death are involved. He found that the underlying symptoms of his PTSD are due to what he saw and experienced in prison and the images that continue to haunt him today. Fernando knew that he carried pain and sadness from his prison experience but he really thought he would recover upon being released and getting back to a life of freedom. He now knows he has hard work ahead of him. He continues to be plagued by PTSD.

"My heart bleeds from this experience and I really was hoping to start recovering and healing from it, you know?" At times Fernando feels as if his PTSD is getting worse. But he manages it. His children help him. Often Fernando seeks refuge in his son's room; a stress-free and happy place. It calms him to spend time with his son.

Fernando missed a good portion of his children's lives. They have grown up without him and he has missed out on some of the necessary parenting that he finds so important. His eldest daughter, Chayla, has started her own family and has given Fernando and Crystal their first grandchild. His second daughter, Carissa, is quite a precocious young lady. She travels with her father on speaking engagements. She is blissfully happy that she has her father at home. She also is so proud of him and so inspired by him that she wants to become a lawyer to help those who are innocent of crimes of which they have been accused. Fernando, Jr., who is studying Tae Kwan Do under his older sister Carissa, is Dad's rock. For now that's just right.

When asked if he's still interested in pursuing his dreams of working in the medical profession, Fernando mentions his bachelor's degree in Behavioral Science. Not quite medical, but related to mental health. These days, becoming a medical professional is a dream Fernando relegates to the memories of his youth. These days he really is just too overwhelmed with life to focus much on the past. Keeping up with house payments and supporting his family is his personal priority. Fernando also is committed to his speaking engagements where he has been able to tell his story and educate his audience on wrongful convictions while earning fees to sustain his family. He has been well supported in these endeavors and wants to continue. Since being released Fernando has spoken around the world, and his speeches about wrongful conviction are well received and so necessary to shed light on this problem and to help him reclaim his place in society.

In 2011, Fernando filed a complaint in federal court against the City of New York and ADA Rodriguez. Now a defendant, ADA Rodriguez responded to the complaint by invoking absolute immunity protections afforded to a prosecutor in pursuing a case and asking the court to dismiss the complaint. In February 2013, the district court agreed and dismissed the case, citing, among other things the ADA's absolute immunity from prosecution.

Fernando struggles with the lack of closure over his lawsuit against the federal government and his compensation claim against the State of New York, both of which continue to be argued. His sense of continued hurt by the system is understandable because the judge hearing his federal complaint is the same judge who denied his writ of habeas corpus in 2004. He is even more disappointed that the Attorney General of the State of New York, someone who has come out in favor of compensating the wrongfully convicted, seeks dismissal of Fernando's compensation claim on a technicality. Under New York State Law, the claimant must sign a statement asserting that he or she has been wrongfully convicted. Fernando's lawyer, after receiving notice of this deficiency in Fernando's claim, failed to provide the missing statement in time. Now, the Attorney General has no choice but to seek dismissal of Fernando's claim. It should be enough that Judge Cataldo found that Fernando is actually innocent but in New York State that is not case.

Fernando has faith that he will prevail against yet another legal battle, even as it exacerbates his PTSD. His faith is in God as the source of his exoneration and eventual compensation from the State and he finds solace in his ministry work. He continues to speak out on wrongful conviction and the problems in the criminal justice system. Fernando is often requested to speak at events and finds those opportunities encouraging and empowering. He feels that distinguishing himself as an exoneree gives him the right to move along with his life and not ever have to say another word about wrongful conviction. He has chosen, however, to do the opposite. Perhaps, if there can be one benefit of those terrible prison years, it is to give the wrongfully convicted a voice. His horrible experience puts Fernando on a path that allows him to be successful, make his family proud, and contribute to society—just like he wanted to do before he was wrongfully convicted.

If you ask Fernando what he missed most while he was in prison, whether he had any food cravings, or whether there was something that he had absolutely been dying to do upon his release, he will tell you he did not have any real desire to go out and eat. He was a finicky eater and he just wasn't that interested. He only really wanted to see his wife, his children, and his mom and dad. The paparazzi were in heavy attendance the day of his release, making traffic conditions more difficult. Still, on the way to his parent's house they did stop at McDonald's. Fernando ordered a Big Mac. It tasted even better than he remembered!

Fernando Bermudez lives with his family in Connecticut. He continues to share his story and educate the public on wrongful convictions in speaking engagements around the world. Carissa Bermudez, his youngest daughter, continues to travel with her father. She was twelve years old when she wrote her story.

CHAPTER 5
Sabrina Butler

In April 1989, Sabrina Butler was seventeen years old and a mother of two children including a nine month old baby boy, Walter Dean Butler. She had been living on her own in Columbus, Mississippi for the past two years. She had been married off by her mother at age fourteen.

"Young and dumb," says Sabrina of her younger years. She's clear and resolved about her life, now. After all there's not much that she can do about her past. But she uses it to inform her life now, day by day, with her children, with her husband, with herself. Her past was really hard. She doesn't want hard anymore.

Sabrina's mother Roszalia Ellen, a victim of incest and gravely affected by her father's sexual molestation, eased her pain by drinking. Her life even after having children was not a stable one. Rose, as she was more often called, had married but separated from her husband when Sabrina and her two brothers were young children. Caring for her children by herself was difficult. She relied a great deal on her in-laws to help with her children. It was very hard for Rose to find a home or keep a home with three children. Many of the landlords she approached would not take even one child and certainly not three. Rose had to make do with the cards she was dealt. The home of her in-laws would be one of the many homes where Sabrina and her brothers would live; the homes of other relatives, friends and strangers, sometimes with their mother and sometimes without her. This would be the makings of the transient life that would become Sabrina's well into her young adulthood.

Each living arrangement brought on different challenges for Rose's children. In one home the children were kept in an attic and were fed barely adequate meals. In another, strange things were happening, unexplainable paranormal things. Sabrina and her siblings were frightened, but as children they found this paranormal activity more weird than dangerous and together they could defy almost anything—at least they believed they could. Once in a while they found themselves in a home where the folks were nice but not often. They were comfortable and happy at their grandparent's home when their grandmother was still alive. Yet no place felt as stable as when Sabrina, her brothers, and their mother could all live together. It didn't matter the type of house or the location or condition. All that mattered was that they were all together.

Sabrina was three years old and living with her paternal grandparents when her sister was born. Her mother was concerned the baby might be treated differently being the child of another man, so she thought it best to put her up for adoption. It would be a long time before Sabrina would see her sister again.

It saddened Sabrina that her mother would do such a thing. Sabrina liked the idea of having a baby sister, but it wasn't to be that Sabrina would get to know her baby sister. This disappointment festered within Sabrina as she grew older. She rebelled against her mother, because of this and so many things. Sabrina hardly listened to her and began to think she should be on her own. Eventually Sabrina decided she could move away if she had her own baby.

At the age of fourteen, Sabrina met an eighteen year old young man who seemed to like her a great deal. At first she wasn't crazy about him, but as they spent time together her feelings began to change and they became intimate. Before long Sabrina was pregnant and Rose was not at all pleased. She was quite angry, in fact, and demanded that Sabrina break ties with the young man. But Sabrina wanted the baby, she wanted the love, and in her rebel yell wanted the chance to be away from her mother and on her own. Because Sabrina was a minor, however, she would be unable to marry unless her mother signed over guardianship to this young man that her mother didn't like. As it turned out, Rose was angry enough to do just that. As Rose left, her parting words to Sabrina were that this man was not the man Sabrina thought he was and that he would not be good for her. Even though Sabrina had dreamt about being away from her mother and on her own, she felt abandoned. She felt her mother gave up on her. She wouldn't be there to help Sabrina with her baby, with her life, with anything important. Her mother was gone.

Sabrina's mother would eventually return when Sabrina went to prison and they would make amends. Until then, this would be a time in Sabrina's life when hard knocks were her only teachers and she would learn the hard way. Her husband would end up being trouble just like her mother warned; a lot of trouble in fact. The marriage didn't last. He went to jail for petty offenses. While her husband was incarcerated, Sabrina knew that she needed to make some changes in her life. She wanted to go into military service. That was her dream job. She wanted to travel, see the world, and learn different things. She needed to finish high school to live her dream. Their young son would live with her in-laws while her husband was incarcerated and Sabrina would attend high school and try to get her life in order. Sabrina's life was briefly on track. She was back in school, but her plans were set aside when she met the young man, a schoolmate, who would become the father of her second child, Little Walter, as she called him. Sabrina was seventeen and about to become a mother of two.

How difficult the struggle must have been for her, this young girl who wanted to be a mother, but had not yet been a child. Sabrina was a party girl. She liked going to clubs and dancing and hanging out with people. She liked the attention she got from young men. She was not a smoker or drinker, she just liked being around people who seemed happy and danced and had fun.

Little Walter's father would end up being another guy not right for Sabrina. He was a philanderer and involved in passing bad checks and other illegal money schemes. He also was terribly abusive; another tragic relationship for Sabrina.

Sabrina lived off and on with her in-laws who tried, at every opportunity, to take away her son. It was difficult for Sabrina to see that they may have been trying to help her. Sabrina was too young to shoulder this life she was leading; trying to be a responsible parent without any guidance or resources, looking for the nurturing that she missed in her early years yet wanting to enjoy the freedom of youth—this was an awful lot for a teenager to navigate. Still it was the life she had and she tried, with whatever strength and inadequate skills she possessed, to make it all work. In the end it didn't work. In the end it fell apart.

***

Just before midnight one Tuesday in early April, Sabrina found herself at the hospital because Little Walter had stopped breathing. At 12:13 a.m. the attending physician pronounced him dead. Over the next two days, Sabrina would tell six different versions of the story of how Little Walter ended up in the hospital. Her first few versions of the story included a fictitious babysitter named Ester Hollis and a fictitious visitor named Steve. In her fifth telling of the story, Sabrina admitted there was no one named Ester Hollis and no one named Steve. There had been no babysitter and no visitor.

Why would Sabrina lie and keep changing her story? She was a frightened teenage mother whose baby had died unexpectedly and alone with her. She was a poor, uneducated, young black woman living in Mississippi. She had left her infant son at home unattended while she went jogging. Any one of these factors would have been enough to cause her to be wary of the authorities. All of them together led her to an ill-conceived decision to lie to the police about what happened. By the time Sabrina told her sixth version of the facts she had resolved to tell the police the truth.

Sabrina put Little Walter to bed on Tuesday night, April 11, 1989 at around 10:00 p.m. After she was certain the baby was asleep, Sabrina went jogging. When she got home she went into the kitchen to get the baby's bottle and then checked on him. He wasn't breathing and Sabrina panicked. She ran to her next door neighbor, Lisa Fowler. Lisa began performing cardio-pulmonary resuscitation (CPR) on the baby, then told Sabrina how to perform CPR and to take over for her. Sabrina took over the CPR, but it was the CPR used on adults, not babies. Frantic, Sabrina picked up Little Walter and began knocking on her neighbors' doors to find someone to take them to the hospital, all the time continuing to perform CPR on him. One neighbor, Brenda Jackson, could not leave her children, but another, Larry Nance, drove Sabrina and Little Walter to the hospital.

At 12:13 a.m. on Wednesday, April 12, 1989, Sabrina carried Little Walter into the Columbus Hospital. For thirty minutes the doctors tried to revive the baby, but with no success. Little Walter was pronounced dead. The police, who were already at the hospital, questioned Sabrina about what happened. That's when she told the first version of her story including the fictitious babysitter and son.

Sabrina agreed to give her statement at the police station and arrived there at around 3:00 a.m. At around 7:00 a.m. a police detective from Columbus, Mississippi heard about Little Walter's death and went to Sabrina's apartment building to find witnesses. He left a message with her neighbor that the police needed to talk to her.

Later that morning, Sabrina went to the detective's office and there she signed the final version of a statement the police prepared for her. In this statement, Sabrina admitted to leaving the baby at home alone while she went jogging. Upon her return she saw that the baby's diaper was wet and when she went to change it, she saw that his rectum was protruding and his stomach was distended. She tried to push the rectum back and when Little Walter wouldn't stop crying, she hit him in the stomach with her fist. When Sabrina finished signing the written statement she was arrested and charged with murder. It would be almost one year before her trial.

Sabrina's six-day trial began on March 8, 1990. The medical examiner who had conducted an autopsy on Little Walter determined that the cause of death was child abuse which resulted in death. Sabrina's defense was minimal and she did not take the stand. The prosecutor mentioned Sabrina's decision not to take the stand more than once in his closing argument:

> "Ladies and Gentlemen, she has not yet told you the whole truth of the torment she subjected her son to. You still don't know the whole story. Incredible, unbelievable evasion from start to finish. Ladies and Gentlemen, is that what an innocent person does?"

On March 14, 1990, the jury found Sabrina guilty and she was sentenced to death by lethal injection. Her execution was set for July 2, 1990. She was moved to a cell on death row. She was the youngest woman in the State of Mississippi on death row. Her cell was six feet by nine feet and she was locked inside of it twenty-three hours a day. She got one hour each day in the yard. On the day she was meant to be executed, Sabrina learned that additional legal inquiries related to her appeal would delay her execution.

On August 26, 1992, the Supreme Court of Mississippi held that the prosecutor's statements about Sabrina not taking the stand violated her constitutional rights, noting that "When an accused exercise his or her constitutional right not to testify, the circuit judge must see that the State makes no direct or indirect comment on this fact." The State Supreme Court called the prosecutor's comments, "... reversible error so egregious in fact that even if there had been no objection at trial, we would nevertheless have been obligated to reverse." The State Supreme Court reversed Sabrina's conviction and remanded the case back to the court for re-trial.

* * *

Death Row Be Gone

As Told By Sabrina Butler

My son Walter, barely three months away from his first birthday, died on April 11, 1989. I was arrested the very next day and charged with capital murder for his death. I was eighteen years old when I was sentenced on March 14, 1990 to die by lethal injection on July 2, 1990. Yes, I was young and naïve and immature, but, I didn't murder my son.

The state of Mississippi provided me with two defense attorneys. I spoke with one of my attorneys briefly. He mumbled something negative to me and left. That was the last I would hear from him until I met my complete defense team two days before my trial. There was no preparation at all and that left me feeling intensely insecure about my trial. Although in hindsight, I'm not sure the preparation would have made a difference. One of my attorneys was drunk throughout the whole trial. I guess he thought the peppermints he constantly popped into this mouth would camouflage the alcohol I smelled on his breath.

Throughout the trial my lawyers kept telling me, "We don't want you to take the stand. We got this thing nipped in the bud."

They had it nipped in the bud all right. The jury came back and said "We find you guilty and we sentence you to death."

Resigned to my fate, I was anxious to leave the county jail and be on my way to Rankin County Correctional Facility. I had no idea what to expect and it was the scariest ride of my life. In my terror, I had completely given up. Why should I care any longer, after the way my attorneys performed; after the way everything played out in court? All my chances were gone and they were going to kill me anyway.

When I got to Rankin County I was cuffed around my wrist and ankles and they were attached with one chain that wrapped around my waist. I had to walk upright for a distance to get to intake. There wasn't much length between the ankle cuffs, so I had to shuffle my feet to walk. It's pretty hard to walk without falling with your body cuffed like that, but I made it. When I got to intake, they gave me clothes, they put bug spray and all this other stuff on my body. They took my fingerprints and pictures of my whole body making sure that they got any scars, or markings. I suppose it was a way to identify me, but honestly, the way they treated me, it didn't make me feel good.

Intake took about two hours. Then I shuffled my way to maximum security. I had to carry all my things, which was doubly hard, being cuffed like that. A security guard walked with me, but he wouldn't help me carry anything—not one thing. He told me, "You see those inmates out there? We tell them when to get up. We tell them when to go to sleep. We tell them what to eat and we tell them everything they have to do." He gave me a cold, hard look and said, "You will die here." When he said that it freaked me out. It was terrifying.

By the time I got to the maximum security check I couldn't even talk. I was out of breath because I was overcome with fear. Already it was hell, and I had just gotten there. I had never been to prison before and I didn't know what to expect. When I got to the next security area, there was a lady there and she asked, "What's wrong with you, girl? You okay?" I couldn't even speak to answer her. She walked me down this long hall. In Rankin County they didn't really have a place for death row inmates. We were housed with the other inmates who had committed similar crimes, but they weren't on death row. There was a piece of tape on the floor; a red piece of tape with the words, "You can't go beyond this point," and they put me in a cell behind the red tape.

It was a six-by-nine cell, no bigger than a bathroom. I sat in this cell for twenty-three hours of the day. I was allowed a one hour yard call which I had to spend by myself. That was very hard and so lonely for me because I had no one during this whole tragedy that knew what I was going through. There was no one who talked with me or told me what to expect or what was actually going on, what I was supposed to do, or give me any legal advice. I cried for two weeks straight. I would sit on the floor in a corner of that tiny cell, rocking and crying. I didn't eat. I hardly talked. I just cried and cried.

There was one other girl on death row with me. Her name was Susan Balfour. She had been sentenced in the same county that I'm from and had been in Rankin for some time. She was housed in the cell right next to mine. She took to me and kind of talked to me and helped me.

When my death day came, I was beside myself. I paced the floor. I was thinking that they were coming at any time to take my life. That's truly what I thought. Every time I heard footsteps or the sound of keys I just knew that I would soon be dead. I was noticeably restless and Susan tried to calm me by speaking to me through the walls. Our toilets were connected through the wall and there was a vent under the toilet. It allowed us to talk as if we were in the same room. She kept telling me they couldn't do anything to me. If they hadn't exhausted all the state remedies, then they really couldn't kill me. She helped me a lot with her words. Nobody had ever told me that the state had to exhaust all remedies before they could actually carry out the sentence of death until Susan did. The day passed and I was still alive. I still believed somewhere deep down inside that they could come and get me, but sometime later I realized that Susan was right and for now I was safe.

Susan helped me a lot, that first day, but I continued to cry, every day. Some days later a guard came down because I guess I wasn't making any progress; there was no relief. The guard opened my door. She walked in and she told me that if I kept on doing what

I was doing, not eating and sitting in the corner and crying as I was, they would send me for a psych evaluation. If a doctor came down I would have to take medication. I didn't want that. I didn't want them to medicate me, or put me on something. So it was at this point that I started trying to figure out what I could do to not go crazy.

Still distressed and upset, I didn't want them giving me whatever drugs they give you. When the guard finally got tired of talking to me, she closed my door and left. Since I had a pencil and paper, I decided to write about my surroundings. I had one little window where I could look out on the yard and see the other inmates walking around and stuff. I would just write. I would try to see what I could learn from whatever I saw, whatever I heard; and I would try to analyze it and see what I would do in their situation. I would watch for a while, then I would write more. This was partly how I managed the whole two years and nine months on death row

Susan was a great help to me during my incarceration. She was much older than me and on death row, too. She knew a lot more about prison than I did. We were the only two on death row in Rankin. We'd spend a lot of time sitting on the floor by our toilets, talking through our vents. Sometimes I would be able to see her shadow in her cell. I wondered if she could see mine. There really was no human contact for death row inmates. We were considered too dangerous to interact with the regular population or one another, but sitting there on the floor talking with Susan was the next best thing. We would talk and talk. She told me about her life and I told her about mine.

Eventually we were able to see each other when they finally allowed us to take our one hour yard time together. The administrator required us to sign all these papers to ensure that we wouldn't hurt one another. Once the paperwork was done we could do yard call. It was the only time we had any actual contact with each other to talk, or with anyone else, other than prison guards. It was worth every minute, though. Having to live twenty-three hours a day without contact in those tiny prison cells was miserable.

I started to teach myself. On Wednesdays sometimes they would let us go to the library where I would read books and learn about law. I started taking Bible courses and things like that to keep myself going. Then one of the security guards was real nice to me and brought me some crochet stuff and I started crocheting. Everybody liked the way I learned how to crochet. I would crochet little baby booties and little hats and stuff like that. It was a way to keep myself busy. I could also draw really well. I made postcards and cards for people and would send them out. Those were the kinds of things I did to occupy my mind and pass the time. I guess that's what kept me going, too. I would also make a lot of stuff for my older son, who my first husband's mother had. I would make him little stuff. I made friends on the yard who knew people outside of the prison. I would send word to them to give my son the outfits I made and other things. My first son was almost two years old when I got locked up. I wanted him to have some things from his mom. I would get outfits sewn or made for him, little short sets, clothes and things because he should get stuff from his mom.

Even though I was able to do creative stuff and it kept my mind off of being incarcerated and on death row, I was angry. I was angry with God for a while because I couldn't understand why He put me through this. I tried to save my son and I was called a murderer. I had a hard time dealing with all of that. I was angry with the district attorneys, with the judges, and with all the lawyers, you know, all that stuff for a long time. I know at least three years. Then one day my sentence got overturned and that gave me a little hope.

My first attorney felt bad about my case so he wrote the brief for my new attorney, Clive Stafford Smith. How I got him, I'm not sure...I really don't know how I got him. I suppose I just feel that he was God sent because he came into the picture with his team and then they started showing up and talking to me and showing me what was going on without me doing anything. They also found out that my son had heart problems, kidney problems, and chronic bowel syndrome. They brought all this to trial. All the witnesses the lawyers didn't call in my first trial, Clive and his team called in my appeal trial. With all of that new evidence, the judge overturned my sentence. What I didn't know was that I was going to stay in jail another three years.

* * *

Sabrina was moved from Rankin to the county jail to wait for her new trial date. Her new attorneys had all the documents and evidence they needed for the trial. All they were waiting for was the district attorney. He asked the court for additional time because he was missing items. The district attorney kept asking and asking and the court kept granting and granting. "He just played it out as long as he could," Sabrina said. It would be three years before Sabrina would see the courtroom again. By this time she was twenty-three years old.

For Sabrina, the county jail was not anything like prison. She was in a larger cell, at times with as many as thirty women; very different from her one-woman cell back at Rankin. She wasn't as distressed, or terrorized as she had been on death row, for obvious reasons. She was fortified with hope. This was very different. She was no longer on death row and it seemed like she had a group of attorneys who were on her side and cared about her innocence.

County jail was different for men and women. The men were separated according to their status; either waiting for court, waiting for sentencing, or waiting for prison. They were separated into two different cells according to their status. Women, on the other hand, were all together, no matter their status, in one twelve-person cell. Sometimes there were up to thirty women in a cell at a time rather than the twelve. Sabrina's experience at county jail taught her that women don't particularly get along well, especially when they've been packed in a cell over-reaching its capacity.

There were a lot of fights, a lot of different attitudes and noises. It was hard for Sabrina to adjust having spent the last two years and nine months in a solitary cell. By now she was used to being by herself, but what could she do? Occasionally the cell count would get down to five or six, but never less than that and never often.

The county jail was a revolving door; always someone in, someone out; so many different kinds of women coming in. There was an order as well. Those women who had been in the cells the longest had the most seniority. They were the ones who set the rules. If you were new and walked in thinking you were going to live by your rules and your rules were different from the current rules, there would be hell to pay. For example, women coming in and out for drunk driving or similar offenses wanted to run the place, but women with seniority were not going for that. Sabrina recalls a night when one of the girls coming in was drunk. Sabrina's television was on the table and this drunk girl wanted to break the antennae. Before Sabrina could say a word, one of the senior women jumped up and started fighting with the drunk girl. This kind of thing happened regularly and it didn't have to be for a big or important reason.

"It was simple stuff. Stuff we take for granted here on the outside; simple sugar and cream, a piece of paper, stamps, food, anything. Those were gold in prison, in jail. People will kick your butt over sugar and cream."

Sabrina had visitors at Rankin. Her mother and her brothers would visit her often and regularly, but they couldn't make it to the county jail. For almost two years Sabrina was on her own. She had to bear the chaos in the county jail for those long years. "I really didn't like being in a cell with all those women, as odd as that may sound. I had been used to being by myself. But that's the way it was." In Sabrina's third year at Lowndes County Jail she would finally meet someone that would help her for the rest of her life. His name was Joe Porter.

* * *

Ask And Ye Shall Receive

As Told By Joe Porter

Back in 1989 I started a job at the Willowbrook Hospital in Columbus, Mississippi. I worked as a psych tech in the psych ward. I had been there for about three years when a new patient was assigned to me. He was in out-patient care so I would see him on and off a few times before I left Willowbrook. I monitored him and helped him through his admission to the ward. Part of my job was to provide what he needed. I was there to listen. He would tell me stories about his depression and stuff like that. He told me about his wife who had been locked up for a serious crime. He said this scarred his life and made him a little nuts. I worked with him for a while. I would see him for two to three weeks at a time, then he would leave, and then I would see him again.

I was ready for a transfer and had applied to the local county jail here in Columbus for a correctional job. I was looking for a better opportunity. Finally about a year or so later I got a job as a correctional officer. At this county facility I somehow wound up meeting the woman that was my Willowbrook patient's wife.

I was her correctional officer. Now obviously at first I had no idea who she was, and never would I have thought that I would be the correctional officer for the same woman who my patient was talking to me about. I arrived at the county jail in 1994 and stayed there until 1996. Sabrina arrived there in 1992. She was there when I got there and then she was released in 1995. I came to realize that Sabrina was a nice lady. I took a liking to her. I also came to believe that all the things her husband told me at Willowbrook were not true. I believed she was innocent and I tried in my power to do all that I could to help her.

It was against county policy for correctional officers to have any physical contact with the inmates. When I did my rounds Sabrina and I would talk; quick conversations as I was passing through. She would talk to me about why she was in jail and that she didn't commit the crime that they said she did. She was up for her new trial and just waiting for them to call her up. She told me it would be soon.

During this time I was in a rough relationship with another woman. We had already been in a relationship for five or six years. But she just wasn't the woman for me. She did a lot of things that she shouldn't have been doing and breaking the rules of a committed relationship. It seemed like there wasn't a whole lot I could do about it except pray for the relationship to end.

I wanted a woman who wanted me for who I am, and would be true in her relationship with me. I prayed to Jesus to send that woman my way. I am a humble man whose faith in Jesus Christ is unwavering. My mama taught us that at a young age. I know that what I ask for in prayer He will provide it for me. So I leave all my needs and wants up to the will of God. I never worry, and trust that He will provide for me. He has in the past and I know He will in my future. I was sincere in my prayers; explaining the difficult times

I was having with this other woman. I wanted something better in my life.

I can't really explain it to anyone who doesn't understand the power of Jesus. I don't need to see things to believe in them. I just know that I trust and believe, and I have never been disappointed. So when I saw Sabrina for the first time I had the feeling deep within me that she was sent to me by God. I liked Sabrina from the first time she shared her story with me. I continued to believe each and every day that this was going to work out for me and work out for her too. I knew that I was to help her in any way that I could.

In the county jail, correctional officers are to have no physical contact with the inmates, nor are they allowed to give money directly to them. At this time Sabrina didn't know that I liked her, but I wanted her to know. There was only one colleague of mine that I trusted above the rest. I didn't have any trusting relationships with most of the people I worked with. I had enough trust in this person to deliver a message to Sabrina. I wanted her to know that I liked her and that I would continue to like her and help her all the way through her release.

I had no doubts about my feelings for Sabrina and I wanted to help her in any way possible. I also had no doubts about her release from the jail. I didn't want any of my co-workers to know that I was helping Sabrina, but I needed to help her. She had no visitors, she was all alone. But she had me, and I wasn't going to let her down. While she was there, since we were not allowed to give money and I had to protect myself. I decided to go through my sister. I would give my sister money and she would be the one to send it to Sabrina. No one would suspect that the money was coming from me. So if she ever needed money, she would always have it. I set up a post office box, too, where she could send me letters and let me know what she needed. That was how we could keep in contact. That way no one would ever know what we were doing. I checked the post office box every day.

I knew that I was going to leave the lady I was living with, so I let her know that. I told her that our time together was coming to an end. Everything I was doing, I was doing out of faith because I knew when I asked for something better than what I had, it would be waiting for me. I wasn't always sure how I would receive it, I really didn't know that, but I never worried about it. She knew that it was over between us and time for me to go. I told her this before Sabrina was released or even before she was to go to court.

I moved out and started getting a place ready for Sabrina. It was still a little while before Sabrina would be released, but that didn't stop me. I knew what God had planned for me. I got furniture, and curtains and everything she would need. I did the girlie thing. If the curtains weren't exactly the way they were supposed to be I would at least try to hang them. And if it still wasn't right she would say so and we could change it. I left all the tags on the furniture just in case.

* * *

Following the instruction of the State Supreme Court, the State of Mississippi retried Sabrina in December 1995 in a different county after the defense request for a change of venue was granted. Sabrina's case had attracted the attention noted civil rights attorney, Sir Clive Stafford Smith, OBE a world renowned death penalty attorney who represented over three hundred death row prisoners in the US alone. Sabrina's retrial was unlike her first trial. Her new lawyer had experience trying death penalty cases and he called witnesses who corroborated her explanation of what happened the night Little Walter Dean died. Sabrina's neighbors testified that she had attempted to perform CPR on the baby. One of the neighbors also attempted to perform CPR on the baby. The defense's medical expert testified that the injuries to Little Walter's body could have been caused by the CPR attempts.

Perhaps the most compelling evidence came from the medical examiner from the first trial. He testified that he had not been thorough in his previous autopsy. He now believed that Little Walter may have died from cystic kidney disease or sudden infant death syndrome. After deliberating briefly, the jury acquitted and exonerated Sabrina and she became the first woman in the United States exonerated from death row. The Mississippi State Senate and House separately approved the State's payment of Sabrina's legal fees.

At Sabrina Butler's retrial hearing the jury returned with a verdict of not guilty. Sabrina fell to the floor crying and releasing the heavy burden that had been hers all those five years. On that winter day in December of 1995 Sabrina stepped foot in the Lowndes County jail for the last time to screams of joy from inmates she'd spent time with. She was finally free. The first thing she wanted to do was see her son Danny, who was already eight years old. He was living with her in-laws. She wanted to regain custody but it would take a while before that to happen.

Joe Porter and Sabrina Butler were married in May of 1996. Joe knew that Sabrina would be released and new that they would be together. Joe has said that he never doubted. "When you ask for it, when you pray for it…you're not supposed to understand in order to receive…" Sabrina was the only woman that stood out in the jail to Joe. He says. "It was just too many signs. How I met her husband, and how I was placed at the jail where she was, and how I liked her and all that. There was just too many signs that was being led to me according to what I asked my Lord and Savior to do for me…" He goes on, "I've been shown some stuff in life with her that no other woman has ever been able to show me. I never would have thought I would have children."

"I went to a convention down in Chicago where all the exonerees [were] and I think she was the only female up on the stage. I had tears coming from my eyes when every one of the exonerees had to get up and say whatever state they was from, and she was the Mississippi state. She said, 'If Mississippi had of had its way, I wouldn't be here today.'"

"Tears just rolled down my eyes, which was the total truth. If Mississippi had of had its way then I wouldn't be looking at my children through her. None of that stuff would exist. That's why man needs to be careful about how quick they sentence people to die."

Joe is Sabrina's angel and has been since he arrived at Lowndes. After Sabrina was released she could not find a job. She never hid her past, and because she had this mar on her record, exonerated or not, nobody would hire her. Joe has taken care of her for all these many years. If it hadn't been for him she didn't know what she would've done.

Sabrina and Joe have three children: Danny, Joe, Jr. and Nakeria. Sabrina was able to win custody of Danny four years after she was released.

Sabrina calls her six-and-a-half year ordeal the "Torture Experience." This experience gave her wisdom and knowledge. First she made sure that she learned how to administer CPR properly. She also is very sure she does not want to enter a prison ever again. She will write, but she will not set foot in a prison again. She wouldn't wish this experience on her worst enemy.

She was angry when she got out of prison. She believes she had to grow into understanding the messages God was trying to give her. "I was angry for like three years. Oh my God, I was such an angry child." If any one were to have talked with her then the conversation would be entirely different than the way she approaches her experience now. Sabrina was also angry with her mother for giving up on her, but that is all forgiven now. It took her a while to get to that point. But her mother has apologized to her and to her brothers. "I just have to love momma for who she is because she's still my momma at the end of the day."

Sabrina has put her anger to rest these days. When asked she doesn't feel she has any severe post-traumatic stress, although when she was initially released she would chronically wake up in the middle of the night and walk through her house checking on her children and husband to make sure they were all breathing. She continues to do that now but not nearly as often, nor with the same kind of urgency. She still lives in the same town and will not risk anything happening to her family on her watch. Sabrina says her husband is always fussing at her to sleep more soundly and rest. Sabrina says, "I'm just not a sound sleeper anymore. "

Sabrina's feels as though she was put in prison to slow her down. She was a partyer and having fun and she just figured the only way she was to hear God's voice was for him to set her down. She didn't want to listen to anything anybody was talking about. She just wanted to do what she wanted to do. The sad thing is that it took the tragedy of her son's death to make her listen.

Sabrina spends some of her time talking with young people now given the wisdom of her own experience. "You know, young people running around here thinking they know everything, but that's not the truth. It's not the truth. I try to talk to them and tell them now that 'You don't need to be thinking about no kids at this young age like this. You need to be thinking about getting your education, going to school, making something of yourself, because babies are not dolls."

Sabrina made a choice when she was got out of jail. "We all got a choice in our life to make. You can decide. You can choose to do the right thing, or you can stay in your rut. I didn't want to stay that way. I wanted to do something with my life so I went back to school and got my GED and I went and got three years of college, you know, in order to advance myself a bit…how can I tell somebody my story and there's nothing positive with it. I wanted to not only for you to hear the bad part but I want you to hear the aftermath, the good part as well.

"The good part is I wanted to change my life and just because I had a bad life didn't mean that I had to, you know [have] my children to experience what I did. I wanted to break the cycle of that in my family. I try to raise my kids differently. They're happy children. I teach them what's positive and I teach them about love. [I] don't want them to hate."

Sabrina advocates and works with Witness to Innocence as an assistant director of membership and training. As the youngest woman sentenced to death row and the first black woman to be exonerated from death row, Sabrina is in demand as a speaker. She travels from state to state speaking to youth, churches, about the death penalty and wrongful conviction. It's important work for her although it's not always easy. In preparation for her speaking engagements she has to go back to that place where she doesn't want to be; those six-plus difficult years of wrongful incarceration and the death of her son. She reaches out as she always does to God for strength and to inform her words, to give her the heart to continue to do this work. It's stressful for her before she speaks and afterwards as well; reliving those days watching all those people trying to take her life away from her and nothing she could do about it, nothing she could say. According to them she was just the worst mother in the world. She has to put herself back in this over and over again. It takes a lot to manage that.

In 2010 the State of Mississippi changed its expungement laws and Sabrina became eligible to apply for expungement. In July 2012, her criminal record was expunged—seventeen years after her release.

Sabrina continues to live in Columbus with her husband and children. She and Joe have been married nineteen years. When asked what she wanted to do when she got out of prison she first wanted to see her son Danny, then she said, "I wanted to watch every movie that came out. I had my husband to go to the store and get me so many movies I think I had my eyes screwed...I had to watch all the movies because I am a TV fanatic." You can hear the laughter in her voice. "When [Joe] was at work I was just in there with that TV. That's what I like. That's what I wanted to get in."

Sabrina Butler-Porter lives in Mississippi with her husband, Joe Porter, and their children. Sabrina is an author and speaks to school, church, and civic groups on wrongful conviction and the death penalty.

CHAPTER 6
Maurice Antwone Caldwell

Before being convicted for a crime he didn't commit, Maurice ('Twone) Caldwell had had brushes with the law. He sold pot from time to time and was arrested, convicted and sentenced to the California Youth Authority for burglary. Everyone who knew Maurice knew he was no murderer. He was young when those crimes were committed and he was placed in juvenile detention rather than an adult penitentiary. Maurice spent a lot of his young life within those confines. We do not know whether he was as bad as his time served would suggest, but we know that he was not a killer.

Maurice grew up in the Alemany Housing Project with his younger brother, Franceil, and older sister, Deborah. His mother was on drugs and his father was in prison for killing a cop. Maurice says, and his family believes, there is a mark on the Caldwell name because of his father's crime. Given the circumstantial evidence on which he was convicted, it seems there may be more than a little something to that. The police abhor cop killers and it can be extremely difficult to implicate a police officer for unprofessional behavior, when the behavior of the accuser is less than stellar. This was Maurice's situation when he found himself the prime suspect in a murder investigation.

One night Maurice was hanging out at Alemany with a few of his partners. There had been a drive-by shooting in the area recently, in which Maurice had been shot and his cousin had been killed. Since then, Maurice and his friends would shoot out the street lights to make it darker and make themselves less visible drive-by targets. That night was no different. They were standing at the bottom of a hill near a street light. They shot out the light. Kitt Crenshaw, a San Francisco narcotics officer with whom Maurice had "history," did not like Maurice. Officer Crenshaw claimed that he and another officer had been standing at the top of the hill watching Maurice and his friends. The young men had not seen the officers when they shot out the street light. By the time the officers arrived on the scene, the gun that had been used to shoot out the street light was safely hidden.

Officer Crenshaw knew about some of the things Maurice had been up to in the past, but there had not been enough evidence against him to press charges. In those cases, Maurice had been arrested, but that was all. On this night, an extremely angry and frustrated Officer Crenshaw was determined to get Maurice off the street and into jail. Officer Crenshaw and his partner forced all of Maurice's friends to lie on the ground, then grabbed Maurice and handcuffed him.

"Okay motherfucker, where the gun at?" Officer Crenshaw shouted at Maurice.

"What you talkin' 'bout, man?"

"Man, don't play me. I'm not trying to hear that shit right now. Where's the gun?"

"Come on Crenshaw, man. Get this way-out shit outta my face, man." Maurice looked down at his partners and said, "Y'all hear all this? This man must be mind crazy. Stupid."

Crenshaw was trembling with rage. No one got away with saying shit like that to Officer Crenshaw, especially in front of other folks. "Oh you think I'm somethin' stupid? You wanna play like this with me?"

Officer Crenshaw snatched Maurice and shoved him into the back of the police car. Then he and his partner took Maurice to the Farmer's Market, a secluded place maybe seven minutes from where they had been. Once they got there Officer Crenshaw pulled Maurice from the back seat and read him the riot act. "Three options," he said, holding up three fingers. "You gonna go to the hospital, to the grave, or the hospital and jail." He grabbed Maurice around the neck and lifted him so his feet were not touching the ground. Maurice gasped for breath.

"You wanna tell me now?" Officer Crenshaw growled, slowly lowering Maurice to the ground.

"Come on man, what you talking about? Why you doing this?"

Furious, Officer Crenshaw shoved his elbow into Maurice's neck, threw him against the squad car door, and then threw him onto the ground.

"Crenshaw, man, why you doin' this? Why you doin' this to me, man?" Maurice pleaded. With each blow, Maurice continued to plead, believing he was going to die at any moment.

"Hey, man." Officer Crenshaw turned to his partner, while moving Maurice so his head was under the car near the tires. "If he don't tell me what I want this time, I want you to drive the car over his head and make sure this motherfucka never speaks again." Turning back to Maurice Officer Crenshaw asked again, "Where's the motherfucking gun, muthafucka?"

Maurice hated Officer Crenshaw, but he didn't want to die. Officer Crenshaw had always been on Maurice's back about something. He also, unfortunately for Maurice, was the kind of police officer who thought about consequences long after taking action. Maurice was not going to give in completely, but he had to get Officer Crenshaw to back off before that man killed him.

"Alright man, alright. It's behind the building."

"What building?"

"Behind the building, man, back there."

"Where? What building? Don't bullshit me! I'll wipe the street wit' yo' ass!"

"I'll show you."

They drove back to Alemany and Maurice was relieved to find that his partners were still there, lying on the ground just like they had been when Officer Crenshaw threw him into the back of the police car. Officer Crenshaw got out of the car, walked over to Maurice's door and opened it. "Let's go. Show me the gun."

Maurice leaned out of the car as far as he could so that Officer Crenshaw couldn't push him back inside the car and slam the door on him. At the top of his lungs Maurice screamed, "Yo, y'all, he's trying to kill me! Officer Crenshaw's trying to kill me, man!" Maurice was pretty banged up. He had scars on his face, neck trauma from being choked, skin scraped away from being cuffed too tightly. Blood everywhere.

Officer Crenshaw found himself in a precarious situation. Maurice had no weapon. He'd been taken away in a police car uninjured, but now was a man who had been seriously beaten. The only thing he could do was uncuff Maurice and let him go, which is exactly what he did. As the police car drove away, Officer Crenshaw glared out the window at Maurice with a look that said, "This ain't over, not by a long shot."

Finally away from the police, Maurice showed everyone his injuries and they encouraged him to file a report on Officer Crenshaw for excessive use of force. His friends and family were concerned that Maurice would turn up dead one day if he did not get his concerns about Officer Crenshaw on the record. Maurice agreed. He knew if he did not file the report this probably would not be the last time he would experience Officer Crenshaw. Maurice filed a police report.

Officer Crenshaw, according to Maurice, is not the kind of officer you should ignore. Maurice describes him as just like Denzel Washington's character in *Training Day*: he owned the streets in every way, terrorizing the innocent and the guilty alike. His law enforcement practices could arguably be considered ethically deficient; he did not like being made to look like a fool. He was vengeful in that way, ruthless; he had to turn things back in his favor; no one could get away with "punking" him. It would not be too long before Officer Crenshaw would have another shot at Maurice.

* * *

Who hasn't heard the quote "The coldest winter I ever spent was a summer in San Francisco?" The temperature in the early morning hours of June 30, 1990 was typically chilly, and especially so in the city's South Bernal neighborhood, not far from the water. Sometime around 2:00 a.m. that Saturday morning, four young men were driving through the Alemany Projects looking to score some crack cocaine.

The driver of the car pulled over to the curb near the middle of the block and not far from a group of men standing under a streetlight. All of the young men in the car got out and one of them, Domingo Bobila, collected the money to pay for the drugs. The men standing under the streetlight walked over to the car and began to talk with Judy Acosta, one of Bobila's friends. After talking it over, one of the men gave Bobila two rocks of crack and Bobila gave the man the money.

"Hey man, this ain't enough!" the seller said ominously.

Alice Caruthers, a resident of the projects, was walking down the street when she saw a local drug dealer, Marritte Funches, arguing with Bobila and his friends. Bobila turned to his friends to collect more money and when he turned back around, one of the men from under the streetlight punched him in the face. A moment later, a gun was fired. Bobila ran back to the car, fumbling to put the key in the ignition. The driver side front window shattered after another shot was fired. The door on the passenger side flew open, startling him. Acosta, clutching his chest, tried to climb into the car. Bobila pulled the passenger seat forward and grabbed Acosta, dragging him into the back seat. As he peeled away from the curb, Bobila heard more shots. The other two young men who had been in the car, Eric Aguirre and Domindar Vivray, ran away unharmed.

Deborah Rodriguez lived upstairs in one of the project's two-story apartments with Maurice's uncle. Maurice lived in a different building and had been visiting along with his friend, Tina McCullum. Tina and Maurice were upstairs when they heard the gunshots. After the shots stopped, Maurice ran downstairs and outside to see what had happened. Deborah, already downstairs, ran outside after him. Other project residents also went outside to see what had happened, but by then Bobila and Acosta had driven away and Aguirre and Vivray were long gone.

Bobila drove around for a few minutes before pulling into a gas station. Acosta was bleeding profusely. "Call 9-1-1!" Bobila shouted to the gas station attendant. He began to perform cardio-pulmonary resuscitation on Acosta while they waited for the ambulance to arrive, but by the time it got there, Acosta was already dead. The coroner filed a report indicating that Acosta died of shock and loss of blood from gunshot wounds and that a bullet wound that traveled through his heart, liver, and spleen had been the primary cause of death.

The police arrived at the gas station and asked Bobila what happened. Bobila was too scared to tell them the truth so he said nothing about being in the projects to buy drugs. A policeman also went to the Alemany Projects in response to 9-1-1 calls reporting the gunshots. The officer called in at 2:51 a.m. to report that it looked like there had been a shooting, but there was no victim. After one of the project's security guards told him the noise was probably fireworks and not gunshots, the officer called in again at 2:53 a.m. to report a false alarm.

Vivray and Aguirre separately arrived back at Acosta's house. A little while later, Vivray returned to the projects to find out what happened. He got nervous when he saw a lot of police in the area and went straight home without stopping. Neither Vivray nor Aguirre called the police that night. Bobila, on the other hand, ended up in the emergency room where the police questioned him about the man who had punched him in the face. Bobila described the man as at least five foot, ten inches, black, with short, nappy hair and wearing a light colored jogging suit. He described three other suspects as wearing trench coats.

Four days later Vivray and Aguirre were at the police station giving their statements. Vivray looked at hundreds of photographs and identified one as resembling the man who punched Bobila. It was not a photo of Maurice. Aguirre did not look at photos, but he did describe the men wearing trench coats and overcoats, stating that one of them was around five foot, four inches.

On July 12, 1990, the police received an anonymous call suggesting they check out Maurice Caldwell. The next day, the police canvassed the projects to find witnesses or anyone with any information about what had happened on June 30. One of the uniformed canvassing officers was none other than Maurice's old nemesis, Kitt Crenshaw. Responding to a knock on her door, Mary Cobbs found herself talking with the investigating detective. When he asked about the shooting, Cobbs said she had seen the whole thing. After a brief conversation with Cobbs, the detective turned on his tape recorder:

> "I was asleep, but the gunshots and breaking glass woke me up. I went to my window and saw two men. One of them had a handgun and one had a shotgun. They were standing under a streetlight. They don't live around here, but I seen them around selling drugs."

Cobbs told the detective she would recognize them if she saw them again. The detective told Cobbs that if anyone threatened her and if she agreed to help the police they would move her out of the projects.

As he was walking around the projects looking for witnesses, Officer Crenshaw saw Maurice. He handcuffed Maurice and took him to Cobbs's door while the detective was still there questioning Cobbs. "I need to put Maurice Caldwell here in the car," he told the detective. "Do you have the keys?"

Why did Officer Crenshaw take Maurice to Cobbs's apartment? He could have waited at the car for the detective to return instead of exposing what looked like a handcuffed suspect to a potential witness. Officer Crenshaw's actions appear even more suspicious because he did not even take Maurice to the squad car. In fact, after leaving Mary Cobb's apartment, Officer Crenshaw removed Maurice's handcuffs and let him go.

On July 26, 1990, Cobbs picked Maurice's photo out of a six-pack saying, "That's him, that's 'Twone." The next day, Bobila picked Maurice's photo out of the same six-pack. He wasn't absolutely sure that Maurice was the guy, but he looked familiar. On October 23, 1990, the police staged a live line-up attended by Vivray, Aguirre, and Bobila. Vivray tentatively identified one of the fillers as the shooter. Aguirre put a question mark by Maurice's line-up number and wrote "maybe" next to it. Bobila wrote an "X" and the word "possibly" next to Maurice's line-up number.

On September 21, 1990, the police arrested Maurice for Acosta's murder. The prosecution's main evidence was the eyewitness testimony of Mary Cobbs and her testimony was full of inconsistencies. She tried to explain away her initial statement that she did not know the names of the shooters because she wasn't sure that Maurice's nickname was 'Twone even though she recognized him as 'Twone on the night of the shooting. She said she knew him from when he lived next door to her. She tried to explain away her initial statement that the shooters did not live in the neighborhood by saying that Maurice had moved and no longer lived in the projects. Betty Jean Tyler, a defense witness, challenged that statement when she testified that Maurice lived in her apartment, which was next door to Cobbs, from 1988 until the day of his arrest.

The other eyewitnesses could not definitively identify Maurice as the shooter or one of the other men with the shooter. Aguirre testified at Maurice's trial that Maurice did not match the descriptions he gave the police of the men who were standing under the streetlight the night of the shooting and was not the man he described as five foot, four inches." Bobila testified that he picked Maurice out of the six-pack and the live line-up because he looked familiar. He also testified that the investigating detective did a dry run-through with him when he looked at the six-pack, before the detective recorded the identification. Bobila said Maurice did not match the height or description of the man who punched him. Vivray testified that he chose Maurice at the live line-up because he had picked Maurice in the six-pack, but he still wasn't sure about the six-pack identification. Each of the witnesses was asked to identify Maurice in court and each of them testified that they could not identify him as one of the men standing under the streetlight and definitely not as the shooter.

Deborah Rodriguez testified that Maurice had been upstairs in her apartment at the time the shots were fired. In a post-conviction statement, Tina McCullum verified what Deborah said. Neither woman heard any more shots after Maurice and Deborah left the apartment. Maurice and Deborah went outside the next morning to find out what happened. Deborah testified that Marritte Funches, someone she knew from the projects, told her he had shot someone. Alice Carruthers testified that she had seen Funches standing under the streetlight with some other men at around 2:00 a.m. that Saturday morning and that Maurice was not outside at that time.

Despite all of the contradictory evidence and the testimony of Maurice's alibi witnesses, on March 19, 1991 the jury found him guilty of second degree murder, attempted murder, and felony discharge of a firearm into an occupied vehicle, as well as additional lesser charges. When the judge polled the jury, however, he learned that the jury foreman had voted "not guilty" on the second degree murder charge. The foreman told the judge that he thought he had to mark "guilty" on the form because of the answers the judge had given the jury to some of its questions. A judge's response from questions from the jury does not dictate how an individual juror must vote. The foreman also told the judge he was not comfortable being the foreman. The judge sent the jury back for further deliberations, but this time they had a new foreman. The next day March 20, 1991, the jury found Maurice guilty of second degree murder.

The defense team immediately filed a motion for a new trial, which the court denied on April 29, 1991. The defense team appealed to the California Court of Appeal, First Appellate District, which affirmed Maurice's conviction. Maurice would remain in prison for nearly twenty-one years before proving his innocence. Mary Cobbs, meanwhile, was moved out of the Alemany Projects as the police promised. She also was honored by San Francisco for her bravery and given a medal of merit, the highest honor the city could give to a civilian.

Even though he was no boy scout, Maurice had nothing to do with Acosta's death. He was angry about being imprisoned for something he had not done; something he could not imagine doing—killing another person. Focusing his anger on his exoneration did not come easily to Maurice, but it did come.

* * *

In The Belly Of The Beast

By Maurice A. Caldwell

Hello everyone, my name is Maurice Caldwell. I am a 2012 exoneree having served twenty years, six months, and four days in prison for a crime I had no involvement in at all. I want to share a very meaningful story about how I was truly able to overcome each day of my prison life without giving up.

When I arrived into the California Department of Corrections (CDC) prison system, I seriously feared I would not make it back home, at least not in one piece. It was all the stories I had heard about prison, the riots, killings, abuse, rape, gambling, drugs, gang-banging, and more, that put the fear in me. As an innocent man going into the prison system, it was very hard, in fact almost impossible to keep my mind right.

At first all I was able to think about was my family and friends and the life that was taken away from me. Living everyday wrongfully convicted, I felt in my heart and soul that I was only going to somehow get through all my losses by adapting to a whole different approach to living my life and altering my state of mind.

I was a twenty-two years young first termer in prison. All new comers to the system were known as "Fish" and if you weren't a strong new inmate then they would address you as "Fresh Fish on the Line." Often some found these labels in many ways disrespectful. That would be a problem because in prison disrespectful can turn into a real serious altercation right then and there.

I already had experience in the California Youth Authority system, when I was younger. The Youth Authority incarcerated juveniles for crimes that weren't too serious. And if you should happen to end up in prison after a stint at the Youth Authority, you would be a little more prepared for prison. They call it Gladiator School.

I knew that if I was to survive in prison I would have to adapt to my surroundings. I was familiar with survival skills and knew that the best way for me to adapt was to be like the others; become a product of my prison environment. I didn't feel I had a choice. But I also knew that, first and foremost I had to get myself out of prison, which required me to focus. With this "new" me I became a respected, focused, and determined innocent guy. I spent my time going to the library and writing many letters to lawyers and media outlet people and some to my family.

I had no serious problems with the inmates when I first arrived. They didn't try to disrespect me or play me. In my mind I wasn't a Fish and therefore I wasn't going to be treated like one. I was a much focused somewhat prepared young guy entering into this prison system, but it turned out I wasn't as prepared as I thought I was.

I was sentenced to a Level 4 prison which is the highest, most deadly level of all California prisons. Level 4 prisons are the places where the most dangerous criminals are held and where the most serious riots and killings take place. The riots are constant. I served almost ten years straight on the Level 4 yards. I was involved in more than sixteen riots, some of which were racially motivated. I witnessed first-hand people getting stabbed, seriously hurt, and even killed. I was in the "belly of the beast" as we called prison back then. So you can see why I was afraid. At no time at all did I ever feel safe or secure when I was in prison. I carried a deep fear every time I left my cell; always worried that I might not make it back. Violence in the prison was at the drop of a dime; suddenly and without any notice at all.

I was really angry too. It was because of this anger that there were confrontations between me and the prison authorities earlier in my incarceration. I really didn't feel that the state had the authority to be controlling my everyday life, since I was an innocent man who didn't really belong there. Every day I was in prison I was so self-conscious about being an innocent man. I was around so many dangerous guilty offenders who had nothing to lose. They would hurt you in any way that they could or kill you and wouldn't give a shit about it afterwards. I guess really I was angry and scared, so when the prison authorities treated me like I was a guilty prisoner it stirred up my anger. Maybe it was an immediate way for me to fight for my innocence.

Here's an example of how it can happen; quick, fast, and deadly! Often uninvolved inmates have no choice but to turn into the "Beast" and defend themselves by becoming an aggressor, even when you didn't initiate or have knowledge that an incident was about to happen. I remember one crowded Sunday morning breakfast at Pleasant Valley State Prison in 2004. It was crowded because in most prisons, Sunday breakfast is the very best of all the breakfasts served so it's the day that almost everybody goes to the chow hall. It was a minor issue that took place at the chow hall window, with a black inmate accusing a white kitchen worker inmate of giving him a half-cooked egg. He and the kitchen worker exchanged negative words, but they couldn't get to each other because they were separated by the food service window. The kitchen worker came out from behind the window where he was serving food. They were some distance from each other and from the crowds all around. Once the inmate in the chow line saw the kitchen worker, the chow line inmate said "hats up" and the kitchen worker threw his right arm in the air in a Nazi hailing Hitler salute. Without any warning or other words, the whites and blacks started fighting, stabbing, and assaulting each other with trays and cups. The riot spread quickly through the yard and inside the buildings. It lasted for what seemed like at least ten minutes but it could've been more. It would stop and then start back up again. During these breaks we would be able to catch our breath and recover from the correctional officers' mace assault; cans of mace shot from a gun called "Big Bertha." Just because of the color of our skin—being black or white—we found ourselves caught up in this riot even though we had nothing to do with it. That's what I mean by having no choice but to become a product of your environment and adapt or play a part in whatever situation happens. Prison life really and truly changed my whole perspective on the power of influence. While in prison, I had very little to no choices, especially when it came down to riots based on race or territory.

Each day that I was in prison I found it very hard to manage the stress. I was stressed in my mind and in my soul. I constantly felt that the life I once knew and missed terribly was just passing me by, giving up on me. The life I once had and planned on enjoying the rest of my days, living and growing old, was now being planned and lived within those prison walls. A tremendous change in the outlook of my life was necessary. In prison, in order to survive everything must change; the need for an adjustment of my mind, my feelings, my attitude, my motives, even my heart. I had to make those adjustments. I had figure out how to survive. But the most important thing I had to do was regain my freedom.

Even though there was stress and drama for me every day in prison I was always able to count my blessings, one of which was that I was able to read and write. You would be surprised at how many inside don't know how to do this. This gift allowed me to communicate with the main people who would come into my life and help me. And this gift would be the very thing that would help me endure the stress of prison life, would help me through the tremendously hard times I faced in prison. Being able to write allowed me to gain some freedom from all those hard times. I used writing as a means to escape all the madness. Every time I sat in my cell and wrote a letter, expressing to anyone, the wrong that was handed to me, anyone who would hear about my wrongful conviction, it was my way of holding onto hope. Every legal letter was one more way to protect myself from the prison life and keep me focused on regaining my freedom. I wrote letters to attorneys and to my family and friends. Writing to my family and friends helped me maintain my sanity and provided me with some means of hope. I wrote to my sister and my uncle. I wrote to television news programs like *Dateline*, *Hard Copy*, *20/20*, *Inside Edition*, and *Front Line*. I wrote to *Montel Williams*, *Oprah Winfrey*, and *Maury Povich*. I wrote to Centurion Ministry Innocence Project and the Northern California Innocence Project. I wrote to whoever came to mind and to everybody I thought could and might help me. I would remain diligent in exposing my wrongful conviction and re-claiming my freedom. Sooner or later someone would hear my cry for help and my claim for justice ... at least I hoped so.

I was so focused on the writing and so determined to get out of jail as an innocent man that I refused to fully indulge in the prison system Job Trade PIA work program. I had a few jobs here and there outside of the prisons' work programs, but I wasn't interested and didn't care about being on a work site, gaining a trade or collecting any of the prison certificates provided when an industry trade course was completed and passed. I would not allow any type of prison work detail to come between me and my fight for freedom. As an innocent man I felt that I would be in conflict by helping the CDC generate political dollars off my back, when I wasn't supposed to be there. I didn't want to be sidetracked from my own meaningful and very important political fight. I refused all CDC jobs that would demand all of my time and create a daily program that would take me away from the most important job of my life—proving my innocence. I said no thank you to a prison job that would tire me and take away all my time. I just didn't want the distraction and wouldn't take the risk of losing interest in my fight, for a few pennies and a certificate.

Prison is full of a lot of danger and is so stressful for the innocent person. The only way I was going to survive and make it out of prison a sane person was to do something positive and consistent. I wrote so many letters, pouring all my heart and soul into them. My determination to regain my freedom and having the ability and commitment to write those letters helped me to survive it all. Certainly in the end the letters were the ultimate factor in my release. I wrote one more letter and someone heard my cry.

Throughout my time in prison, I was known as a convict "who functioned" which meant I was able to understand and work within the structure of prison life. At the same time I also fully represented myself as a determined man, focused on proving my innocence and regaining my freedom. I was well respected by all my prison peers. They saw in me, my ability, no matter what, to stay true to my claims of innocence. They also saw my strength to continuously deal with the negative surroundings in the "belly of the beast."

Now that I am free, I have restored my sense of security, and I appreciate being able to reject political situations at my choosing. I have learned from my experience how the prison system works; that those in charge aren't interested in rehabilitation. The staff is more concerned about their paychecks than what they are paid to do. They abuse their jobs by being selective about what they do and don't do; which rules they enforce or ignore, depriving the incarcerated of their prison rights and their security. These correctional officers have neither the time nor the patience, or in point of fact the will, to invest the effort to turn the negative mind-set of the prison population into one that is constructive and rehabilitated. I'm thankful, finally, to be out.

* * *

It took nearly eighteen years for a court to consider Maurice's writ of habeas corpus. On February 18, 2009, his post-conviction legal team filed the writ with the Superior Court of the State of California. It had taken them over a year to build a case that included two new eyewitnesses to the shooting who contradicted Mary Cobbs's testimony and corroborated the testimony of the defense witnesses. They also located Marritte Funches in a Nevada prison. Funches, who admitted to being the actual shooter, provided an affidavit that was attached to the writ. Funches also admitted that the man with the shotgun that night was not Maurice Caldwell and, further, that Cobbs could not have seen Funches standing under the streetlight because he had not been standing under the streetlight that night. Funches had been living in Nevada since the shooting and while in Nevada he murdered another person. Funches claimed that until he was contacted by Maurice's post-conviction legal team, no one, not even the police, had spoken to him about the events of June 30, 1990.

In December 2010, Superior Court Judge Charles Haines set aside Maurice's conviction and ordered a new trial. Initially San Francisco prosecutors announced they intended to retry Maurice, but by this time Mary Cobbs had died. When the judge ruled that Cobbs's testimony would not be admitted as evidence, the prosecutors decided not to retry Maurice. The charges against him were dropped and he was released on March 28, 2011. Even though Maurice had been found guilty, the trial testimony of two defense witnesses should have caused the San Francisco Police Department (SFPD) to investigate whether Funches was in fact the shooter. Had they done this, there is a good chance they would have learned in 1991 that Maurice was innocent and he would have been spared the horror of spending more than twenty years in prison for a crime he did not commit. Even when faced with new eyewitness testimony that corroborated the testimony from the 1991 trial, and Funches's own confession by affidavit, the SFPD still did not investigate Funches as the shooter and to this day, inexplicably has not conducted any investigation involving Funches. Perhaps if they had investigated Funches back in 1991, the taxi driver he killed in Nevada would still be alive.

During the more than twenty years Maurice was in prison, he lost many members of his family. Fortunately for him his sister, Deborah, was there for him so he would keep fighting for his freedom.

* * *

I'm Still Here

As Told By Deborah Caldwell

It was unbelievable. Nothing was really right about his case. They didn't have the gun that killed the victim or any strong evidence. The men who were with the victim at the time of the murder couldn't positively identify Maurice. The only eyewitness didn't really know Maurice and falsely identified him for gain. They gave her a trip to Disneyland and a new apartment in a different place. It was just all mixed up, I don't know, it was like they were targeting him. That's how I looked at it.

Nothing worked out like it should have. Maurice's attorney was referred to him by a friend, but he was a drug lawyer not a murder lawyer. He had never tried a murder case in his life and he took Maurice's. I don't think by law he was supposed to, but they said since the murder occurred during a drug deal it was okay. I guess that's why he took the case. The whole court system just looked like...I don't know. I was sad because I knew he didn't murder anybody. Maurice had a past, but he wasn't a murderer.

Maurice was bad when he was young, but not to the extreme. He wasn't so bad that he would kill somebody. He wasn't like that. Every kid makes stupid mistakes when they're young. He did stuff he's not proud of, but people shouldn't label him. Yet that behavior followed him. When you're young and doing stupid things and bad things it all gets combined together. They could've been looking at all the stupid bad stuff he did, and knowing that made him a suspect.

We all grew up in Alemany Public Housing in Bernal Heights. When we were young my mother was on drugs which made me grow up fast. I had to care for my two brothers. My grandmother was around helping us too, but at eight years old, I was cooking dinner, washing the dishes, and making sure my brothers were okay. I was the big sister and the mama and everything else. I thank them for that, though. It made me strong and a better person to deal with what I am going through now. But it was Alemany where all the bad stuff started to happen with 'Twone. We all called him 'Twone back then; we still do.

I was so sad for him. I went to every court hearing he had. I was there when they convicted him and I was shocked when they handed down his sentence. 'Twone was given a sentence of twenty-seven to life. That is a long time to be in jail for a crime you didn't do. It just wasn't right. I knew that my brother was not the murderer. And the circumstances by which he was found guilty were so weak.

I had no doubts that he would come home. I just didn't know when. I prayed on it every day. I wrote him letters and tried to visit him every other weekend, hoping I was keeping his spirits up. It was kind of hard getting used to all the prison rules for visitors. They didn't treat visitors very well in the beginning. What was even harder was when we went to visit and he couldn't leave with us. I know that was hard for him at the end of our visits, and we were saddened because we knew how much he wanted to be out of there and at home.

As time went on, it became more difficult to get there when our mother got very sick. I couldn't get there as often as I wanted, but I continued to support him through letters and phone calls. He would call often and talk with all of us. You could hear his stress when the call started, but after he talked to all of us you could tell he was feeling a little better.

One of the bad things about being in prison is that a lot of stuff happens outside that the prisoner misses, and it's even harder when they're in jail but shouldn't be. Our brother and mother died when 'Twone was in prison. That was the hardest thing to deal with. I found it so difficult it took me almost a month before I could tell 'Twone that our mother had died. I didn't know what to do. I knew it would be hard for him to hear the news. When they talked to each other his spirits would rise, so I knew this sad news would be a jolt. I just didn't want him to have more stress and be more depressed than he already was. But I told him...finally.

I tried to be as much support to 'Twone as I could. He could count on me and I wanted to make sure I was there for him. I helped him write letters to everybody. He wrote letters. I wrote letters. It was one of the ways I could support him—especially when our mother's illness got worse. He needed this support and I was there for him in every way I could be. When he was released from jail he began

111

speaking on wrongful conviction. I even did a speaking engagement with him in support of this effort. I didn't really like it though, it was just ooh...I get so nervous in front of people, and I don't like the way that feels. But it was for 'Twone, so I did it for him.

Sometimes I felt like I was not doing enough. Often I would break down. When I could get in my own little space I would think about all the stuff that was going on, around me and my family, like my family members passing away, and 'Twone being wrongfully convicted. I would cry and cry. I cried a lot and it was hard, but I had to be strong. I was always the one they would call, whenever something had to be done. I was the one who took care of it. I'm still the one who takes care of things, but I don't have a problem with it. I loved my momma dearly. I took care of her until she died. I took care of my grandmomma. She passed from cancer. I was there to take care of my brother and I am still here to take care of him and anyone else who needs me.

It's been a blessing to take care of my family, especially my momma and grandmomma. I didn't think I would do it for anyone outside of my family, but I'm now in home health care, professionally. Taking care of my family has been a good thing for me. It prepared me for this kind of work. It's been a blessing. I guess it's just in me to take care of people.

I don't blame the justice system for what happened to 'Twone. It was that girl who identified my brother mistakenly. There was this other 'Twone in the neighborhood back then. She didn't know who she was talking about. In some ways it may have been a blessing because he was bad in his younger days. It may have saved him from getting deeper into the life he had before. I am truly thankful that the Northern California Innocence Project had faith in him and knew he was innocent. They went out of their way to help him. They did the footwork, talked to witnesses, and different stuff that his original lawyer didn't do. Doors were opened because of this support.

'Twone didn't belong in prison. He didn't commit the crime he was accused of, but he remained safe in prison and he made it home safely. Not too many make it home. He came home to some family. It was sad that there were those who passed away while he was in prison and he didn't get a chance to see them before they passed, but that's just a part of life. I'm so glad he's home. He's doing okay. He's got a family and they live in a new place away from Alemany. It gets better day-by-day, just seeing my brother home, living his life like he should have been doing a long time ago.

I'll always be there for him. It's just me and him now, basically with his kids and my kids. We are each other's family. We are each other's support.

* * *

TRUE fact!!

Some of the men and women who have been released from prison after living a sentence that should not have been theirs have processed their feelings through various kinds of therapy traditional and unconventional. Unlike them, Maurice is still reckoning with his wrongful conviction. He wants people to realize that his trip to prison, and he is convinced that this is how it happened, was at the hands of someone who in a perfect world should have served and protected him rather than used his power and influence to throw him into the "belly of the beast." Maurice did not commit the crime and no matter how one looks at it, regardless of his past brushes with the law, he should not have been imprisoned for that crime. No man, woman, or child should spend time in prison for crimes they did not commit.

Maurice vowed when he was released that he would not step foot back into the Alemany Housing Projects. He wanted a new and different life. He did not ever want to be at risk of imprisonment again. At first, with limited options in living arrangements, Maurice moved in with his sister, Deborah, and her fiancé, Danny. He stayed with them for eight or nine months. Danny was very generous and supportive and for a good while helped Maurice acclimate himself to the new world he found upon his release. Unfortunately, Danny passed away. Maurice didn't want to be a burden on his family and decided to move. He called everyone he knew to get a lead on a job and eventually was connected with someone through the Northern California Innocence Project. He found a job in a warehouse and worked for a while, until injuries, developed while in prison, kept him from doing his job. Maurice recently underwent surgery on his hands for carpal tunnel syndrome but continues to be plagued with back pain.

Maurice still struggles with employment. He receives disability income, but he would like to be responsible for more of the financial load. Maurice currently speaks to a wide variety of audiences around the country on wrongful conviction and the death penalty and is always available to be a voice for these issues which is sorely needed and for which he stands strong. One of the bright spots in Maurice's life since his release is Pamela Haynes. They became inseparable and now have a healthy baby boy named Maurice and a daughter named Amaya.

While he is grateful to be out of prison, Maurice has experienced sorrow as a free man. "The saddest two days out of my life as a free person," he says, "were when the Lord unexpectedly took my brother-in-law, Danny Milton, from me and my family, and when me and my sister and our family were forced to give up our apartment and be torn apart as a family once again."

In 2012, Maurice named three officers, including Kitt Crenshaw, in a civil suit filed against the City of San Francisco for their involvement in the unreliable testimony of Mary Cobb resulting in his wrongful conviction. In 2013, Maurice filed a claim for compensation with the California Victims Compensation and Government Claims Board for $731,400 for his wrongful conviction and incarceration. Maurice, his family, and his defense lawyers are waiting for decisions in both matters.

If you ask Maurice what he wanted to do as soon as he was released, after making sure that he was able to see all his family, he will tell you he wanted a Big Mac from McDonald's. His lawyer took him to McDonald's where he swooned saying that it tasted as good as he remembered.

Maurice Caldwell lives with his family in Northern California. He travels around the State speaking out against wrongful conviction and advocating for the rights of the wrongfully convicted. Deborah Caldwell, his sister, is a health care professional.

CHAPTER 7
Arthur Paul Carmona

Arthur Carmona celebrated his sixteenth birthday on February 5, 1998 with his family and friends. Like most teenage boys, Arthur loved riding his skateboard, playing video games, and hanging out with his friends and cousins who were his age. His mother, Ronnie, occasionally asked Arthur to babysit his twelve year old sister, Veronica. Most teenage boys would complain about having to babysit their little sister. Arthur never did. He always kept an eye on Veronica, even when she was in the yard playing with her friends. He liked babysitting her, but he sometimes bugged Ronnie to hurry up with whatever she was doing so he could go skateboarding with his friends.

Arthur had been protective of his little sister from the day she was born. One evening, not long after bringing the baby home from the hospital, Ronnie was sitting on the sofa feeding her when Arthur, age five, ran into the living room and jumped on the couch. "Mama, somebody's trying to break in my window!" Ronnie laid the baby down on the couch next to Arthur and went into Arthur's room to see what was happening. Ronnie thought it was her husband coming home drunk and trying to sneak in undetected.

"You idiot!" Ronnie said as she entered the room and heard the window rattling. "You're scaring Arthur." Ronnie opened the window blinds and saw a stranger standing on the other side of the window, trying to lift it up. Fortunately it was locked.

"I'm calling the police!" she shouted to the stranger outside and ran back into the living room to be with her children. She heard pounding on the kitchen door as she grabbed the phone and dialed 9-1-1. "A man is trying to break into my house!" Ronnie yelled into the phone. "He's trying to kick the door down!"

Ronnie ran into the kitchen and threw her body against the door and stayed on the phone with 9-1-1 until the police arrived at the door. By then the man had run away. Ronnie let the police in and went to check on Arthur and baby Veronica. They weren't on the sofa where she left them. Before she could panic one of the police officers pulled the sofa forward and there sat Arthur, wrapped in a blanket, cradling Veronica and rocking her so she would not cry. Brother and sister remained close until prison changed everything.

On February 10, 1998, shortly before 2:00 a.m., a Denny's in Costa Mesa, California was robbed. The robbery was witnessed by two Denny's servers—Casey Becerra and George Algie. Becerra was standing at the cash register when a man wearing a baseball cap pulled down over his face came in and pointed a gun at her. Becerra gave the robber the money and, at the gunman's order, got down on the floor with Algie. The robber left and Algie stood up in time to see a truck speed out of the Denny's parking lot.

On February 12, 1998, Ronnie asked Arthur to stay home and keep an eye on Veronica. At around noon, Veronica went to visit their grandmother. Arthur took a short nap before calling his friends to figure out what they were going to do that afternoon. Meanwhile, at around 1:00 p.m., a young Latino man wearing a black LA Lakers baseball cap was seen peering through the window of a juice bar in Irvine, California. Two employees noticed him because of the distinctive design of the baseball cap—purple letters with a gold basketball in the background. At around 3:30 p.m., the robber entered the juice bar and asked the cashier to change a dollar bill. When the cashier opened the register to make change, the robber pointed a gun at him and demanded the money from the till. The cashier put the money from the register into a black backpack the robber had placed on the counter. The robber shouldered the pack and told everyone in the store to lie down on the floor. Three employees and two customers dropped to the floor and the robber ran outside to a gas station across the street. The cashier called 9-1-1. Two men at the gas station across the street from the juice bar saw the robber as he quickly fled the scene. One of them described the robber as "a Latino person, about five foot six or five foot seven and skinny," about "seventeen or twenty years old" who "didn't have any facial hair." They saw him jump into a truck parked at the gas station. The other gas station witness described the getaway driver as "a male Hispanic in his thirties." He thought something was up and wrote down the license plate of the getaway truck as it sped around the corner. When the police arrived, he gave them the license plate number.

Arthur had called three of his friends between 1:00 p.m. and 3:00 p.m. and left his home in Costa Mesa to go to the home of his friend, Roy Bueno, at around 3:45 p.m. Before Arthur could make it to Roy's house, also in Costa Mesa, a policeman stopped him on the street and took him into custody. The first time the officer saw him, Arthur was riding his bicycle down the street, at about 4:15 p.m. The officer did not think Arthur fit the description of the robber. Arthur wasn't wearing a helmet so he quickly left his bike at another friend's house. Money was tight at home and he didn't want to upset his mother by getting a ticket for riding without a helmet. Arthur was only sixteen years old, not seventeen or twenty or in his thirties. At five feet eight inches he was a little taller than the description and at a hundred and sixty five pounds he would not have been described as "skinny." Furthermore, Arthur's thin moustache was facial hair, contrary to the description of one of the gas station witnesses. A few minutes later a police helicopter directed the officer to where Arthur was walking down the street. Although Arthur wasn't wearing a baseball cap or carrying a backpack, he did have on a dark shirt and witnesses had described the robber as wearing dark clothes. That flimsy description was enough for the police to arrest him.

The police thought the robbers were responsible for both crimes as well as a number of other armed robberies in the area. They ran the license plate number and discovered it belonged to Shawn Kaiwi. The police went to Kaiwi's address and found the truck parked outside of the apartment. Inside were the black LA Laker's baseball cap, the black backpack, and a nine millimeter handgun with ammo. While the police were at Kaiwi's apartment building, a woman in Costa Mesa saw a young man jump the fence behind her house and start running across the yard. She called the police and when they arrived, he was gone, but the woman described him as a "Hispanic teenager wearing a baseball cap and dark clothing." It would take someone about ten minutes to get from Kaiwi's building to the woman's house, but he would have to cross at least three lanes of freeway traffic to do it.

The police proceeded to gather eyewitness evidence from the people in the juice bar and the evidence was mixed at best. First the police drove three of the juice bar robbery witnesses to Kaiwi's apartment building. One of the gas station witnesses identified Kaiwi as the man waiting in the truck, but none of the witnesses identified him as the robber. Next, the police took the witnesses to another address where they saw a "[s]hort, stocky, old" person who they did not identify as the robber. Finally, the police brought the witnesses to the street where they were holding Arthur. None of the witnesses identified Arthur as the robber. One of the witnesses asked to see Arthur wearing a baseball cap. The police put the LA Lakers cap they found in Kaiwi's truck onto Arthur's head. The cap matched the description given to the police by the juice bar cashier and, after seeing the hat on Arthur's head, the cashier identified Arthur as the robber. The police did not tell the cashier that the hat was not found on Arthur, but was in the getaway truck. Another juice bar employee could not identify Arthur even with the hat on his head. At trial this employee explained that he thought Arthur was the robber because of the baseball cap. He said that without the hat he couldn't tell it was Arthur but with the hat, "it made more sense to me."

> *Witness*: Well, when I first saw him I wasn't for sure that was him, but then he put the baseball cap on, the Laker's hat, then I said that's him.
>
> *Question*: So the hat made the difference to you?
>
> Witness: Right.
>
> *Question*: So you ID'd the hat as being the one you saw, or a Laker's hat with a Mexican kid under it?
>
> *Witness*: Right. Like the face I can't do it by the face. I couldn't identify him, just the face. I told the cop that, too.

The woman who watched someone climb her fence also needed the hat to make an identification. "When they took [Arthur] out of the car, the hat was not on his head, and I asked the police officer if there was a hat, and there was a hat in the car and they put the hat on his head when they took him out of the car. It was the same baseball cap... It had a design, same design on the front." Like the other witnesses, the woman was identifying the cap and not the person wearing the cap. What no one told her was the cap was not the same one that the fence jumper was wearing because at the time he was jumping the fence, the police were collecting the Lakers cap from Kaiwi's truck.

The four remaining juice bar witnesses did not participate in a field identification. Instead, they came to the police station to view photo lineups. Not one of them identified Arthur and two of them, the customers, identified someone other than Arthur as the robber. After Arthur's arrest for the juice bar robbery, the police charged him with the Denny's robbery and tried to charge him with ten other similar robberies in the area. Becerra did not identify Arthur's picture in a photo lineup, but she did identify him two months later when Arthur, wearing an Orange County Jail jump suit, appeared in court next to his attorney. The other Denny's employee, Algie, chose Arthur's photo from a six-pack because Arthur "was the closest" of the six pictures to the guy who robbed Denny's but that he "looked younger than the robber." A month later, Algie could not identify anyone in the photo lineup as the robber. Aside from the shaky eyewitness identifications, there was no other evidence linking Arthur to Kaiwi or these two robberies or the ten other similar armed robberies Kaiwi and his accomplice had committed.

Despite the lack of evidence, Arthur was charged with twelve counts of second-degree robbery and one count of assault. School records showed that Arthur had been in class at the time of ten of the armed robberies. The charges related to those armed robberies were dropped. At trial, only two witnesses of the nine witnesses to the remaining two armed robberies identified Arthur. The cashier at the juice bar stated that he was only eighty percent certain until the baseball cap was placed on Arthur's head. Becerra from Denny's also identified Arthur. The woman who saw someone jump her fence identified Arthur, stating that she recognized the face and the eyes but that she wasn't close enough to see any facial hair. The defense did not question how she was too far to see facial hair but close enough to see the man's eyes and face. In fact, Arthur's attorney did not call any of the logical alibi witnesses—the friends he called from home that afternoon. The prosecutor made a point of mentioning this in his closing argument:

> "The failure of the defense to call the logical witnesses or [Arthur's friends], you can consider that... [I]t's illogical that those people would not be able to come in and testify to you under oath as to supposedly talking to the defendant on the phone which would provide him with a possible alibi."

On Thursday, October 22, 1998, the jury found Arthur guilty on all counts. Despite being only sixteen years old, Arthur had been charged as an adult. He would remain in the county jail until his sentencing. Until Arthur's arrest and wrongful conviction, Ronnie's faith in the justice system had been unshakeable. Like many, she believed the truth would prevail, the system would work, and Arthur would come home. She soon learned that truth can be a victim of the system and even a good kid with no record could be labeled a felon through no fault of his own. Arthur's conviction shook Ronnie's faith to the core.

* * *

A Lazy Saturday Afternoon With Mijo
By Ronnie Sandoval

This recipe was handed down to me by my son, Arthur Carmona. Arthur was wrongfully convicted when he was only sixteen years old, but the State tried him as an adult. He was sentenced to twelve years in state prison.

After Arthur's release, he never spoke to me about his experience in prison. The first few years after his release he spent lost in his anger. After the Northern California Innocence Project found him and united him with other California exonerees, Arthur found a love for cooking. His specialty was grilled veggies lightly seasoned, medium rare porter house steak cooked slowly, and brown rice. I remember one particular Saturday afternoon. I was cleaning the house and washing clothes. I asked Arthur to make me some soup. He smiled slyly and it was then that he made me "The Spread."

I remember that day well. After a long morning of household chores, I was exhausted. I sat down on the couch and put my feet up—lifeless, in a daze, watching television. I looked over to my right, and there he stood at the kitchen sink; his expression was solemn. I could see steam rising up from the sink, obscuring his face a little. I curiously watched him gently breaking ramen noodles in the package. What in the world was he cooking? I yelled over to him, "Hey goober, I like the long noodles!"

He looked up and said, "This is better than regular soup." I had no idea what he was preparing and I got even more confused when I saw him at the sink draining the water from a bowl. Who makes soup without any liquid!?

A few minutes later, Arthur walked over to where I sat on the couch and handed me a bowl on a plate surrounded by crackers. The bowl was filled with some sort of tuna noodle spread. He sat down next to me and watched as I took my first bite. Whoa! It was delicious. I was hooked. Arthur nodded knowingly, almost smugly, "I told you."

He put some of the spread on a cracker and took a bite. We sat silently for a few moments, just crunching and eating. A feeling of contentment rippled through me. As we sat eating the spread, I asked Arthur where he learned to make this.

"In there. Prison," he said in almost a whisper.

I didn't know you could cook in prison, so I asked, "How do you cook in prison?" I'll never forget his answer.

"You'd be surprised what you can do in there."

I was surprised because Arthur never spoke about the time he did in prison. I sat quietly eating and listened to him. I still can't think about him in that awful place without tearing up a little.

"This stuff reminded me of when I was young," he said wistfully, "before everything. I remember you cooking whatever we had to eat, mixing things together until they tasted so good you would forget how simple the dish was."

"Mijo," I replied. "You know what I think? Someone was trying to make tuna casserole."

Arthur nodded. "Yup."

As we sat and I ate, he talked. He told me how nothing in there went to waste. He never said the word "prison." He just called it "in there." Arthur explained how an inmate once made a placemat out of paper gum wrappers. He explained how to make fire using lead from pencils and a small wad of toilet paper. I was amazed at what they could do in there with very little. Imagine what some of those men could do if given a chance. After a while, Arthur stopped talking and we just sat there on a lazy Saturday, watching television and eating The Spread with jalapeños. I share this memory of my son with you and hope you will remember him as I saw him that Saturday—happy and at home with people who loved him.

Arthur's Tuna Ramen Casserole (a.k.a. "The Spread")

Ingredients

1 package of ramen soup (chili—if you like spicy, chicken, beef, or oriental)

2-4 tablespoons mayonnaise

1 can of tuna

Crackers (your favorite brand or flavor)

Jalapenos (fresh or pickled)

Boil some water according to the instructions on the package of soup. Take the noodles out of the package and set the seasoning packet on the side. Break up the noodles and put them into a bowl with a lid. Cover the noodles with boiling water and put the lid on the bowl.

While the noodles cook, drain the tuna and put half of it in another bowl. Mix in the mayonnaise. Sprinkle in the seasoning packet to taste. Drain the noodles and gently fold them into the tuna mixture.

Serve with your favorite crackers and the jalapenos as a spread. As a variation, you can break up the crackers and sprinkle them on top of the casserole.

* * *

Immediately after Arthur's guilty verdict, his inept counsel was replaced and his new counsel filed a motion for a new trial. Over the next few months the eyewitness identifications, including Becerra, were recanted. Becerra claimed the police told her they found the gun, baseball cap, and backpack and that they were Arthur's. She said they also told her Arthur had been seen in the truck. Despite the recantations and extensive media coverage of the case, on June 10, 1999, the trial judge denied Arthur's motion for a new trial. The courtroom was filled with people who wanted to speak on Arthur's behalf. After a number of people had spoken up for Arthur, Judge Everett Dickey sentenced Arthur to twelve years in prison instead of the twenty-five years Ronnie was expecting. Even though he had been tried as an adult, Arthur was sent to Norwalk Youth Authority. Nadia Davis, an attorney and close family friend, appealed to prison authorities to house Arthur in a youth facility. About one week after his sentencing, the law firm of Sidley Austin Brown & Wood agreed to take on Arthur as a pro bono client. One of their first actions was to have Arthur transferred to the Preston Youth Correctional Facility until his eighteenth birthday. He had been assigned to Pelican Bay Prison, a Level 4 facility for housing the most dangerous adult males. Over the next fourteen months Arthur would be transferred back and forth between multiple prisons.

In January 2000, Arthur's attorneys filed a habeas petition in Orange County Superior Court. Only hours before a court hearing to determine whether Arthur would be granted a new trial, the prosecution offered him a deal. If he would sign a stipulation that there was no misconduct by the Irvine Police Department or the Orange County District Attorney's office his habeas petition would be granted, his conviction would be vacated, and his record would be expunged. The case would be dismissed with prejudice and Arthur would be free to go. Arthur did not want to sign the stipulation, but Ronnie wanted her son home. She no longer trusted the legal system. She feared for Arthur's life. In the fourteen months since his sentencing Arthur had lived through two riots and what else she did not know. What she did know was Arthur had an opportunity to get out and come home and she was going to make sure he took it.

By this time Arthur was eighteen years old and could sign on his own behalf; he wanted to prove his innocence. Despite Arthur's resolve, Ronnie prevailed upon him to take the deal and on August 21, 2000, Arthur signed the stipulation and was released. The next day, Judge Dickey did exactly what the stipulation required. He granted Arthur's habeas petition and ordered Arthur's release. The district attorney did not apologize to Arthur for the shoddy police work or for the time that Arthur spent in prison. Instead he sanctimoniously stated, "Arthur, it's a rare event that a convicted defendant gets this kind of break. You are getting a second chance. Don't let yourself or your supporters down. When you get out, find a job, improve your skills, have a good and productive life—do not commit any crimes!" Arthur would find out a few years later that his record had not been expunged. He was picked up on a misdemeanor and when the police saw the two robberies on his record, they arrested him on a three strikes violation. Fortunately, Nadia Davis remained in Arthur's life and was now the wife of Bill Lockyer, the Attorney General of the State of California at the time. Attorney General Lockyer demanded that Arthur's record be expunged as promised. Two weeks after his arrest, Arthur was released.

When Arthur was in prison, Ronnie did everything she could think of to get his sentence reversed. She spent every waking moment worrying about him. It was as though Ronnie was right there in prison with him. Fortunately for her she had someone on the outside supporting her just as she was supporting Arthur.

Being There

As Told By Della Reyes

Ronnie and I have known each other for about seventeen years, since a little before Arthur's arrest. I met Ronnie through my neighbor. We were going out to this nightclub that we always went to and she said, "Maybe we'll invite my friend Ronnie," and then she introduced us. Ronnie and I hit it off right away; there was a connection. We were both alike and had a lot in common. We're not very trusting people, at least not right away. We like people that are truthful. What I really like about Ronnie is she keeps it like it is. I like that about her, her strength, her ability to come out and say what she feels to anybody's face. I'm not so much that way only because I'm a little more quiet and reserved. I'm not the type to speak out like she does. I admire that about her. I bite my tongue before I say anything.

I didn't know Arthur very well. I had met him a few times. Most of what I knew about him I learned from Ronnie. I was around a couple of times before Arthur was arrested. We were all shocked when Ronnie told us what happened to Arthur. We couldn't believe it and I think at the time we just all felt they were going to realize they made a mistake and let him go. Instead, everything just went in the opposite direction—from bad to worse.

Ronnie struggled constantly with wanting to get Arthur out of prison, and how difficult it was to wait for the conviction to be overturned. It consumed her life, but it also helped her. Being consumed in her efforts to get him out of prison, doing whatever she could, talking to different people, and going to group meetings kept her busy and made her feel like she was doing something to help Arthur. She met Nadia Davis through these efforts. I remember saying to Ronnie, "I think Nadia is really going to help you." Nadia seemed so interested in Arthur's case. She was doing everything she could.

There were a number of events and people that helped Arthur. There were fundraisers, and awareness events. Even Esai Morales, the actor, was supportive and visited Arthur in jail, which brought in additional support. It all seemed so promising, and gave Ronnie and Arthur hope. Knowing that someone like Esai believed he was innocent was very encouraging. Through these events Ronnie felt she was accomplishing something, but it was also one of those situations where every time you took two steps forward you took one step backwards. It just always seemed like that.

Ronnie worked tirelessly to get Arthur's conviction overturned. She had some help on the political side, but things just didn't go the way she thought they should. Sometimes Ronnie would get discouraged, particularly when they were suing to get some kind of support and compensation for Arthur after his release. There was no compensation for all that he went through. No monetary anything after the wrongful conviction. It was like "No he's guilty. You're just lucky that he got out because we're not going back to court."

The hardest times for Ronnie, when Arthur was still incarcerated, were the holidays. That would be very difficult for her. I remember feeling guilty for having my son with me. Ronnie would look at him and it would upset me so. My heart would break because she couldn't be with her son, and there I was with mine. Now magnify that by the stuff you hear that goes on in prison. That's hard to bear especially as a mother; when bad things can happen and there's no way to keep them from happening, no way to have any control. There's nothing you can do.

I tried to be there for Ronnie when she needed me. I did a lot of listening and would encourage her to talk about Arthur as often as I could. Most of the time I felt like I wasn't doing very much. But I knew if I was there for her that would be as helpful as anything else I could do. If she would tell me, "I'm thinking of doing this and that" on Arthur's case, I would tell her if I didn't think it would work. If I thought it would work I'd say, "Great, go with that." Anything Ronnie wanted to do to help Arthur I would be there to support her. She could call me or text me whenever she needed me. Sometimes I would not be able to answer the call or get the text right away, but she knew I would be there eventually. She would say "Just being able to leave you a message, knowing you're going to hear it and get back to me whenever..." that seemed enough. You could tell with that kind of connection that a lot of times, just hearing each other's voice was comforting; familiar and true.

Ronnie has been equally as committed to our relationship and has been there for me, too. When she moved here she was already dealing with Arthur's wrongful conviction. My son had just been born and I was having difficulties with his father. Despite everything Ronnie was going through, she managed to be my rock. She has always been here for me as I have been for her. She's a very good friend. She's the type of person that is always there for everybody. If you need Ronnie, she will be there for you.

When we met, Ronnie was having trouble with her husband. He was a carpet layer. I met him once when he came over to measure my floors. He never did the work though. Ronnie told me about their situation and I thought she was better off without him. Fortunately, she was strong enough to get out of that abusive relationship. It's tough for some women to make that move, but I was glad Ronnie was strong enough to do it. When she and her husband separated, Arthur was very protective of his mom and sister, Veronica. Ronnie shared with me how upset Arthur was with how her new boyfriend was mistreating her. From Ronnie's stories about Arthur it was clear he loved his family and felt like he had to protect them and be the man of the house. We had a lot of conversations about him. It was always Arthur this, Arthur that.

Eighty-five percent of the time Ronnie was talking about Arthur. Our conversations would usually be about what she was going to do to help him, or who she was going to try and contact to help him. When someone is constantly talking about something sad or bad, the easy thing to do would be to retreat. You might run in fear because what more can you do with the same conversation over and over again. And truly, in my experience not everybody is going to be there to listen to all of that and try to get you through it because it's hard when you can't do more for that person than just listen to them. I didn't mind though because I wanted to help her and I thought if that's all I can do, then that's what I'll do. Of course there were fundraisers and other events that I would go to, to support Ronnie. I just did anything I could to help her.

Many times I'd call and say, "Come and meet me and let's go out. Let's just go to the movies. Let's go to dinner." I thought at least if she gets out and she's around people instead of just being home it would be a release for her. Ronnie often felt guilty about being out, as though every waking moment should be spent on Arthur's release. Somehow I would get her to come with us and not feel guilty about it. It was helpful for her, I think, for her own sanity, to do things to keep moving forward; to keep helping Arthur and just be strong for him. It was something Ronnie simply had to do. I was not directly involved so I was able to see her situation more clearly than she could. Sometimes when you're on the outside you can see people's needs better than they can see for themselves. I could see that convincing her to take a break and get out of the house would be helpful. It would be an opportunity for her to get a bit of normalcy back in her life. I'd think, "What would she be doing if all this wasn't going on? I was trying to bring some balance into her life. I wanted her to do these things because she needed them.

Ronnie brought Arthur over to the house after he was released. Nadia also gave a small get-together for family and friends after his release. These were really the only times I saw Arthur. I didn't really get a chance to know him. Ronnie shared a lot about Arthur with me. I was with Ronnie every step of the way, from her stories of Arthur as a teenager to the boy who was released from prison, and how he had changed from the boy who went to prison to someone often unrecognizable. He went through a lot of changes and Ronnie, unfortunately had to bear all of them. When Arthur came out he didn't talk about his prison experience, or his release. At times he would be understanding, other times not. He would treat Ronnie well at times but would treat her bad too. It was clear he had a lot to get out, and Ronnie was always there to listen. But Arthur wasn't always willing to talk. Through every one of those challenges I made sure I was there for her. Arthur at one point was so angry that he went to live with his father and his father's girlfriend, but he eventually came back home.

Arthur eventually got involved as an advocate for the wrongfully convicted and justice reform. These issues gave him an outlet for his anger. He began to realize what an ally Ronnie had been to him. People would tell him "Gosh what your mother did!" It calmed him down and it seemed that he and Ronnie were getting close again. Then the unthinkable happened and suddenly he was gone.

It was the weekend and Ronnie and I were going out to dinner. Ronnie and Arthur were checking in with each other when she was over my house before we went left for dinner. Ronnie called me the next morning but I didn't get her message until I woke up. Arthur was the victim of a drunk driver early that morning. I could hardly understand what Ronnie was saying through the tears and her crying, but I understood clearly that Arthur had died on the spot. Listening to my friend in so much pain was awful. I went to her house to be with her. I know I couldn't bring back Arthur, but I could be there for Ronnie. Arthur had just started liking his life and was so involved with his advocacy work. He and his mother had become closer to each other and then this. It took so much out of Ronnie.

Ronnie was always very strong, fiercely independent and smart. She was in school before her husband left. She had to drop out to support the family. She had talked about paying back by going back to school and even becoming an attorney. I always told her, "You would be a great attorney, because you bring up some good arguments." She was feisty and strong and always honest.

Ronnie would have been a great attorney, but I think everything took a toll on her, especially when Arthur passed away. It drained her emotionally and physically; maybe that passion wasn't there anymore. The last time she talked about it was a little over a year ago, and she did bring it up once again recently, but nothing came of it.

Ronnie has changed. I still see her as a strong woman but I think that all of this has been so difficult for her. I'm used to her being feisty and strong, and I don't see that in her as much. I'm very hopeful for Ronnie. She's had to deal with more than one person can handle, but I think she just needs time. She's also dealing with some health issues which have required her to step back from some of her scheduled events and rest. When she starts feeling better physically, she'll start feeling better emotionally. When your body's not working well, everything else sort of goes with it.

Ronnie won't stay down for long; it's not in her nature. She gets most of her strength and energy by going to events and speaking on behalf of wrongful conviction and justice reform. She'd text me "Okay, I'm flying out here or I'm flying out there," and when she'd get there she'd tell me, "Gosh I feel so good about being here."

I'd tell her, "That's because Arthur's with you. He's right there with you." She'd really sound empowered and that would be where she would get her second wind. Ronnie mentioned to me just recently that there was a dinner that she wanted to go to that was in support of eliminating the death penalty. Arthur was really passionate about this cause. Ronnie wants to continue to support this cause on his behalf. And hopefully she will. Knowing that now she would be doing something that Arthur would've been doing. She's there representing him.

When Ronnie gets back on her feet, I will be there for her as I have always been. She's my friend, my good friend. And I am her friend. I am there for her, and as her good friend she should expect and get nothing less from me.

* * *

In the first few months after his release, Arthur was unhappy that he had signed away his right to sue the police department and prosecutors for their misconduct in handling his case. Gone was the carefree young man he had been. His relationship with his sister, Veronica, was different, too. Where they had been almost inseparable before his conviction, they were now like strangers with each other. It took a while, but they eventually found their way back to each other. Ronnie was worried that Arthur might be angry with her for insisting he sign that stipulation. He was not. Arthur told her, "Yeah, Mom, I'm angry. I don't know who all to be angry at, but I was never mad at you. I'm sorry if I made you feel that way."

The path Arthur walked to set aside his anger started with a call from the Northern California Innocence Project at Santa Clara University School of Law (NCIP). Having won its first exoneration, NCIP invited a number of California exonerees to the Santa Clara University (SCU) campus to talk with law students. Cookie Ridolfi, a criminal law professor at SCU and co-founder of NCIP, invited Arthur and other exonerees to speak at the law school. Through Cookie, Arthur met other people involved in judicial reform in California. One of those people was Natasha Minsker, an attorney with the ACLU in Northern California. Natasha helped Arthur develop public speaking skills and signed him up for the ACLU's Faces of Wrongful Conviction project. He began to speak at law schools and events around the State to raise awareness about wrongful conviction and proposed solutions to reduce them. His work as an advocate for the wrongfully convicted helped Arthur focus his anger and energy. He was excited about this work.

Through his advocacy work Arthur began to find his voice again. He had missed out on so much when he was in prison and, like other exonerees, he was finding it difficult to just step back into the life he had before prison. Even though Arthur had been in prison for less than three years, during that time his friends had moved on with their lives. They had attended prom, graduated, and many were already in college. Arthur, on the other hand, had spent that time getting beaten up, watching his back, and simply trying to survive in prisons and youth facilities. Spending time with other men and women who had been wrongfully convicted helped Arthur; he knew he was not alone.

With the encouragement of his mother, Natasha, and Professor Ridolfi, Arthur got involved with supporting legislation to make it easier for the wrongfully convicted to find justice in California. He supported three bills in the California State Senate, all three of which were passed by the State Legislature and all three of which were vetoed by Governor Schwarzenegger. Arthur was undaunted and continued to speak to groups about how wrongful convictions can be avoided and to endorse new legislation.

Arthur had enrolled in college and was training to become a fire fighter. He was slowly recovering his life when tragedy struck again. He celebrated the end of his first week of training by attending a party in Santa Ana on the night of February 16, 2008. When a fight broke out after midnight the partygoers scattered into the street. Arthur ran outside with everyone else and tried to avoid a gray pickup truck that was intentionally being driven through the crowd. The truck hit Arthur on his right side and he rolled across the truck's windshield and back onto the pavement. The driver drove over Arthur's body as he sped away leaving Arthur dead in the street. The family learned later that the initial hit broke Arthur's ribs, severing his heart and killing him instantly. The driver, Felix Abreu, avoided arrest for over ten months until the police were able to break his alibi.

Ronnie does not remember much about Arthur's funeral. She recalls seeing another California exoneree Arthur had been working with on advocacy issues, Herman Atkins. Herman also was Arthur's mentor and they both were members of the Council of the Wrongfully Convicted. Ronnie remembers seeing Natasha and a few other people. It is hard for her to think about that day. She learned later that there were many more exonerees at the funeral. Looking back she wishes she had known they would be there. "I would have asked them to carry Arthur's casket," she says wistfully. "They're the ones who helped him find his way back to life."

Despite the misfortunes, 2009 ended on a good note for Arthur's memory. In October, Governor Schwarzenegger signed into law a bill that will make it easier for the wrongfully convicted to get justice, including being able to sue an incompetent defense attorney and an extended period in which to file a claim for compensation. On December 18 Abreu pleaded guilty to gross vehicular manslaughter. He might have gotten off with probation and time served, but Ronnie was having none of that. She insisted on finding justice for Arthur asking the judge, "To whom will you grant justice? Felix Anthony Abreu or the victim, Arthur Carmona?" Although the judge responded by saying that his duty was to remain dispassionate, on May 11, 2010, Abreu was sentenced to six years in prison. He served less than two of them. Before his death, Arthur founded the Arthur Carmona Center for the Wrongfully Convicted with Ronnie's support. Since his death Ronnie has kept the organization going and continues Arthur's legacy of advocacy for improvements in the law and support of the wrongfully convicted.

Arthur Paul Carmona lived with his mother and sister in Southern California until his untimely death. He was an advocate for the wrongfully convicted and for the repeal of the death penalty. Ronnie Sandoval, his mother, continues Arthur's work by sharing his story with the public and raising funds to provide post-exoneration support to exonerees. Della Reyes is long-time family friend.

CHAPTER 8
Antoine Maurice Goff

Turf battles between rival San Francisco gangs in the Sunnydale and Hunters Point neighborhoods were common in 1989. In March of that year the violence escalated when Sunnydale gang members attacked a Hunters Point gang member and his mother. Retaliation by the Hunters Point gang resulted in the shooting death of a member of the Sunnydale gang. In April the Sunnydale gang retaliated by driving through Hunters Point and shooting up an intersection full of people heading home from a late-night party. Two people were killed in the drive-by shooting and eleven others were injured. The police investigated the shooting, but were unable to identify the gang members in the car. Antoine Goff and some of his friends from the neighborhood were in and around that intersection as the Sunnyvale gang drove by and some of his friends were shot. Antoine was among those questions by police investigators, but he had nothing to tell them about the shooting.

As the summer wore on, the number of gang-related killings mounted. On the morning of August 19, 1989, long before the sun came up; Roderick Shannon was driving through Hunters Point. Chante Smith was sitting in her convertible with three male friends in the parking lot of a liquor store when a pick-up truck drove into the parking lot followed by two more cars. Smith's boyfriend, Luther Blue, and his two friends, Mark Anthony and Lavista Ricard had been drinking. Anthony and Ricard walked over to the pick-up truck to talk to some guys they knew. After drinking for a while, everybody decided to head over to the 7-11 on Bayshore and continue the party. Smith was not in the mood for drinking all night, but she agreed to drive her friends to 7-11. Shortly after they arrived, Smith saw a family friend she knew from Sunnydale. She didn't want to be involved in another gang battle. She told the guys with her that he was not from Sunnydale, but then warned him, "You better leave before they figure out you from Sunnydale." He left quickly and another car almost identical to his Skylark came around the corner moments later. The guys in the pick-up truck thought they recognized the driver as someone from Sunnydale and began pointing and shouting excitedly.

"Remember that party back in April? The one where those bangers from Sunnydale shot up all those people?"

"Yeah?"

"That's the car!"

Ricard grabbed his 12-gauge shotgun and jumped into the back of the pick-up truck with some other guys. Everyone jumped into their cars and tore out of the parking lot, tires squealing. They chased the Skylark with the pick-up in the lead. Ricard was drunk and thinking about his friend, Cheap Charlie, who had been shot and killed recently by a rival gang. Looking for a little payback, Ricard took a shot at the Skylark, hitting it on the driver's side right behind the door. The driver of the Skylark sped desperately through the streets trying to get away from the chasing cars and truck. Smith lagged behind the other cars. She had heard the shotgun shots but did not see who fired them. She pulled to the curb and let the chase cars pass her. The driver of the Skylark faked a turn and threw the car into reverse. The driver of the pick-up followed suit and chased the Skylark in reverse, Ricard shooting as they drove. The rest of the cars continued the chase, but not driving backwards. The Skylark barreled up onto the curb backwards and crashed into a fence unable to go further. The driver stumbled out of the car and started running. The pick-up and the other cars skidded to a halt. Young men leapt out of every door and the back of the truck to continue the chase on foot. Anthony, who had been in Smith's car, jumped out and ran to catch up with the crowd chasing the driver of the Skylark. As she drove back to the action, Smith sighed with relief when she saw that the driver of the Skylark was not her family friend.

Rose Marie Dowd was in bed in her apartment when the squealing of tires jarred her out of a sound sleep at around 1:00 a.m. She was barely awake when she heard a shotgun blast. She peeked out of her window and saw a young black man jump out of a car at a full run towards the parking lot of the convenience store shouting, "Don't shoot. Don't shoot him, man. Don't shoot him." Not much later she heard a single shotgun blast come from inside the parking lot. Suddenly, young men were racing out of the parking lot into waiting cars that disappeared in moments. She didn't see anyone else in the area.

As Dowd was getting out of bed, Bernardo Santos was coming home. He had just gone inside when he heard the screeching tires. Santos looked out the window and saw the Skylark screaming backwards down the street until it crashed into a fence. He saw the driver climb out of the wrecked car and start running uphill towards a convenience store parking lot. Santos watched as a pick-up truck careened backwards down the street, following the Skylark. The pick-up drove right past Santos's home, close enough that he could hear the four or five guys in the back of the truck screaming and yelling. Santos saw another car arrive and called the police. While he was on the phone he heard a shot. He didn't see any girls in the area on foot.

The driver of the Skylark was Roderick Shannon. The young men chasing Shannon eventually caught up with him and took turns punching and beating him. When the pick-up truck stopped, Smith saw Ricard get the shotgun out of the truck. He walked toward the crowd that was gathered around Shannon. As they watched Ricard approaching with the shotgun, everybody backed away from Shannon. There were too many people for Smith to actually see Ricard shoot Shannon, but she heard the single shotgun shot. Then she saw Ricard return to the pick-up truck and climb into the back while still carrying the shotgun. Smith didn't see any other females in the area.

The police investigated Shannon's murder. At first no one came forward, then, a few days after the shooting, two young girls contacted the police claiming to be eyewitnesses to the shooting. Twelve year old Masina Fauolo and her fourteen year old friend Pauline Maulina told police investigators that Fauolo was driving them in a stolen car the night of the shooting. The girls told police they followed the car chase for a while and then got out and ran on foot to the convenience store parking lot along with the rest of the crowd. Over the next few weeks Fauolo and Maulina would make a series of conflicting statements to the police investigators. Maulina's statement conflicted with Fauolo's statement and the statements of both girls were at odds with some of the material facts and evidence in the case. Eventually, through a photo line-up, Fauolo identified John Tennison and Antoine Goff to Inspector Prentice Sanders and

Inspector Napoleon Hendrix as the guys who killed Shannon. Maulina also identified a photo of John but failed to identify Antoine. According to the girls, John held Shannon while Antoine shot him. On October 4, 1989, well after Fauolo and Maulina had given multiple statements to the police, Investigators Sanders and Hendrix requested $2,500 to offer as a reward to encourage witnesses to come forward. Before John and Antoine went on trial for Shannon's murder, Maulina recanted her previous statements. She told District Attorney Butterworth that she was not there when Shannon was shot. She recanted her previous statement four times saying that Maulina had coached her on which photo to pick, but eventually, after some encouragement by the police investigators and her friend Fauolo, Maulina recanted her recantations and went back to her initial statement.

The only evidence connecting Antoine and John to Shannon's shooting was the eyewitness testimony of the two girls. On the basis of that testimony and in the absence of a rigorous defense, the jury found Antoine and John guilty of murder on October 3, 1990. Antoine was sentenced to a term of twenty-seven years to life.

* * *

I'm The One That Runs The Show

As Told By Antoine M. Goff

messed up

When I was arrested for Shannon's murder I had no experience of prison or juvenile hall. My mom had been really strict with me growing up. I wasn't out in the streets getting into trouble. By the time I turned eighteen, Mom said I had to be in school or move out on my own. I decided to go to school but I also decided to move to my grandmother's house where things were less strict. I started running the streets with my buddies and ended up with the wrong people in the wrong place at the wrong time. There was always something going on and one day, it was something pretty scary. I was hanging with some friends and we were talking to some girls when a car from another neighborhood drove by and shot up the group.

One of my friends and one of the girls ended up getting killed. A bunch more people had gunshot wounds, but they survived.

The cops came around asking questions. There were these two detectives who started doing their investigation. They talked to a lot of people and finally got around to catching up with me. They asked me about the case, about the shooting. They asked me if I saw who did the shooting. I told them I didn't see who did it. They pretty much tried to get me to say I saw someone and I refused to do that. I think from me refusing to go along, they had it in for me. I wouldn't cooperate with them and from then on they had bad blood for me. A few months later, when Shannon got shot and killed, I was on their radar. I wasn't worried though, because I wasn't there.

I was naïve. I didn't know to take it seriously. I was arrested and put in county jail I figured, "I'm innocent and they'll figure out what's going on and come get me up out of here." That's what I thought. They tried me and John Tennison together. I had never dealt with a lawyer before, so when my lawyer told me to say yes to this and yes to that, I did what he said. He was the expert, right? I did what my lawyer told me and before I knew it, I was convicted and sent to San Quentin! Too late I realized just how serious this was and San Quentin was not county jail. I trusted the system and I was innocent so I figured it would turn out all right. I didn't tell my parents or my grandparents anything about what was happening to me. It wasn't until I was convicted that my grandfather stepped in and told me my attorney was a waste of time. "Nah," Grandpa said, "He ain't dealing with none of this. We're getting you a paid attorney." In the meantime, I was going to prison. Fortunately, and you might not think this was fortunate, I had some uncles who had been in and out of jail. They schooled me about the street code—the respect of the streets, how to survive on the streets. Well, it was the same in prison. Don't disrespect anyone and don't step on anyone's toes. In prison, though, there was something else. In prison you learn how to adapt and how to adapt quick. You turn from a little boy into a man, just overnight.

Everyone goes through San Quentin when they're first convicted. You get classified based on the crime you were convicted of and whether you've been in prison before. I was in San Quentin for two months before they moved me to a Level 4—Pelican Bay. Level 4s are dangerous. People in there are lifers or people that have more than fifteen years on their sentence or been in and out of prison, back and forth, or been bad guys in prison or just got out of the hole—solitary. I was put right in the middle of all of that. First thing you do is find your people. You get affiliated with your race and then with your neighborhood, maybe even people you grew up with. Even if you don't know anybody, you probably know somebody from the neighborhood who knows them, so you have somebody in common. You build a bond and that can save your life in prison. It's a scary thing, but it's like that commercial—never let 'em see you sweat. That's one way you have to adapt. Don't let your fear show. I could sense the fear in some people. The tough guys, the predators prey on the fearful. In prison, you turn into a man or stay a little boy and get preyed upon.

In the end, it's all about respect. I respected everyone and they respected me, until they didn't. Then they would see another side. That's just how prison is and back then it was dangerous. There were lots of race wars going on in prison. Pelican Bay was almost always on lockdown. I was there for five years from the end of 1990. During most of that time there were race riots and we were almost always on lockdown. We would be locked down for twenty-three hours every day. During that one hour when we weren't on lockdown we could have a shower and maybe get something to eat. Sometimes, when the riots were really bad, they would bring the food to the cells and we only got out for a quick shower. I just tried to stay out of trouble so I would get good behavior points and get moved to a lower security facility. Level 3 prisons, the next level down, had fewer restrictions, more time in the day room and longer visitation time. Some people, once they get to a Level 4, don't care anymore. They figure, "This is where I'm gonna do my time so I don't care how many points I get." That wasn't me. Eventually I earned Level 3 status and moved to Solano. It was closer to home and had a bigger law library. It wasn't always on lockdown so I could spend time in the law library talking with jailhouse lawyers.

Once I got to Solano, my mind eased up a bit and I relaxed a little. I was able to focus on getting out of prison. When I was at

Pelican Bay all I could focus on was staying alive. I had no time to think about getting out. At Solano I could spend more time in the law library and figure out what I needed to do to get my case looked at. I ended up meeting a guy at Solano who would end up being my mentor. He talked to me about life and history. He prepared me for coming home and counseled me on many things. After I started talking to him, I began to have a more positive outlook on my situation. I had a really bad taste in my mouth for attorneys and he helped me see that not all of them were bad. My first attorney never took a murder case to trial before mine. He always did a plea so he didn't know much more about defending me than I did, but I didn't know that at the time. I thought, "He's representing *me*. He's *my* attorney." Whatever he told me, I believed it. If he told me something and it sounded good, I went for it. I didn't know any better. When it was our turn at trial we only had two witnesses, but I didn't know any better. My next attorney, the one Grandpa paid for, wasn't any better. He took my family's money, over twenty-thousand dollars, and paid another attorney to write an appeal that was denied. I found the name of another attorney in one of the law library books. My family paid him about four thousand dollars to read over my case. He told us there was nothing he could do. Three lawyers didn't do much for me, so no surprise that I had a really bad taste in my mouth about lawyers. But my mentor helped me understand that there were better lawyers out there.

There was another guy who I met while I was at Pelican Bay. We became good friends. Later we were both transferred out of Pelican Bay. I transferred to Solano and figured I'd lost a friend. But, after some time had passed, he ended up there, too. It was great to see a familiar face and have a friend in Solano. He is the one who encouraged me to spend a lot of time in the law library. He believed I was innocent and that I should be working on my case. He really motivated me. I would go to the law library every day. I didn't really know why. I was just going.

They say everybody in prison claims to be innocent, but guys in prison know if you're really innocent. Some guys are in and out or just know people on the street they can check with to see if your story checks out. My story checked out. People on the street knew I was innocent. By now, Tennison had this lawyer who was working on his appeal. Tennison's lawyer had people to do news articles on us. This one guy from the Bay Guardian did a big article on us and that opened things up in San Francisco, in the whole Bay Area in fact. When that article came out, the whole prison system knew about me and my case and that I was innocent. There was a guy in the prison law library who was what you call a jailhouse lawyer. He started helping me and told me to pick lawyers from the lawyer directory in the library. He also told me to make copies of the *Bay Guardian* article. "I'm gonna type up something for you," he said. He typed up a letter and I made twenty copies of it and the newspaper article and sent them to twenty attorneys in the Bay Area—names I picked out of the directory.

At first I didn't hear anything back from anybody. I lost heart but my mentor told me to wait a while. "It'll take some time," he said. "Lawyers get lots of letters from people in prison. It'll take some time for them to read up on you and decide what to do." The first lawyer I heard back from was John Burris. He wrote to say he was sorry about my situation but he was too busy to take on my case. I took that letter to my mentor and asked, "Why did this dude even respond to me if he couldn't help?" My mentor told me to just keep the faith and if no one responded we'd pick twenty more lawyers and send out more letters. I prayed that I would get a woman attorney. I figured I might have better luck with a woman attorney since the men attorneys hadn't helped me at all so far. In that first batch I also sent a letter to Tony Serra. It was around 1999 or 2000 when got a letter back from Diana Samuelson, a woman in Serra's office. She sent me a letter telling me that Serra didn't do post-conviction work. "I checked you out," she wrote. "I heard good things about you. Everybody had positive things to say about you and Tennison. I would like to visit you, but you need to sign a release so I can get the attorney paperwork."

I figured she was blowing smoke. After all my bad luck with attorneys, I didn't put much faith in her actually showing up...but she did. She visited me and brought a couple of interns with her. We talked for a while and then she broke it down for me. "I'm gonna teach you the law," she said. "We're gonna walk through this together. I'm gonna teach you what an attorney is supposed to be. I don't know what kind of experience you may have had, but I'm gonna show you and teach you what a righteous lawyer is supposed to be." Then she had us all stand up and hold hands. We all looked at each other. Diana said, "We're gonna make a pact. We're gonna be with you until we get you out of here." When they left, I felt like I had a shot. I told my mentor I thought I had a real shot at getting out of there.

Diana started sending me these little cases and I'd read them. I started putting two and two together about the law related to my case. I really started to understand what had happened and then I started to really believe that I would get out of there. "I'm coming home," I thought. I couldn't wait to get into that courtroom. Things were different now. I was the one running the show. Diana taught me that she was working for me, but I was in charge. She gave me the motivation to really believe that now, now, now I'm about to go home. Things were heating up on the outside as well. More articles were being written about my case, me and Tennison—not just newspapers, but television, too. I knew it was going to happen. I didn't know when but I knew it would happen. I felt it. I went from a Level 3 to a Level 2—Solano was Level 2 as well as Level 3. In Level 2 you went into a dorm setting. I went into Level 2 at around the end of 2002 and I stayed there until I got out in 2003.

* * *

Antoine Goff and John Tennison had been tried together and sentenced together, but their appeals would be handled separately. John started his habeas petition earlier than Antoine and was through the California state court system by the fall of 2002 when the California Supreme Court denied his petition without comment. While Antoine's habeas petition worked its way through the California state courts, John appealed the California Supreme Court's denial in federal district court. Around the same time, Antoine's habeas petition was being heard before the California Superior Court in San Francisco.

The primary argument in the habeas petitions was a violation of due process rights granted by the Fourteenth Amendment, also known as a Brady Violation. The basis of the violation was actual innocence and the prosecution's suppression of evidence of actual innocence. The prosecution is obligated to disclose any exculpatory or impeachment evidence and has a duty to learn of any exculpatory or impeachment evidence known to anyone acting on behalf of the government—like police investigators. The intention of the prosecution in withholding the evidence also is irrelevant. It does not matter if the prosecution did not have ill will or did not intend to convict an innocent person. The prosecution's duty to disclose information and to learn whatever information it could have learned is absolute.

A treasure trove of exculpatory and impeachment evidence existed in Antoine's case and the prosecution withheld almost all of it. The statements of the young girls who claimed to have witnessed the whole series of events from before the car chase started were inconsistent with the physical evidence and internally inconsistent. Fauolo claimed, for example, that she saw John Tennison in a car behind her through the rearview mirror, but it would have been difficult for her to see anyone clearly at night driving into or parked in a dark parking lot. She also claimed that Shannon was beaten with a baseball bat as well as fists, but there was no physical evidence that a baseball bat was used to beat Shannon. In his questioning of Maulina, Investigator Hendrix suggested material facts which she had not offered . The statements of both girls were inconsistent with the testimony of other witnesses whose testimony was consistent with the physical evidence, but this was not the most egregious behavior regarding Maulina's statement.

Maulina recanted the testimony she gave at the preliminary hearing. She explained to the investigators that Fauolo told her what to say and which photo to select. Fauolo was her friend and had helped her out of jams in the past, so when Fauolo asked her to lie, Maulina agreed. The investigators tried to discourage Maulina's recantation but she insisted that she had been lying at the hearing. They gave her a polygraph test and the tester suggested that she go back to her initial testimony. When Maulina insisted that she hadn't been at the scene and knew nothing about the events, Investigator Hendrix arranged for Maulina to have a private phone call with Fauolo. After that phone call with Fauolo, Maulina went back to her original statement. The prosecution did not tell the defense about any of the recantations or the polygraph results.

The police investigators did not disclose to the defense their request for reward money. They claimed that no funds had been paid out and therefore no disclosure was required. Unfortunately, they could not account for what happened to the $2,500.

Chante Smith gave her statement to the police nearly nine months before the start of Antoine's trial. In that statement Smith identified Ricard as the person with the shotgun. The defense was not made aware of Smith's pre-trial statements nor her identity. The police investigators used Smith's statements as the basis for further investigation and questioning of people mentioned by Smith. This suggests that the police found Smith's statements to be material and credible. Luther Blue's videotaped statement also was withheld from the defense and Blue contradicted Fauolo's statements and testimony. Had the prosecution and the police not withheld any of this evidence, the defense might have been better able to impeach the testimony of Fauolo and Maulina.

Once the trial was over and Antoine and John had been found guilty and sentenced the police investigators probably thought the case was done. Little did they know their case was about to blow up. Ricard was arrested in connection with an unrelated crime and the police investigators in that case videotaped Ricard confessing to shooting and killing Shannon and confirming that neither Antoine nor John were present at the time and were not involved in the planning. The prosecution did turn over Ricard's videotaped confession six months after the police obtained it, but by the time they did it was so late in the trial that it could be of little use to the defense. Had the prosecution turned over Smith's statements, the defense would have had corroboration of Ricard's confession.

Judge Wilken found that there was substantial and material exculpatory and impeachment evidence that had been withheld from the defense by the prosecution. For a case as weak as the one against Antoine and John, the probability was high that, had the withheld information been made available to the defense in a timely manner, the results of the trial might have been different. Judge Wilken did not discuss any of the other claims, stating "Because the Court's confidence in the outcome of the Tennison's [sic] trial has been undermined by the Brady violations, the Court need not reach Tennison's [other] claims." Judge Wilken granted John's habeas petition, vacated his prior conviction, and instructed the prosecution to re-try him in sixty days or release him. Because the two cases were inextricably linked, the judge viewing Antoine's habeas petition in superior court waited for the district court decision before granting Antoine's habeas petition.

Around the same time Judge Wilken was considering John Tennison's habeas petition, Earl Sanders, now the San Francisco Chief of Police, was being indicted along with nine other police officers in a scandal known in San Francisco as Fajitagate. Sanders ultimately would be acquitted of the charges against him, but his behavior along with that of Inspector Hendrix and District Attorney Butterworth called into question other murder investigations and convictions with which they were involved.

Back at Solano, everything seemed to happen all at once. One afternoon Antoine returned to the dorm from the yard and one of the dorm mates said "your colleague going home."

Antoine didn't believe it. "Man, quit playing me," he said.

"Look at the news," his dorm mate said right back.

Antoine turned on the news and there was John Tennison on the news being walked out of the prison. It was pretty late in the day on Friday and Antoine knew if he hadn't heard anything by then it would be Monday before he'd hear anything. A court had to order his release and the courts were closed already and would not issue an order over the weekend. Antoine was ready to get that order on Monday morning, but no order came. He went to the law library to kill some time and then came back to the dorm. The guard desk was out in the open and the phone on the desk started to ring. Everyone in the dorms could hear the phone. Antoine was sure it was for him, thinking "The phone call is for me! The phone call is for me!" It was all he could do to keep calm. Then a woman's voice announced over the intercom, "Goff, report to the office. Goff, report to the office." Antoine went to the guard desk and the guard handed him the phone. The warden's secretary was on the other end. "I assume you know what this is all about. We got an order of release from your attorney for you to be released. It might be a couple of hours but you're going home."

Antoine went back to his dorm but after a while the guards announced that legal mail was in the main office. He passed two guards on the way to the main office. The guards were headed to the dorms to get him, but first they took him back to the dorms to get his belongings. Antoine only took his legal files and phone book. He gave the rest of his property to his friends. Back in the main office Antoine was waiting to be released. After two hours, the guards explained that there was a lot of press in front of the prison and they were waiting for the crowd to disperse. A few more hours passed and then it was too late for him to be released on Monday. The guards took him to another dorm and locked him up by himself. Now Antoine was no longer an inmate and the prison, and the State of California, would be liable if something happened to him before they released him. Early the next morning one of the black guards saw him. "Man, you still here? What are you doin' still here?" He went to find out what the holdup was and then made sure Antoine was released. They gave him two-hundred dollars and after another couple of hours, took him out to the front of the prison where his mother was waiting for him with Diana and his other attorneys.

When he saw that Diana was there, Antoine was relieved. "When I saw Diana, that's when I knew there were attorneys you could count on, people you can count on, people you can believe. With Diana, I trust her with my life."

* * *

We Prevailed

As Told By Michael McGee

When Antoine was a toddler, before I was born, our uncle Jerry used to call him Popcorn. Over the years Popcorn became Pop and we all called him that for as long as I can remember. Pop and I grew up together. As young boys, we would go cherry picking together.

Our uncles would take us hunting and teach us how to shoot guns. We did a lot of activities together when we were kids. We also spent a lot of time at our grandmother's house; all of us did. When we'd stay overnight there and Pop, and I shared a bedroom. We had a good time growing up together. We were very close.

Pop was two and a half years older than me. Even though he wasn't technically the oldest he was the oldest of those of us who spent a lot of time at our grandmother's. He and I were like brothers. We were always together and we always knew where each other was. Pop had a younger brother but he was much younger than us, and as much as his brother may have wanted, he was just a little too young to hang with us.

We all looked up to Pop He was smart and he was very talented in sports. Pop was also a very stylish guy. He liked his clothes and he was always together in that way. At one short point in our lives Pop and I actually wore the same size. He would let me wear some of his clothes, once in a while but I also messed up some of his clothes. I didn't mean to, but sometimes that's what would happen. I bet he was glad when we no longer wore the same size

When Pop was arrested it just shut our family down. My grandmother's house was the house that everybody came to. We all loved it and looked forward to being there. But the feeling in the house after Pop's arrest just wasn't the same. Once Pop was found guilty it became so hard for all of us. Pop was a good guy. He was never in trouble for anything. It was hard for us to believe this was happening.

At the time Pop was arrested and then incarcerated our family was going through so much stuff. My son was born, right after Pop left. Our great-grandmother was sick and hospitalized. She eventually passed away. Five to six months after Pop was incarcerated his father passed away. Then my mother passed and our grandfather passed. All these incidents along with Pop's incarceration sent shockwaves through us all. We didn't know how we would recover from all of this. We were going through some hellish times.

We all wanted to help in any kind of way we could, but whatever we tried it just didn't work out. We spent a lot of time going back and forth to court for Pop's case—and just couldn't believe it when they found him guilty. The decision was shocking. Pop was the last guy that should be going to jail. The terrible thing was, I couldn't really help him with his case. I knew for a fact Pop was innocent. You see, the guy Pop was accused of killing was a partner of mine. I had been with him the day he was killed. In fact, he was dropping me off at my grandmother's house. We said a few words and then he left. When I went into the house there was Pop in the bed asleep. So, obviously he didn't kill that guy and everybody in the family knew it. Pop was there with me and we were at our grandmother's. Pop's mom started drinking after that. She was hurting so much she was killing herself hurting. My other aunt Bernitha also was drinking, it wasn't good.

We all tried to do stuff to help Pop get out of prison. Pop's mom tried. Our grandfather tried by providing money for the appeal attorney. Pop's dad tried. I tried. I wanted to help. I would've been the perfect witness but the defense team came to the house and told me that they didn't need me to testify. So I didn't go. I didn't know why at the time, but over time I realized it was because I had been in jail. I would've been a good witness if I hadn't been previously arrested and incarcerated. I was right in the middle of it. Imagine, my partner is killed after he drives me home to my grandmother's house. Then they are accusing my cousin of killing him while my cousin was asleep at our grandmother's house. Then they send my cousin to prison for twenty-seven to life. Wow! I mean Wow! I honestly believe they wanted Pop in jail, so they railroaded him. And there he was doing the time for a crime he didn't commit.

At first he had a public defender, but he didn't do a good job at all. Seemed like they wanted to throw him under the bus. Then there was the appeal. Our grandfather paid for an attorney to represent Pop for the appeal, but he was useless. The attorney was a guy who went to school with Pop's dad. Nobody saw him and he still got paid. Easy money for him. He did a shitty job, too. Who could Pop trust to get him out of prison after that?

Pop always called me to find out what everybody was doing on his case. He'd call to see if anyone talked to those girls who lied on him in court. He wanted me to check on that and get those girls to go and tell the truth. Pop would call me for everything or try to find out if I was trying to help him. He called everybody, though, to see what was happening to get him out of prison. Even when our grandfather died, Pop was calling and wanting me to be doing stuff for his case and saying I wasn't doing anything for him. It wasn't the right time for us to be having that conversation with me trying to tend to our deceased grandfather. I mean I get it. Pop shouldn't have been in prison and he wanted more, needed to see there was action to get him out. It took him coming home to really see all that I was doing or could do; to see what we all were doing.

Maybe it was hard for Pop to understand how badly the whole family was taking his incarceration and especially with everything else happening how the family was falling apart. I was trying to keep it together. I think I even helped his mom some. She took this real hard. I would go over and talk to her and help her get stuff off her mind. She was drinking a lot because of this terrible thing. Still, it was easy for Pop to get mad being in prison. He could be a little extra grouchy at times. Sure, being in prison when you ain't supposed to be, well you probably would be a little grouchy. Still we were all trying to figure out what to do and we really thought we were on the right track

The best it seems we could do was be there to talk with him on the phone, and boy did we talk. He talked with everybody, our grandmother, his mom, his aunts, all the cousins. I don't even know how he could stay on the phone that long. I wanted to say something about the calls because they cost a lot, but you know he was incarcerated and shouldn't have been. What could I do?

When Pop got out he was on the news with the other guy. They asked them, "Well how does it feel?" Pop said something like, "I stayed solid and I prevailed." He came home militant; the other guy was crying and Pop was sitting up there like the Terminator. Pop was mad with the police, but he told me, "Man," he said "Mike, I ain't trippin' I just want to come home."

When Pop got home, all I could think of is man I am so glad them times are over. All them phone calls. All the suffering and pain. O God! When Pop got home he realized all we had tried to do to get him out. And when you think about it, he just wanted to get out of there and there is nothing anyone can do to move fast enough or soon enough to make that happen. You realize that it's the heart that counts. You can't put a value on the heart.

* * *

When Antoine got out of prison the first thing he wanted to do was go to his grandmother's house. His grandfather had died while he was in prison, but his grandmother had continued to be Antoine's lifeline to the outside while he was inside. He didn't have any particular meal he wanted to eat. In fact, he had given up beef and pork while he was in prison, prompting his grandmother to remark, "I don't know what to cook for you no more." Antoine had been in prison for over thirteen years. Things were different when he came home. His cousins had all been babies when he was convicted. Now they were teenagers. His brother, nine years old when Antoine went to prison, was a stranger. Even though Antoine was the big brother, his little brother didn't look up to him in the usual way of little brothers. They're working to rebuild their relationship and recently went to Puerto Rico to celebrate Antoine's forty-fifth birthday. He describes his youngest cousin as having an "in your face" kind of personality. She won't let him mope around and withdraw from family activities. He says she opened him up a bit.

Antoine knows the worth of true friends and he only has a few of those. Some people who he expected to be there for him, to support him, forgot about him. But even though some did forget about him, not everyone did. There were people from whom he would never have expected support. Mike, another guy from the neighborhood, stepped up. They didn't live on the same block growing up, so they didn't run in the same circles, but that didn't stop Mike from visiting Antoine and sending him things now and then. If Antoine asked Mike to send him something or to come visit, Mike was there for him. Diana, his lead attorney didn't let Antoine down either. Antoine also has an unbreakable bond with John Tennison. They knew each other from the neighborhood before they were arrested, but they didn't run in the same circles. John is four years younger than Antoine. Now that they're out, they've become best friends. They share a common horrific experience. They understand what's happening to each other when no one else understands. They call each other up to talk about crazy things that happen to them just to make sure they're not crazy. It's the same bond they share with other exonerees and Antoine knows a few, some of whom he was friends with before prison. He understands what they're going through—especially the ones who are recently exonerated. Like Antoine, they thought they could just come out and insert themselves back into society, but it doesn't work that way.

While time sort of stood still for Antoine while he was in prison, life went on for everyone outside. The world changed. Friends got married and had children. Recent exonerees don't always understand that and, like Antoine, make the mistake of trying to jump right in like nothing has changed, no time has passed. Like a big brother, Antoine takes the time to tell them to slow down a bit and not try to make up for the lost time all at once. He chuckles when he says he knows he'll have to say this more than once or twice, but he smiles as he remembers that he did exactly the same thing. He says he had "a few" girlfriends in the first ten years after he got out of prison. He didn't have one before he left. He says he was too afraid of his mother to bring a girl home without her permission, but he's been with the same woman for the past three years. They're taking things slowly, no need to rush.

One of the activities Antoine took up to work his way back into society was a late night basketball league. To play in the league you also had to attend the monthly workshops on job searching and general life lessons. A speaker at the workshop from a San Francisco company talked about taking the initiative to find a job. Antoine was unemployed and the next day he went to the company to find out what job openings they had. They turned him away. The next time there was a career workshop a representative came from University of California at San Francisco (UCSF). After she gave her spiel about taking the initiative, Antoine spoke up. "You all come to our neighborhood, telling us what to do. You tell us to take the initiative and when we do, y'all don't do nothin' for us." She asked him for a resume. Antoine went to his car and returned with a resume. He called her a few days later to follow up and eventually he was hired at UCSF in a six-month temporary job in the mailroom. That was in 2005.

One year earlier, the California Victim Compensation and Government Claims Board (the "Board") inexplicably denied Antoine compensation for his wrongful conviction. Under California law a wrongfully convicted person is entitled to compensation of a hundred dollars for each day of wrongful incarceration. Antoine asked for $489,800 and the Board rejected the request. The state court and the federal district court had determined that Antoine and John Tennison were factually innocent, a determination to which the San Francisco District Attorney stipulated. The California Attorney General, on the other hand, disagreed with the factual innocence determinations stating to the Board that, "Goff and Tennison have not proven that they did not commit this murder as is their burden under [law]." The Attorney General recommended that the Board deny the claim, which the Board did, concluding "Claimant Goff has failed to establish by a preponderance of the evidence that he is entitled to compensation...and his claim is denied."

In 2008 Antoine and John filed a civil suit against the City of San Francisco, the District Attorney, and the SFPD lead investigators in their case. In January 2009, the city settled with both men. Antoine received two million nine hundred thousand dollars and John received four million six hundred thousand dollars. Everyone expected Antoine to quit his job at UCSF, but he didn't. He put the settlement funds into an annuity and continues to work at UCSF where he has been hired full-time as a member of the custodial team.

Even though Antoine Goff and John Tennison were putting their ordeal behind them, the City of San Francisco had no such luck. In 2006, San Francisco District Attorney Kamala Harris appointed George Butterworth, the lead prosecutor in Antoine and John's case, as head of the homicide prosecutors on her staff. In her order reversing John's conviction, United States District Court Judge Claudia Wilken called Butterworth's actions "troubling" and his questioning of a witness who subsequently recanted her testimony as "artful" and suggesting that Butterworth "...may have been aware of the polygraph examination..." the results of which "...cast doubt on the credibility of a prosecution witness." When Antoine and John sued the City of San Francisco, Butterworth, Sanders and Hendrix, the two investigators in the case, Sanders and Hendrix asked in a motion for summary judgment for the district court to throw out the complaint. The district court denied the motion for summary judgment. Sanders and Hendrix appealed the decision arguing that they were entitled to immunity from prosecution. The United States Court of Appeals for the Ninth Circuit upheld the district court's denial noting that the investigators were not entitled to qualified immunity or absolute immunity.

Antoine Goff lives in Northern California. He speaks out across the State of California against the death penalty and is an advocate for the wrongfully convicted. Michael McGee is his cousin.

CHAPTER 9
Tabitha (Pollock) Hershberger

Tabitha Pollock was fearless, well, pretty fearless when it came to stuff like her older brothers tossing her into the pool or tossing her back and forth between them in a strange game of catch where she was the ball. When it came to following her passion, however, Tabitha was not nearly so fearless. She wanted a career as an auto mechanic. She got that from her father, who worked on cars. When Tabitha bought her first car, her father taught her how to do basic maintenance on it. Tabitha discovered that she really loved working on her car at her dad's side. To the young Tabitha, her father knew everything. "My dad was a great and wonderful guy," she said. "He knew everything there was to know."

Even though Tabitha wanted to be a mechanic and fix cars, she did what her mother expected and went to school to study nursing like her sister Suenjae. As the youngest girl, perhaps she felt she had to please her mother. Tabitha had an older sister, two older brothers, and one younger brother. Tabitha's mom wanted her to be a nurse and that's what Tabitha went to school to become.

Tabitha's cousin introduced her to his girlfriend who had a brother named Scott English. Before long, Tabitha and English were dating. They broke up but eventually got back together in August 1995. The couple had a two year old son, David, and Tabitha had three other children—eight year old Jack, five year old Preston, and three year old Jami Sue—from previous relationships. Tabitha moved into English's place temporarily with three of her children (Jack was living elsewhere) and shortly thereafter, in late September, all five of them moved into the home of English's parents. Also living there were English's parents and his brother's girlfriend, Pam, and their young son.

The evening of October 9, 1995 was no different than most other evenings in the English household. At around 6:30 p.m. Tabitha called the children to dinner. About thirty minutes later, Pam came home with her son and all of the children had ice cream. They fin-

why they work at sit down

ished and ran off to play in the living room. "All right," Tabitha told her children just after 9:00 p.m., "It's time for bed."

She took them upstairs, but the children were not ready to go to sleep. "Mom can we watch TV?" they pleaded. At first she said no, but eventually Tabitha let them all pile into her bed and together they watched television for a couple of hours. At around 11:30 p.m. the children started falling asleep. David, the youngest, wasn't feeling well so he would be sleeping in his parents' bed. After she put the other children to bed in their room, Tabitha went downstairs to do some laundry. She checked on the children a little after midnight and they were sleeping.

Tabitha heard the children making noise just as English arrived home at around 12:40 a.m. When she checked on them, she found English standing at the foot of their bed. "Get back to sleep you guys," he told them. English went downstairs to the kitchen to get something to eat and brought it back upstairs to his and Tabitha's bedroom. They talked while English ate, and then got ready for bed.

"I'll just jump in the shower first," Tabitha said. To get to the bathroom, she had to walk through the bedroom where the children were sleeping.

After taking his shower, English checked on the children again. "They're fine," he said as he climbed back into bed to watch television with Tabitha. At around 3:30 a.m., English went to the bathroom before going to sleep. "Jami was wrapped up in her covers again," English told Tabitha as he climbed back in bed "but I fixed them."

Sometime later that morning, David's crying woke up his parents. He had a fever and his father gave him some Tylenol, which David threw up immediately. "Ugh," English groaned, "I'm going to clean myself up." He went to the bathroom again and returned to bed a few moments later to a sleeping Tabitha. Soon after, Tabitha felt the bed jostle as English climbed out of it again. Groggy, she sat up moments before English ran into the bedroom shouting. "Wake up! Tab, wake up! Jami's not breathing! I heard a noise and went to check on the kids and found Jami wrapped up in her blankets again and she wasn't breathing!"

Tabitha ran into the children's bedroom and brought Jami into her bedroom, where she started performing cardio-pulmonary resuscitation (CPR) on her daughter. "Call 9-1-1," she screamed at English. He called the paramedics and said, "I already tried doing CPR on her and it didn't work."

At 4:58 a.m. the ambulance arrived and paramedics rushed upstairs where they found Tabitha performing CPR on her daughter. Although Jami was unresponsive, the paramedics found her body was still warm and her skin had a slightly bluish tone. One of the paramedics took over CPR from a "frightened and shaken" Tabitha. She rode in the ambulance with Jami and held her hand as the paramedics continued to perform CPR. The ambulance arrived at the hospital at 5:05 a.m. and CPR duties were taken over by the head of the hospital's emergency room.

Tabitha was asked to wait outside while the emergency room team worked on Jami. She frantically paced the floor waiting for word on her little girl. Just after 6:00 a.m. Jami still had not been resuscitated. The doctor pronounced her dead and the coroner was notified. Tabitha suffered a complete emotional breakdown when she heard the news. The hospital staff let Tabitha say goodbye to her baby. She sat rocking Jami for a long while and when they took Jami away from her, Tabitha collapsed to the floor and cried inconsolably.

The emergency room doctor testified that he had seen Jami three days earlier for a cut on her head that required stitches. English had brought Jami to the hospital explaining that she hit her head when she fell off of a box while brushing her teeth. At the time, no one in the emergency room considered child abuse because they often saw children with this sort of minor injury. Pronouncing Jami dead only three days later, however, prompted the emergency room doctor to ask one of the nurses to make a detailed inspection of Jami's body and catalogue all of her injuries. After Jami's death, the nurse who checked her body found eleven marks of various sizes, most of which were not thought to be the result of abuse.

That afternoon, Jami's body was autopsied and additional injuries were discovered. The coroner determined that those injuries had occurred minutes or, at most, hours before Jami's death. Some of the injuries indicated Jami had been suffocated. These included her pale face, ruptures of tiny blood vessels in her face and neck, and clawing marks she had made on her chest when trying to remove whatever had been suffocating her. Other injuries indicated Jami had been hit extremely hard on her head. These included various areas of hemorrhage that caused her three year old brain to swell to the size of an adult brain. The coroner concluded that Jami's death had been caused by suffocation and blunt force trauma to the head, either of which on its own could have killed her.

The following evening, Tabitha and English went to the police station where they were questioned separately. In one interrogation room Tabitha described what had happened at the English home the previous morning. Meanwhile, in another interrogation room, English told the police that after he cleaned himself up from David's vomit he went back through the children's room and saw Jami tangled up in her blankets again. English admitted he had hit Jami on the back of her head, stating "...I yelled at [Jami] and I hit her twice in the back of the neck or head..." He described the first hit as a "hammering motion" and the second as delivered "...with the palm of my hand." According to English, Jami cried softly and he didn't think he had hurt her.

"[I] didn't mean anything. I just wanted to let her know that she shouldn't be covering up like that. Then, I pulled the blankets up and she spun and there was no movement. She was lifeless and I proceeded to do CPR after that. I leaned down to listen if she was breathing or if she had any pulse and then I did CPR. I didn't want this to happen. When I corrected her I never knew that I was going to hurt her that bad."

"When the police asked English if he performed CPR because he had hit Jami, English responded, "Yes, because that's the only thing that I have done to her. I have never laid a hand on her. I loved her so much." English denied ever hitting Jami other than the two times he admitted to hitting her that morning.

The police told Tabitha that the autopsy report indicated that Jami had died from being hit on the head and suffocated. The officer conducting the questioning testified that Tabitha appeared shocked and astonished when she heard this and found it difficult to understand what he was telling her. She did not understand how Jami had been hurt because no one in the house had ever hurt her or the other children. The police then told Tabitha that English had confessed to hitting Jami in the head. Tabitha insisted that she had no idea English had done anything to Jami. Now that she knew this, though, she understood why English had told her that morning that he was scared. "They always blame the one who finds the dead child," he told Tabitha, "and I'm just scared I'll get blamed."

English was arrested on October 12, 1995 and charged with murder and aggravated battery of a child. On the same day, investigators for the police and the Department of Children and Family Services (DCFS) went to the home of Tabitha's parents, where she was now staying. They questioned her about some of the other bruises and injuries found on Jami's body. Tabitha recalled instances when Jami had suffered accidents such as falling down the stairs and falling off of a box when brushing her teeth. In each instance, English had an explanation of what happened. Some of the accidents had been witnessed by other people living in the house. Tabitha knew that Jami sometimes called English "mean," but she thought it was because English made Jami stand in the corner when she misbehaved. There also was one incident when Preston told his mother that English had choked him causing abrasions on his neck. He later told her that some boys had thrown rocks at him.

In November, a grand jury returned indictments against Tabitha and English for felony murder and aggravated battery of a child. In 1996, English was found guilty and sentenced to life in prison, which was affirmed on August 18, 2000. Later, his sentence was reduced to fifty years. He will be eligible for parole in October 2020.

In its opening statement at Tabitha's trial on June 17, 1996, the prosecution said that prior to Jami's death on October 10, 1995, Jami had been abused and that Tabitha "...either murdered Jami herself or allowed her boyfriend, Scott English, to murder Jami by giving him access [to] and control over Jami when she knew or should have known of his abusive nature and his danger to Jami." Over the course of the trial, the prosecution called witnesses who testified that English had been abusing Jami and Preston and that Tabitha was in denial that he was not abusing her children. For its part, the defense called witnesses, including Tabitha's mother and sister and English's mother and father, who testified that the incidents characterized by the prosecution as examples of abuse were actually accidents. English was present during some of these incidents. All of these witnesses said they were not aware of any abuse of Jami prior to learning of the statement English made to the police on October 11, 1995. A report written by an investigator from DCFS, filed in response to a neighbor's allegation that Tabitha had been neglecting her children indicated that there was "environmental neglect," but found no indication that Tabitha had been physically abusive to her children. A doctor who was asked by DCFS to examine Preston and David after Jami's death did not find bruises on the two boys that would indicate abuse.

In its closing argument, the prosecution again told the jury that Tabitha "...knew or should have known what was going on here. And that's important: knew or should have known." The prosecution reiterated to the jury that Tabitha was accountable for Jami's death:

> "She should have known. She should have done something. Because any loving reasonable, caring parent would have seen it; they would have done something about it.

> "But not Tabitha Pollock. All she did was continue to allow Scott English to have control over Jami. She continued to give him access and allowed him in the end to do what he ultimately did. And for that, she's as guilty as Scott English of murder and aggravated battery of a child. Because for [sic] without Tabitha Pollock, Scott English could not have carried out this murder. Without Tabitha Pollock, Jami Sue Pollock

would have never been at 720 Pleasant Street, and she would have never been murdered."

After both sides rested their cases, the trial judge instructed the jury. In addition to the standard instruction on accountability, at the request of the prosecution the trial judge gave the jury three non-standard instructions.[†] After only three hours of deliberations, the jury found Tabitha guilty of felony murder and aggravated battery of a child. The judge sentenced her to thirty-six years in prison for the felony murder stating, "[T]he finding of guilty was based not upon her own direct action, but upon her failure to act to protect her child from the actions of her live-in boyfriend."

Still grieving the death of her baby girl, Tabitha somehow had to find the resolve to survive prison and continue fighting for her freedom. She did not know whom to trust in prison and it took her some time before she began working in earnest on her exoneration. Fortunately, there were other people who kept nudging her and kept her going.

wow but english would've dve life of 55 yrs

Sunshine

By Tabitha Hershberger

You were just a little girl
By the name of JAMI SUE.
You were only three years old,
With eyes of the purest blue.

You had such a beautiful face,
And such a pretty smile
I'm so sad…
You were here such a short while

You loved all living things, big or small,
Although your favorite was the butterfly.
You could light up a room with your presence;
Even though you were rather shy.

You will always be mommy's SUNSHINE
And No-One can ever take that away.
You are in my heart Always,
And Sweetie-Pie that's where you'll stay

- Mommy

* * *

The Kite That Saved My Life

As Told By Tabitha Hershberger

Supposedly I had an appeal, and I had a court-appointed lawyer, who told me they could do this, this, that and the other, and I had no clue what they were talking about. They weren't explaining the process to me. They never filed the appeal, so I ended up contacting with Center for Wrongful Conviction at Northwestern University. It didn't happen all of a sudden. The whole time I was in county jail, every time I talked to my mom, she'd say, "Oh, some lawyers in

160

Chicago, they just got someone else out of prison." I'd ask, "Who are they? Where are they?" She had no idea.

It was a little over a year before I figured out who these lawyers were and got in touch with them. By then I was in Lincoln, a co-ed prison. I didn't know there were co-ed prisons. I was in a dorm with three roommates—another white woman, and two black ladies. One of those black ladies said, "I want you to meet somebody."

"Uh, who am I meeting, first of all?"

"Oh this guy that comes over, and he a plumber."

"I don't want to meet him. What are you thinking? I'm in here because of a guy. I don't want to meet a guy."

Eventually, I let her introduce us. We got to talking, and after a while he said, "Why are you in here?"

"I have yet to figure that one out," I replied. "If you know something I don't know I'd be more than interested to hear it." I told him that I was trying to contact this law school in Chicago. I didn't know which law school or the address or anything. I asked him if he could help me get a hold of the law school and he agreed to help me. After a while I got this kite from him telling me who I needed to contact. I thought about it and I wrote Northwestern a letter, then in two weeks I had a letter back from them. They told me to get my case files and documents together. It took me a while to get my mother to send me the documents. By the time I got them, the folks from Northwestern already had them.

Jane Raley, the Northwestern lawyer, came to visit me in prison and brought a couple of her students with her. I was telling them my story, and every time I'd tear up, Jane would tear up as well. As they were preparing to leave, I asked Jane if they would take my case. She didn't want to commit, saying "I don't know. We've got such a big caseload, I can't say." She explained they were so busy that she didn't know if they would be able to fit my case in with so many cases they were responsible for already. Even though they had not agreed to take my case, I left the visiting room knowing that they would. It was just a feeling I had because of the way Jane responded when I was telling her what happened to me. I called my mom and told her I had a new lawyer. Good thing they decided to take my case! Jane called me about a month after they came to visit me in prison. It didn't take them very long to get my appeal filed, but because we missed a filing date, they had to jump through some hoops before the court would even listen. I was in prison a little over seven years all together from being locked up in county jail until the day of my release.

While I was in prison two things really got me through the time—being a teachers' aide and crochet. I never thought I'd be crocheting as much as I did, but it helped me tune out the noise and chaos that is prison. I made a coat for my sister and an afghan for my parents. I also made afghans for my boys. I have three sons. Crochet saved my sanity and on more than one occasion it saved my butt. There was this male prison guard who used to try to get me to meet him in the guards' bathroom. I was always busy working on a crochet project though, for family gifts, so he knew I had a time deadline. I also had some pretty tough friends on the inside. I made friends with the biggest women I could find in there and they protected me. Nobody messed with me and especially not that guard.

Being a teacher's aide gave me something to do with my time. I had my GED and a couple of years of college before I went to prison. The teacher I worked with taught fourth and fifth grade level courses. I only taught math and the teacher taught everything else, but I knew that I loved it. It would be great if I could be a teacher after all of this, but it won't happen unless I'm granted a certificate of innocence. I took some college courses while I was in prison, but I did that to pass the time and it was more productive that just sitting around. Now that I'm out, I think I might be able to do something positive with my training and experience. Only time will tell.

* * *

When Tabitha went to prison, her parents adopted two of her three sons, Jack and Preston, and her youngest son, David, stayed with his father's parents. Tabitha wonders whether her mother just couldn't face David after his father killed Jami. Tabitha's parents left Illinois and moved to Florida, taking Jack and Preston with them. After they moved, they were able to see Tabitha only once a year. Tabitha's sister, Suenjae, was her main visitor while she was in prison. Tabitha's father died while she was in prison. The rest of the family spread out and scattered. It was in prison where Tabitha first learned she had multiple sclerosis (MS)—she thought she'd had a stroke. That's all Tabitha needed—having to deal with MS and prison and the break-up of her family all at the same time. The training she got with her brothers tossing her back and forth helped her keep her fearlessness in prison.

In May 2002, Tabitha appealed her conviction to the Illinois Supreme Court (Court) after her conviction was upheld in December 1999 by the Illinois Appellate Court for the Third District. The Court sought to determine whether Tabitha could be held legally accountable for her daughter's death, which is required for felony murder. After reviewing the trial court records, including the jury instructions, the Court found that the non-standard instructions contradicted the standard instructions. These would have required Tabitha actually *know* English had been abusive to Jami or was likely to abuse and endanger her. The Court found that Tabitha's jury could not "...perform its constitutional function," because the instructions were made unclear by the contradiction created by the non-standard instructions. The Court went on to explain that without knowledge of the need for action there could be no duty to act and Tabitha could not be held accountable for Jami's death.

Specifically, the Court found that there was "...insufficient evidence to support the inference that, prior to Jami's death, [Tabitha] knew Scott was abusing her children or that [Tabitha] sanctioned the abuse of her children by Scott." The Court further noted that the other injuries to the children presented by the prosecution as evidence of abuse "... did not establish that Scott was engaging in an on-going pattern of abuse against [Tabitha's] children" and that "... the injuries sustained by [Tabitha's] children were never so extensive or severe that [Tabitha] was put on notice that Scott posed a serious threat to her children." The Court concluded:

> "...the evidence does not establish that [Tabitha] intended to promote or facilitate the aggravated battery which caused Jami's death. The evidence simply does not support the inference that Jami

was the victim of an ongoing pattern of abuse that the mother knew about and sanctioned."

The Court reversed Tabitha's convictions without sending the case back to the trial court for a new trial. Perhaps no one was happier about Tabitha's release than her big sister Suenjae, called "Sue" by her family and friends. The sisters had always been close despite the difference in age and prison did not change that.

* * *

There's No Crying In Prison

As Told By Suenjae "Sue" Ostrowski

I'm ten years older than Tabitha. She was born in August of 1970, and I was born in August of 1960. I still live in Kewanee, Illinois. That's where Tabitha lived when all this happened. That's where our whole family had always lived, but I'm the only one left here. I didn't know Scott English's family at all and I'd only met Scott one time. Tabitha and Jami would come to my house all the time, and a lot of times Jami would just stay all night with us. One day Tab had come to visit, she had Scott with her, and I had never met him. We went to the park with the kids, and that's basically the first and last time I saw him until Jami's death.

We were surprised when Tab was charged with killing Jami. After she was arrested and charged, she was sent to county jail. She was there for a long time before the trial ended. We figured it was some sort of mistake because Scott had confessed. Tabitha had been going to court and I was there to support her. I was going to the courthouse alone. Our parents had moved to Florida by then. When Tab was found guilty and was convicted, we couldn't believe it because she had never hurt her kids. She was not like that, but they convicted her of murder.

After the verdict, there were reporters crowded together outside the courtroom. My mom and dad were there with me. My brother Bill was there. I don't remember who else. I just remember them. All the reporters were out there, and we did not want to talk to them at all. We weren't talking to anyone. Bill went out and told the reporters, "My family does not want to talk to any of you people, and we'd appreciate if you'd just leave us alone." They didn't, of course. They followed us all the way down the steps in front of the courthouse; all the way down. They were lined along both sides of the steps. It was not a good thing.

To this day I still don't know how that jury found her guilty. They should not have convicted her. The prosecutor said there's a law when there wasn't. Tabitha did seven years, but she shouldn't have done any time at all.

We didn't know what to do. Mom used to watch *Oprah* and we thought she might be interested in Tabitha's story. It seemed like just the kind of story her viewers would like. The justice system did this terrible thing to my sister. She hadn't hurt anyone, especially not her kids. How could they convict her? The law they convicted her under was that as a mother, she should have known that Scott was going to harm her daughter. We didn't understand how anybody could have known. Even all the people that lived in the house with them didn't know. Nobody knew. How could anyone know anything like that? We thought Oprah would get a lot of people who would agree with us, so Mom and I decided we should send a video. We would make a video and send it to the Oprah show. She was somebody that we thought could help. They sent us back a letter that said something like they weren't interested at all in that. We were very upset that Oprah didn't want any part of Tabitha's story. After the people from Northwestern got Tabitha released, Oprah's show sent a letter saying they wanted to interview Tabitha. We thought, "Well, isn't that something. She didn't want to help us when we wanted help, but now she sure wants Tabitha on her show." We thought she'd be interested in a story where a woman, a mother, had been treated so poorly by the justice system. She'd been such a strong advocate for women. I haven't felt the same about Oprah since.

Before our parents moved to Florida, they already had adopted Tab's son, Jack. They hadn't adopted Preston yet, but they would soon. Not too long after our folks moved, Tabitha was transferred out of county jail to Dwight Prison. I had been able to visit her weekly when she was in county jail. Mom's brother, Uncle Charlie, would go with me and my kids to visit Tabitha. We tried to go every month, but sometime we didn't have enough money and Mom would send us some money so we could still go and visit Tabitha. I remember the first time we went to visit her in prison. When it came time to tell her goodbye, it was just hard to do. She was leaving the visiting room. She was going back to her cell. She was ready to cry; I was ready to cry. I don't think either one of us wanted to show each other we were that upset. I was trying to be strong for her. She was trying to be strong for me. We'd always say to her, "Well, it will get easier as time goes on," but it never did. Every time we visited her it was hard to just leave her there.

When we got nowhere with Oprah, we realized we had to do something to try and get Tabitha out of there. Mom and I wrote letters to people on her behalf, but nothing ever really came of them. We visited to keep her spirits up but also to keep up our own. On those visits, we tried to stay upbeat, but it was tough to see her in prison when we knew she hadn't done anything wrong and she didn't belong there. Tab seemed to deal with it better than we did. She had a job teaching. Some of the women inmates couldn't even read. She taught them math. She was always really good at math. She studied to be a nurse, but she never finished because of the conviction. Tab was only twenty-five years old when she went to jail. It seemed like she was going to spend the best years of her life behind bars. Fortunately, the lawyers from Northwestern were able to win her exoneration after she'd been in prison for almost seven years. We thought she'd avoid spending her best years in prison, and then we learned Tab had MS. In an ironic twist of faith, the years she spent in prison were her last healthy years.

The doctors gave Tabitha an MRI of her brain and found that MS already had caused some deterioration. I know it's serious, but Tab's had too much serious in her life already. I tried to keep things light by telling her, "We always knew you were an airhead, Tab." It's been great having her home. Back in 2005, almost ten years ago I had a liver transplant. Tab came back to Illinois to help me for the first week I was out of the hospital. When she was exonerated, Tab moved away. I'm the only family member left in Illinois. When Tab came to visit it was like it used to be when we were kids. We made fudge, lots and lots of fudge. Then we took a whole platter full of fudge into the bedroom to watch movies. Tab gained eight pounds on that visit!

Tab used to come to visit two or three times a year, stay a few weeks, and then return home. I think it was very difficult for her. When Tabitha was convicted, our parents adopted Preston and Jack. They didn't adopt David, Scott's son, so Scott's parents let David come and live with them for a while. We don't know what happened, but David ended up in foster care with a family in Moline or Quad Cities or Rock Island. We think they're the family that eventually adopted him, but we don't know. We lost contact with David over the years. My brother, Rock, tried to reconnect with David a few years ago, but David wasn't interested. He said he had his life and that he didn't want to talk with us. He was only two years old when Jami died and probably doesn't remember anything about his real mother and father or his sister and his brothers.

Once Tabitha had been found guilty, people we had known forever started acting strangely. My daughter was eight years old at the time. She and her little friends used to have slumber parties. After the jury verdict, parents wouldn't let their girls talk to my daughter anymore. People just assumed Tab did it because she was found guilty. One day at the grocery store, I saw the mother of one of my daughter's playmates. We weren't close, but we had been friendly because of our daughters. She looked at me and said, "She did it, and guilty is guilty."

I couldn't let it slide, so I responded, "I don't believe I saw you at any of the court proceedings. I don't believe I saw you anywhere or that you know what is going." It's like everyone was going out of their way to say something nasty to me. Even people who never met Tabitha assumed she was a murderer. How could they say things like that about her when they never even met her?

Of course, after Tab was exonerated, they were saying how unfair the system was. Suddenly they were on her side. The woman I ran into in the grocery store came up to me again and said, "Sue, I think about what I said to you in Galva at the grocery store. I thought about it and you're right. I really didn't know anything."

I know I should have let it go, but I couldn't. Instead I said, "Oh, ten years later you're gonna tell me this." Then I just sighed and told her "okay" because it didn't really matter.

This whole experience got me to thinking, there's probably hundreds more people in prison that don't belong there. What's worse, some of the innocent people in prison are on death row. Fortunately for us there are people like the lawyers at Northwestern who help innocent people get out of prison. We need more of them.

* * *

When Tabitha won her freedom Sue came to drive her home. The two sisters walked out of prison together. As they walked to Sue's car, Tabitha's son Preston ran to greet his mother. Preston picked up his mom and swung her around like she weighed nothing. He was only twelve years old at the time, but he was strong and muscular.

In the years since Tabitha's release Jack, her eldest son, moved to China where he married. They have a young son, making Tabitha a pretty young grandmother.

Although Tabitha has been exonerated, she is still waiting on a certificate of innocence to completely clear her name. Tabitha, like many exonerees, just wants the entire ordeal to be over. She likes to say, "I have Warden on my side. I have Marshall on my side. I have God on my side. How can I lose?" She's referring to Rob Warden and Larry Marshall, senior lawyers with Northwestern's Center for Wrongful Conviction.

Tabitha Hershberger lives with her husband, Abe. Suenjae Ostrowski, her sister, is the only family member still living in Illinois.

---

†At the end of a trial, the judge gives the jury instructions that help explain how the jurors should apply the law to the facts in the case. The judge should have given the standard instruction on accountability: "A person is legally responsible for the conduct of another person when, either before or during the commission of an offense, and with the intent to promote or facilitate the commission of the offense, he *knowingly*

solicits, aids, abets, agrees to aid, or attempts to aid the other person in the planning or commission of the offense." (Emphasis added.) Instead of delivering the correct instruction, the trial judge gave the jury three instructions related to accountability, each of which overreaches and which, collectively, contradict the standard instruction. Instruction Number 10 incorrectly confirmed the prosecution's theory of "should have known" as the standard for determining accountability: "A parent has a legal duty to aid a small child if the parent *knows or should have known* about a danger to the child and the parent has the physical ability to protect the child. Criminal conduct may arise not only by overt acts, but by an omission to act where there is a legal duty to do so." (Emphasis added.). The trial judge also issued instruction Number 11: "Actual presence at the commission of the crime is not a requirement of accountability." The trial judge also issued a third instruction, Number 13: "For accountability, intent to promote or facilitate crime may be shown by evidence that the defendant shared a criminal intent of the principal or by evidence that there was a common criminal design.").

CHAPTER 10
Gloria Goodwin Killian

Some people have their lives decided for them almost from birth. Others never seem to figure out what to do with their lives. Gloria Killian took a few years and a rather circuitous path, but she discovered her passion and it was the law. Although she had not attended college, Gloria intended to start law school. When the school she applied to would not enroll her, Gloria challenged the administration and won admission. She started the evening program and worked hard to keep up with her homework while holding down a full-time job.

Gloria was spending all of her time working, studying, or attending classes. Her already troubled marriage fell apart. Before long she started dating one of her classmates. From the beginning it was a tempestuous relationship. Gloria's boyfriend delighted in messing with her already fragile psyche. Things would happen that he would deny, instead telling Gloria, "It's all in your head. That never happened." Looking back on that period, Gloria recognized she was not being herself. In that relationship she allowed herself to be emotionally abused, something she had experienced off and on throughout her life. "He gaslighted me," she said, "and I just took it."

Gloria was in her third year of a four-year program when she ran out of money and had to put her legal education on hold. Some might say thirty-five years old was a bit late for law school, but Gloria was undaunted. She took a job in a coin shop and tried to save up enough money to finish her legal studies. The job wasn't much, but it gave her time to figure out where she was headed and what she needed to do next, time to get her bearings.

Ed and Grace Davies were proud of their collection of silver coins and medallions. The rather large collection was stored in six suitcases in their home when it was not out on loan or exhibition. Perhaps they should have stored the collection at a bank or some other secure location, but there had been no problems with keeping it at home.

Ed and Grace were preparing for bed one fall evening when there was a knock at the front door. The woman standing outside looked anxious. She asked to come in and use the phone to call a tow truck. For some reason, the Davies did not let her inside, which turned out to be fortuitous. The couple went to bed and forgot about their evening visitor until two months later.

On December 9, 1981, Stephen DeSantis, dressed as telephone repairman, entered the Davies' home in Rosemont, California, a suburb of Sacramento. He handcuffed Ed and Grace and hogtied them as well. After the Davies had been securely tied up, he let in his cousin, Gary Masse. The two men proceeded to ransack the Davies' home searching for the silver. They found the six suitcases. Before they left, one of the robbers shot Ed and then shot Grace in the head. Miraculously, Grace survived, but Ed was not so lucky. He died of his gunshot wounds. After the two robbers left, Grace managed to crawl out of her home to the front lawn where she was found the next morning.

The Sacramento area had been plagued by a series of coin shop robberies that year. The murder of Ed and the attempted murder of Grace were so grisly they made the local news that evening. Gloria recognized Ed from his visits to the coin shop where she worked. "Oh, my God," Gloria gasped when she saw the news. "He used to come into the shop."

On December 14, 1982, the police received an anonymous tip identifying DeSantis and Masse as the robbers and Gloria as an accomplice. The officers went to Masse's home to arrest him, but he was not there. His wife told them a woman had planned the heist. When one officer said "You mean Gloria," she agreed. Three days later, the police brought Gloria in for questioning. On that same day, Masse surrendered himself to the police. Gloria cooperatively answered questions until the police charged her with felony murder, attempted murder, burglary, robbery, and conspiracy. As a former law student, Gloria knew to remain silent after being arrested by the police; she knew to ask for an attorney. Because the crime was a capital offense, she was held without bail. Nearly five months later, Gloria was released after a preliminary hearing failed to establish any connection between her and the crime. The charges against Gloria were dropped and the case was dismissed. Gloria was elated but her ordeal was not over yet.

Masse was tried and convicted of first-degree murder in May 1983. On May 16, he was sentenced to life without parole. Masse immediately contacted the Sacramento Police Department (SPD) asking whether it might be possible to get his sentence reduced. He claimed to have evidence that could help SPD identify other accomplices. On May 20, SPD interviewed Masse but, at the instruction of the prosecutor, did not promise him a reduced sentence. Masse wanted his sentence reduced to twelve years in exchange for his testimony against DeSantis and Gloria.

In June 1983, Gloria was re-arrested along with DeSantis. This time she was not subject to the death penalty because a 1983 law excluded the death penalty for murder accomplices. Gloria and DeSantis were tried separately. At Gloria's preliminary hearing in August 1983, Masse testified for three days, implicating Gloria and the DeSantis brothers. On September 6, Deputy District Attorney Christopher Cleland wrote a letter to the judge in Masse's case, asking him to recall Masse's sentence because Masse was cooperating in the prosecution's case against Gloria. Under California law the court has 120 days during which it can recall the previous sentence for the purpose of re-sentencing the defendant. Prior to this letter, Cleland had never sent a letter asking a judge to recall a sentence. Masse's sentence was recalled on September 8, 1983. Cleland gave Gloria's defense team a copy of the September 6 letter.

DeSantis was tried first. He testified that he did not know Gloria Killian and she had not been involved with planning the robbery. He also testified that Masse's wife, Joanne, was the woman who asked to use the Davies' phone in the earlier robbery attempt. DeSantis's brother, Robert, had driven Masse to the Davies home on the day of the robbery and he also testified that he did not know Gloria. Robert DeSantis was charged for his role in the Davies robbery. He agreed to a plea deal in exchange for testifying at his brother's trial. He did not testify at Gloria's trial and his testimony was not introduced as evidence at her trial. It was, however, introduced during the habeas hearing before the district court.

On April 18, 1985, before the jury began deliberating, Cleland wrote another letter to Masse's judge asking for leniency in Masse's sentencing because of his testimony against DeSantis and his anticipated testimony against Gloria. Masse had not been re-sentenced since the judge recalled his initial sentence in 1983.

Masse testified at Gloria's trial in 1986. He implicated Gloria as "the master planner" behind the robbery and stated that after she realized the robbery had happened, she called him and demanded "her share" of the loot. Even though Masse's testimony was the only direct evidence linking Gloria to the robbery, the jury found her guilty. At her sentencing, Cleland asked for the maximum sentence. He acknowledged that Gloria had no prior arrests or convictions and had been, so far as he knew, a law-abiding citizen who was planning to be a lawyer. He argued that someone like Gloria should get *more* time because of who she was and that's exactly what happened. Gloria was sentenced to thirty-two years to life on February 26, 1986. She was not the only person in the courtroom shocked by the severity of her sentence. She recalls hearing a gasp from the sheriff's officer who escorted her to court that morning. Back at the jail where Gloria had been held during the trial, the inmates learned of her sentence. As word spread, murmurs of "wow" and "damn" rippled through the public areas.

Masse's sentence was reduced from life without parole to twenty-five years. He was responsible for Ed Davies's death and Grace Davies's injuries and his sentence was for less time than Gloria who was not even present at the time of the robbery and shootings. Still, Masse was disappointed because he thought he had a verbal agreement with the police that his reduced sentence would be twelve years. On April 21, 1986, Masse wrote a letter to Cleland's investigator expressing his anger at what he saw as a repudiation of their deal. Masse wrote:

> "...as far as I'm concerned, there was a verbal agreement of no more than twelve years. I been upfront and honest as I could be. I gave you De-Santis and Killian. I did my part all the way to

the end. I even lied my ass off on the stand for you people."

Cleland did not disclose this letter to Gloria's defense team.

Gloria Killian would spend another sixteen years in the California Institute for Women in Chino before she could prove her innocence. At first she fought for her freedom. She met many women who were in prison for having fought back against the men who abused them. Eventually Gloria became resigned to living out the rest of her life in prison. She decided to make as much as she could of her situation. Gloria was assigned to the prison law library where she could use her legal education to help other prisoners prepare their appeals. She built a community of friends at Chino—friends who would help her survive the next sixteen years.

One of Gloria's closest friends was a fan of the French National Holiday, Bastille Day. She also had been wrongfully convicted. Gloria wished she could help her friend with her case, but there was nothing she could do. They focused, instead, on creating a Bastille Day celebration. Gloria remembered her friend sitting at a table with plastic cutlery—she was coloring the spoons purple with a marker. Neither of them could recall what purple had to do with Bastille Day, but they sat together at a table in front of a pile of white plastic cutlery and a handful of purple markers and got to work.

* * *

Waiting For The Revolution
By Gloria Killian

Bastille Day is a national holiday in France commemorating a day during the French revolution when the citizens of Paris stormed the Bastille, the French penitentiary, and freed the prisoners. This French holiday is little known in the United States, but it seemed to me to be the most appropriate holiday for us to celebrate at the California Institution for Women where I was serving a sentence of thirty-two years to life for a crime that I did not commit.

For a brief few minutes I experienced delusions of grandeur, envisioning the entire prison wildly celebrating one of the few historical victories of the incarcerated, but fortunately I concluded that discretion was a better idea. I discussed the upcoming holiday only with my closest friends and we decided that the perfect celebration would be a picnic lunch in the grassy area known as "the circle" overlooked by the Administration Building. Each of us (forever enshrined in my brain as "the Bastillettes") would bring as many delicious goodies to eat as she could cook, conjure up, steal, or save from her quarterly package.

I decided to make tamales for our first "holiday" lunch and so we began our traditional celebration of Bastille Day, which continued for the sixteen and a half years that I was wrongfully incarcerated. Sadly, the local citizenry surrounding the prison never came to my aid, but the annual gathering of "the Bastillettes" was the highlight of each of my prison years.

Bastilles

6 bags of tortilla chips, finely crushed

3 cans of roast beef

1 can jalapenos

1 small box Velveeta cheese

2 cans green salsa

Salt to taste

1 large white laundry bucket

4 stingers (immersion heating implements)

10 clear plastic bags cut into small oblong shapes

1 tin can lid

Most women crushed the chips by hand, but I discovered that it was much faster to triple wrap the bags of chips in plastic bags and jump up and down on them. It was also great for my feelings of frustration as well as good exercise.

> Boil a small bowl of water and mix with the crushed tortilla chips to make masa. Place a tablespoon of masa on an oblong of plastic and pat into a slightly smaller oblong until half the masa is used.
>
> Use the tin can lid to chop the roast beef and jalapenos and mix together. Place a spoonful of meat mixture along the center of each oblong of masa and top with another tablespoon of masa. Pat masa to cover the filling and seal the masa layers together. Triple-wrap each tamale in plastic wrap.
>
> Fill the laundry bucket half full of water and use the four stingers to heat the water to a low boil. Place the tamales in the laundry bucket and cover the bucket with a towel. Cook for four hours, and then unwrap the tamales and place on a plate. Chop half the box of cheese and place the cubes in a bowl. Mix in the two cans of salsa and place the bowl over a larger bowl of boiling water until melted. Mix well and pour over the tamales which can also be served plain if desired. Recipe makes about 15 tamales.

When I left prison, I left the Bastille Day picnic inside with my friends. They continued the picnic for a couple of years after I left.

* * *

From the time of her initial arrest until the time she was released, Gloria spent nearly twenty years in prison. When she thinks about how her wrongful conviction affected her life, she looks at the entire period, including the time she had to deal with the case when she was not imprisoned—over twenty-five years. While she would rather not have spent any time in prison, Gloria believes a person, especially an innocent person, needs to find some sort of personal benefit to being in prison in order to survive. "Not only survive," Gloria explained. "It's a lot like the foxhole mentality. You're basically in a mode to survive every day of your life. Women don't have all the violence and that kind of stuff, but just because you're paranoid doesn't mean they're not after you. When you live under such tremendous stress you need a lot of the little defenses that we all put up to protect ourselves. As a result, you can make and have the most amazing friendships in prison. It's very much like people who have been through a war together."

Gloria seemed to find her mission while in prison. She became an advocate for women prisoners, particularly for the reform of the prison system and how women are treated in it. "Being involved in prison reform absolutely saved my life," Gloria explains. "It really did because if it hadn't been for that I don't know what I would have done." It also was a good thing she didn't know at the time that she'd be in prison for as long as she was. She did have moments of despair and depression even as she helped other inmates fight for their rights. Her friend Barbara died in prison. They formed a pact between the two of them. If ever there came a time when one of them could not take being locked up, she would, as Gloria put it, take herself out. When Barbara was diagnosed with cancer, she went through chemotherapy treatment. When the diagnosis was colon cancer, she refused treatment. Gloria did not blame her friend for refusing medical help. "I told her I understood what she did," Gloria says sadly. "She was life without the possibility of parole."

Gloria's advocacy work included helping women with their cases. Each year when the inmates were assessed for job assignments, Gloria was assigned to the prison law library. She was a law clerk for nearly fifteen years. No one in the State prison system had ever held a job for that long. For all intents, Gloria was running a law practice from inside the prison. She helped staff as well as inmates. "I used to help staff," she says with a twinkle in her eyes. "Well, some I would help and some I wouldn't. If I didn't want to help, I just told them I didn't know." Gloria was so busy working on inmates' cases and on legislative reform that she never had time to work on her own case. Her friends used to get on her for neglecting her case. "Work on your own case they would tell me," she said. "But I couldn't for one simple reason—I didn't know what had happened."

Gloria was surprised at who stood by her through both trials and who did not. "There's nothing like getting arrested for murder and having it on the front page of the local newspaper to show you who your real friends are...and are not," she said sadly. Her ex-husband was one of those who surprised her. He was an officer in the Sacramento Police Department and he stood up for her with his law enforcement colleagues. "It was odd," she mused. "People I thought were my friends disappeared in a hurry. People I thought would disappear didn't." Some of Gloria's closest friends today are the women she met in prison.

Gloria was not alone in wanting to help women inmates. In the early 1990s, Gloria met Joyce Ride who had dedicated much of her adult life to helping imprisoned women through an organization called Friends Outside. Joyce met Gloria on one of her visits to the prison in Chino and they became friends. As their friendship grew, Joyce began to wonder if Gloria might be innocent. Joyce hired a private investigator to find evidence of Gloria's innocence. After years of denied appeals, Gloria did not want her friend to waste her money on what she saw as a hopeless case. Joyce paid no attention to Gloria and good thing she did not. Her private investigator found Masse's letter admitting he lied on the stand. He also discovered the second letter Cleland wrote to Masse's judge asking for a lighter sentence because of Masse's cooperation in Killian's trial. In all, Joyce's investigator unearthed three letters that had been withheld from Gloria's defense team. Together the three letters, along with the fourth letter requesting a delay of Masse's sentencing, suggested an agreement between Masse and the prosecution team for a lighter sentence in exchange for his testimony against Gloria—at least that's the way the United States Court of Appeals for the Ninth Circuit (Ninth Circuit) saw it.

Don't Fence Me In

As Told By Joyce Ride

I didn't know Gloria until I met her in prison. I'd been invited by my Presbyterian women's group to hear a speaker. She talked about visiting women in jail and what she said appealed to me, so I asked her if I could meet her at the jail and if she would train me as a jail visitor. That was back in the 1970s and I've been visiting women prisoners ever since. I'm not there to preach or proselytize. I'm just there as a friend, someone trying to bring a little normalcy and humor. Sometimes I think we forget that they are just people. That's how I see them, as people, not as criminals.

I met Gloria because of another woman I had been visiting in jail. She had been serving a three-year sentence but was released early because she was diagnosed with a brain tumor. She moved home to Indiana to be with her family. It was during our last visit that she suggested I talk to Gloria. I was preparing for a meeting in Texas to discuss issues facing women in prison and she thought Gloria would be the perfect person to give me some background information. I wrote to Gloria. We exchanged a few letters and I asked, "Would it be all right if I visited you?" She didn't say yes right away. She had me checked out first and then decided that I was all right.

I visited Gloria without knowing much about her background. We just talked and enjoyed one another's company. After about a year of meeting and talking with her, it occurred to me that I hadn't been spending all that time with a criminal. I asked her why she was in prison. She remembers it as me blurting out one day, "Why the hell are you here?" I never thought I'd ask an inmate what she was in for and it took me a year to ask Gloria. I had to because I just had a feeling that she was innocent. She told me her story and when she finished I said, "Oh, would it be all right if I hired a detective to go up to Sacramento and check out the story?"

"Sure," she replied, "that would be all right."

I hired a private detective and after several months he reported back to me that Gloria wasn't guilty. I told her what he said and asked if it would be all right if I hired an attorney. "Well," she replied, "you'd be wasting your money, but it would be all right." I didn't think it would be a waste of money, but I also didn't think it would take so long to prove Gloria's innocence. After so many years of appealing her conviction and having court after court affirm her conviction, Gloria wasn't very optimistic. Hope was not her middle name, but I believe our friendship gave her some kind of hope—something to be thankful for, to be hopeful for.

I got the name of a good defense attorney in Santa Monica and went to his office to meet with him. Before I called him I had already talked to a couple of attorneys who didn't want to go out to the prison to meet Gloria. They said they'd take the case, but they didn't have the time to even meet with her. The lawyer from Santa Monica, Bill Genego, was interested in Gloria's case, but he wanted to talk with her before he'd decide whether to take her on as a client. He went out to the prison and talked to her. I think he went out there a couple of times. She liked him. When we met, he told me he didn't think Gloria was guilty and he agreed to take her case. It took him five years and many different courts, getting turned down over and over, before he finally got Gloria's conviction overturned. There have been all sorts of news reports about how much I paid Bill, but he wasn't doing it just for the money. At one point he was as invested in the case as we all were and he continued to work pro bono from then on.

Over time Gloria and I became friends. Right off the bat we noticed we have a lot in common. We are both kind of short, the same height, both of Norwegian background. Gloria can talk a lot on almost any subject. Me too. She has the same sense of humor that I have. We both work with women in prison. Gloria was helping inmates when she was in prison and she continues to work on issues affecting women inmates since her release. She's been out around twelve years, but she feels like this is something she has to do—go back and help the women she left behind. An amazing thing happened on the day Gloria was released. I went to pick her up and everybody was in the visiting room. They all had gone to the visiting area, inmates and visitors, and all of them were standing there waving and cheering. They were really happy for her.

I can't imagine what Gloria felt when I went to pick her up from prison, but as we left, I was singing "Don't fence me in." I looked over at Gloria sitting in the passenger seat, smirking as I sang. We drove about twenty miles away to Rancho Cucamonga to have dinner at a nice Italian restaurant. Gloria had her first glass of red wine in almost seventeen years.

Gloria had no living relatives. Her mother died when she was in prison. The only relative was an uncle up in Washington. He sent her money regularly and he has since died. When Gloria got out of prison I asked her to move in with me. She's still here.

I continued to visit the prison and especially enjoyed spending time with one of Gloria's friends. I visited her for quite a while, until she died of cancer. While Gloria was in prison, we started a Christmas gift program where we would put together a gift package to deliver to the women. Gloria has taken over the program. She's been doing it every year and there are more and more people getting involved. The sheriff's office thought the program was such a good idea they got involved.

Since we're housemates we have a lot of time to talk about things. We've discussed the underrepresentation of women in terms of getting support for exoneration, or even support for defense, or just to have people listen to their cases. I used to do a bit of public speaking, trying to convince people that these women are people, not criminals. I spoke to a lot of women's church groups. When I started visiting jails I had no preconceived notions about the justice system. I never really gave it much thought until the day I realized I needed to. I still don't ask for details about their imprisonment, but I am able to accept them as fellow human beings. In the early 1990s I promoted myself from jails to prisons. The pressure was slightly less and I wasn't getting any younger. On jail visits we'd see fifteen or twenty women and leave with fifteen or twenty requests. In prison you're only permitted to visit one person at a time.

Usually I get requests for things like books—law, poetry, biographies. One woman wanted everything I could find on Elvis. Gloria has a list of the women on death row and we send Christmas packages to them. They really appreciate it when someone thinks about them even a little bit. When she was in prison, Gloria did legal work. She had a few years of law school and used it to help everyone. She always said, "I can help everybody but myself."

My church friends used to have a hard time understanding why I visited prisons. My neighbors didn't know what I was doing. They didn't belong to the same church. My daughter knows what I'm doing and she's very supportive. She's a Presbyterian minister, but she's no more evangelical than I am. She's also got a great quirky sense of humor. I think it runs in the family.

I'm so proud of all that Gloria has accomplished, and her advocacy of women's rights. She's written a book that tells all about her life before and after her wrongful conviction. She's the same age as my other daughter and a book just came out about her life as an astronaut. It's called *Sally Ride*. Before she died she started a foundation, Sally Ride Science, which encourages children, and especially girls, to be interested in science.

I'm very happy that Gloria is my friend. Sometimes I'm asked where Gloria would be if we hadn't met. Would she still be in prison? I don't know, she might, but I don't have to think about that because we did meet and she's a free woman.

* * *

In 2002, the Ninth Circuit found that Masse lied on the stand at Gloria's trial stating "...one cannot deny that Gary Masse gave perjured testimony at Killian's trial." The Ninth Circuit also discounted Masse's insistence that there was no agreement with the prosecution for his testimony. The letters from Masse talking about his understanding with the prosecution's investigators and Cleland's written leniency request to Masse's judge were withheld from the defense team. Withholding such damaging and potentially exculpatory evidence convinced the Ninth Circuit that some sort of agreement existed between Masse and Cleland. When confronted with the evidence of his perjury, Masse admitted to lying on the stand. He explained, "I couldn't tell the truth because there would have been no more deals. I wouldn't have come through for them."

In addition to Masse's perjured testimony and the prosecution's failure to disclose exculpatory evidence, the Ninth Circuit found that the prosecution also violated Gloria's rights when it implied at least eight times during her trial that by invoking her right to remain silent, Gloria had something to hide. The court held that Gloria's silence was a protected privilege established by no less than the United States

Supreme Court, noting specifically that "...Killian's silence is squarely within [established law]." The Ninth Circuit explained its decision to grant Gloria's writ of habeas corpus. It described Masse as a "make or break" witness for the prosecution and the cumulative effect of the errors at trial as devastating:

> "The collective presence of these errors is devastating to one's confidence in the reliability of this verdict and therefore requires, at the very least, a new trial."

On March 13, 2002, the Ninth Circuit reversed the district court's previous denial of Gloria's writ and expressly instructed it to grant the writ or immediately grant Gloria a new trial. It took over four months from the time her writ was granted for Gloria to be released. The delay was caused by the prosecution filing motion after motion, stalling tactics designed to keep her locked up. Gloria almost laughs when she thinks about it. "The way I got in there was really strange and the way I got out was equally strange." On August 8, 2002, Gloria was released from prison and all charges against her were dropped.

Her good friend Joyce was waiting to pick her up at the gate. Joyce might have been happier than Gloria. While she had been imprisoned, Gloria lost all of her family, so Joyce invited her to move into Joyce's Southern California home. The friends have been housemates since then and both continue their work with women prisoners. Gloria founded the Action Committee for Women in Prison, advocating for improvements in the living conditions in women's prisons, the release of women who have been unjustly imprisoned, and changes in the laws that imprison victims of domestic violence for protecting themselves.

* * *

Gloria's case is one of only a handful where the prosecutor who engaged in misconduct was actually charged for his misconduct. Prosecutors enjoy almost absolute immunity from punishment related to their actions in connection with a trial. In 2008, the State Bar of California charged Cleland with five counts of misconduct. With a straight face, Cleland testified that he did not know to whom he should give the letters. He confessed to being "stymied" and "giving up." He relied on the California Supreme Court to sort it all out on appeal, smugly stating "...and that's what happened." Of course it happened sixteen years later, but to Cleland apparently that qualifies as justice. The State Bar Judge, Pat McElroy, found Cleland had behaved improperly on only two of the charges. Of the three letters that Cleland failed to disclose to Gloria's defense team, Judge McElroy surprisingly found only one to be relevant and containing exculpatory evidence. He disagreed with the Ninth Circuit's characterization of the letters as important to understanding why Masse lied about Gloria's involvement. Not surprisingly, Judge McElroy found that Cleland improperly commented on Gloria invoking her right to remain silent.

It is obvious that Judge McElroy understood the duty of prosecutors, stating that "Prosecutors have a constitutional mandate to disclose material, exculpatory evidence to defendants in criminal cases." It is undisputed that Cleland did not share Masse's letter in which he claimed to have lied on the stand about Gloria. Additionally, if Cleland had not made an agreement with Masse for his testimony, why did Cleland fail to send the defense team a copy of the 1985 letter he sent to Masse's judge asking for leniency in sentencing? Despite clear evidence that Cleland had withheld exculpatory evidence, Judge McElroy saw fit only to admonish Cleland for his behavior. An admonishment is neither exoneration nor discipline. Judge McElroy explained his lenient approach to punishing Cleland's obvious misconduct by referencing the many character witnesses who testified on behalf of Cleland at the hearing. It seems ironic that the testimony, ultimately perjured testimony, of a convicted felon would weigh so heavily against a woman who had no prior criminal record and no other evidence linking her to the crime. Whereas a prosecutor who, allegedly, had not committed any prior acts of misconduct was given every benefit of the doubt and his character references led Judge McElroy to be lenient when his misconduct was irrefutable and led to the wrongful conviction and sixteen year imprisonment of an innocent woman. Failing to appreciate the irony of the situation, Judge McElroy wrote:

"In light of the presence of compelling mitigation, including respondent's thirty-eight years of practice without prior discipline, good faith, cooperation with the State Bar, demonstration of excellent character, passage of considerable time since the misconduct occurred and excessive delay in conducting disciplinary proceedings, any discipline would not further the objectives of attorney discipline and would be punitive in nature."

Judge McElroy did not seem to understand, or simply refused to acknowledge, that the reason it took so long to bring Cleland's misconduct to light was that Cleland himself hid the evidence of his misconduct. Discipline "punitive in nature" is exactly what was called for here. Cleland should have been punished for what he did to Gloria. Instead, no consideration was given to the fact that if Cleland had shared Masse's letter about his perjury with the defense as soon as he received it, Gloria might have spent only one or two additional years in prison instead of sixteen!

So long as prosecutors who engage in blatant violations of their constitutional mandate and defendants' rights are not held accountable for their actions, they tarnish the professional reputations of hundreds of law-abiding prosecutors and weaken the public's faith in the fairness of our judicial system. Until misbehaving prosecutors are held accountable by, at the very least, the bar associations that license them, we cannot hope to reduce the number of wrongful convictions that occur in our justice system.

Gloria Killian lives in Southern California and is a dedicated advocate for the rights of women in prison and battered women and children. Joyce Ride, her friend, is dedicated to improving the lives of imprisoned women.

CHAPTER 11
Larry Lamb

Sometimes bad things happen. Sometimes terrible things happen. For Larry Lamb at the age of forty-two the inconceivable happened. Larry was arrested for crimes he did not commit five years after the crimes occurred. Some people believe things happen for a reason and even an inconceivable occurrence can be rationalized by true a believer. Larry is such a believer. What happened to him looked bad, felt bad, and it was bad. Still, deep within his soul, despite the terrible situation he was in, Larry found a glow of light that took away his fear, his anger, and his confusion and in their absence he found peace. Despite his inconceivable situation, being an innocent man in prison, Larry found himself bathed in the light of the blessed. There was a time that "blessed" would not describe Larry's situation and how he lived his life.

Leamon Grady was a bootlegger in Duplin County, North Carolina. People used to drop by his home unannounced at all hours of the day and night to buy some of his white lightnin'. If you had the money, Grady had the liquor. Sometime early on the morning of Saturday, February 28, 1987, Grady had some drop-in customers. They came to purchase liquor, but something went wrong. By the end of the transaction Grady was dead of a single gunshot wound to the chest. On the other side of town, Larry was finishing his shift at the factory. He clocked out at 12:06 a.m. and went home to get a good night's sleep.

At around 2:00 a.m., one of Grady's neighbors drove past his house on her way home from work. She saw two unfamiliar cars in his driveway and recognized Grady's car under the carport. When another neighbor drove by at around 3:00 a.m. the two visitor cars were gone and Grady's car was still under the carport. During that time two friends, Larry Buckram and Simon Lofton, stopped by Grady's to buy some liquor. Buckram waited in the car while Lofton went inside to make the purchase. Shortly after Lofton went inside, Buckram heard a single gunshot. Lofton came back to the car and they drove away. Lofton would later tell Buckram when he asked

Grady for the change from his twenty dollars, Grady reached for his .25 caliber pistol. Lofton claimed he shot Grady before Grady could shoot him. Shortly after 3:00 a.m., two more of Grady's customers stopped by and found him dead on the kitchen floor. Not much later, Sheriff Dalton Jones arrived on the scene and noticed an unopened can of cold beer on the kitchen table. It was 4:00 a.m. Half an hour later, the medical examiner arrived and noted that Grady's body was still warm and pliant—rigor mortis had not set in at the point. This meant Grady died between 2:00 a.m. and 3:00 a.m. on Saturday morning.

The police investigated Grady's murder and came up with nothing—no suspects, no leads, no evidence. Although they found Grady's .25 caliber gun on his bed, they never found the gun that killed Grady. After three years of no progress, a four thousand dollar reward was offered for information leading to an arrest. Up until that point Lovely Lorden, like everyone else in the neighborhood had repeatedly told the police she knew nothing about Grady's murder. Once the reward was on the table, however, she changed her story and told police that her ex-boyfriend and two of his friends, one of whom was Larry Lamb, had murdered Grady. According to Lorden, she and the three men drove to Grady's house at around midnight with the intention to rob him. Lorden said she stayed in the car while her then boyfriend, Levon "Bo" Jones, and the other two men went inside. She said she heard two gunshots just moments before the three men returned to the car and drove away. Jones had been carrying a gun when the three men entered Grady's house.

Lorden's story changed at least five times over the next two years. Her descriptions of what happened were inconsistent with the evidence. In November 1990, the North Carolina State Bureau of Investigations (SBI) had Lorden wear a wire and set up a meeting with Larry Lamb. The authorities wanted to corroborate Lorden's prior statements and thought Larry might implicate himself. Lorden tried to get Larry to admit to being at Grady's that night or having something to do with Grady's death:

Lorden: The night...the night that...Leamon did get killed, I don't know whether you can remember or not. You, me, Tootie...was together.

Lamb: No, we wasn't.

Lorden: We were together.

Lamb: Uh-uh.

Lorden: And they are giving me...

Lamb: Not me. You got me mixed up.

Lorden: ...a lot of hassle.

Lamb: You got me mixed up with someone. It's not me.

Lorden: You Larry Lamb?

Lamb: Yes, I'm Larry Lamb. But that night...I was at work. That's right, I was at work...I don't know nothing about it. I wasn't with you. You got me mixed up with somebody, but it weren't me. I was working at night then.

Larry is the youngest of eight children. He had six sisters and one brother. Since he was the baby, Larry's sisters always took care of him, but he never veered far from his mother. It would be safe to say that he was a spoiled little boy. He learned quite a bit from his family. He learned how to plant a garden with his mother, and he learned how to take care of his belongings and himself, having watched his sisters manage the house and him. He learned a lot living with a whole lot of women, all of which would become handy later in his life.

On August 13, 1992, more than five years after Grady's murder, the police arrested Larry and his two friends and charged them with first degree murder, robbery, and conspiracy to commit murder. Lorden was paid the four thousand dollar reward. Larry went on trial first and on day one of his trial he was offered a plea deal of six years on the condition that he testify against Bo Jones. Larry refused to "lie on Bo," even in the face of a possible life sentence if he was convicted, which is exactly what happened. Larry was convicted in 1993 and sentenced to life in prison. Throughout the arrest, trial, and his incarceration, Larry declared his innocence. When given the opportunity to speak to the court before sentencing, Larry again proclaimed his innocence saying to the judge, "I will take whatever time you give me and I will go with it with pride, but to let you know you haven't solved this case by locking me up."

Larry would remain in prison until Judge W. Douglas Parsons ordered his exoneration and release on August 8, 2013, over twenty years after his wrongful conviction.

* * *

Two Short Rows

By Larry Lamb

Life in all of its twist and turns will carry you places where you never thought possible. I felt somewhat comfortable with my life on the morning of August 14, 1992, until a knock came on my front door around 10:30 a.m. The sheriff at my door asked, "Are you Larry Lamb?" and when I said "I am he," the sheriff said, "You are under arrest for murder." All I could think was, "This is a mistake" and "When we get downtown we will get to the bottom of this issue."

Well, getting to the bottom of this issue didn't happen when we got downtown; in fact, it took twenty-one years to get to the truth. I learned that for most of us, we live in the here and now, not thinking of what our lives could be like tomorrow. I was taking life for granted, thinking "I'm comfortable to a degree, and life is okay."

The detectives held me in a room for many hours, trying to get me to tell them what they wanted to hear. They charged me with first degree murder. They took all my possessions except my underwear, pants, and shirt. I was put in a single-man cell where I couldn't see or hear anything. It was like I was in a world all alone. I stayed in that cell for more than a week before being moved to a two-man cell. This cell was located in the main jail area and I could talk with the guys in the cells around me. It was a relief to be able to communicate with others because most of the time I was in that two-man cell by myself. The men that had weekend time to serve were put in there with me occasionally. Byrd, a young guy I met a year or so before I was arrested was put in the cell with me one weekend. He knew I was innocent and he wanted me out of there. He told me he had several weekends to do and he would be back the next weekend. He also said he had some hand grenades at his house and if I wanted him to he would bring me a couple. Wow, the minds of young folk! I laughed for a good while when Byrd said that and smiled every time I have thought of him over the years.

After a few weeks I finally understood I wouldn't be going home any time soon. I wouldn't be running down to the corner store to purchase a "coke cola," a bag of chips, or fruit. My life was turned upside down. I spent more than a year in county jail, locked up for something I didn't do. It made no sense. Being taken from my warm comfortable bed to sleep on hard cold steel didn't make any sense to me either. Just a couple of months earlier I had purchased a new set of Posturepedic queen size mattresses.

My comfort was gone, replaced with a slab of steel. I wrestled with this for a minute, wondering why this was taking place. I asked myself, "Who can I talk to, to reverse this harsh ordeal?" My pastor visited with me and assured me he would do all he could to make it comfortable for me. The co-pastor came to encourage me and to let me know that God had led them to me to strengthen me for what I was about to go through. Then my mindset changed and I began to see God's hand at work around me and through me. A man from Jones County named Benny was brought over to Duplin County for trial, because his case had been highly publicized in Jones County and they were seeking the death penalty. Benny was put in the cell with me and we got along fine. Benny knew he was fighting an uphill battle and he didn't want to get a death sentence, but that's exactly what he got. What a sad time it was when they brought Benny back to the cell to get his belongings. I thank God for the time He allowed me to spend with Benny, praying together and reading scripture. God even allowed me to talk with Benny a few times in the prison before they executed him. When I accepted the reality of God being in control of every situation in this universe, my life became so much simpler. Many of the situations He allowed in my life were too large for me; I needed a greater power than myself. There were times when God flooded my life with folk to try my patience. I know now that during those times He was teaching me without me even knowing what was going on.

After Benny went to death row, they put Ernest, one of my co-defendants, in the cell with me. It was known on the street that Ernest was a snitch. The detectives had been taking him in and out of his cell to talk with him. I let it be known in the beginning that I knew nothing about this crime they had charged me with committing, so I used what they call reverse psychology with Ernest. Instead of waiting for Ernest to ask me about this crime, I asked him what he knew about it and how he thought he got involved in it. I told him I didn't know how I got tangled up in this mess. I even told him a time or two not to be saying things that he didn't know to be a fact. Ernest stayed in the cell with me for a month or so before he was moved to a larger cell.

I didn't know that the two-man cell I lived in at county jail was right next to the female cell. A young lady named Juanita was sent to jail for auto theft and driving without a license. She came in talking loud, even hollering at times. She was broke, without a dime, and with a smoking habit she couldn't afford. We started talking through the wall and I learned where she was from and she wanted to know how much time I thought she might get. Juanita became my "jailhouse girlfriend" as she called herself. One morning shortly after breakfast I heard a woman's voice singing an old gospel song and it sounded so good. I tapped the wall to see who was singing and it was Juanita. As I complimented her on how beautiful she sounded, she told me that she used to sing in the choir at her mother's church. I found out that Juanita was full of gospel songs and that's when I put her to work. When they dimmed the lights at night I would tap on the wall and tell Juanita to sing us to sleep. The whole jail would be quiet, for you could hear her all over the jail. When new women were brought to jail, Juanita would put them on notice that there was a man in the next cell and I was *her* man.

Juanita's trial was in November, where she received time served along with three years of probation. Lenoir County also had charges against her; therefore she wasn't released after her trial in Duplin County. I was working on a jewelry box one evening and the matron for the women prisoners, Ms. Rosemary, brought me a phone number and told me to call Juanita. When I called her, Juanita told me that her three years of probation had been revoked. She went to prison and served twelve days on the three years from Duplin County before they decided to send her home after all. A couple of weeks before Christmas an officer brought me a few packs of cigarettes and told me that my woman sent them to me and that she would be back here shortly. I felt Juanita did things to get arrested because she knew I was in jail there and that I would look out for her. Can you picture a one hundred and ten pound lady with biker shorts and a halter top trying to steal two cartons of cigarettes? As Christmas was approaching, I thought about Juanita being in jail with no one to send her anything. God put it in my spirit to make her a purse out of a Newport cigarette pack; I even put her initials in it. There were two more women in the cell with Juanita. It appeared that they were going to be there for Christmas as well, so I made them each a small jewelry box so they would have a little something for Christmas. On Christmas Eve I sent Juanita and the other two ladies their gifts. They were really surprised; they thanked me and wished me a merry Christmas. Over the next few months, Juanita was in and out of jail, but when she was out she would call me to see how I was and to keep me up with what was going on with her.

The food in the county jail wasn't too bad. Ms. Mattie was the head cook and she did the best she could with what they gave her. At least whatever they served would stop a growling stomach. Breakfast probably was the best meal they had, especially when we had bacon, eggs, and grits. The fried chicken was edible from time to time as well, but none of the jail food was worth writing home about. After being in county jail for almost eleven months my attorney came and asked me one day did I want to go to Dorothea Dix for a pretrial evaluation. He said I would be there ten to twelve days. I saw it as a vacation and I told my attorney that I needed a break from this madness.

When it came to my trial, the judicial system was only going through the proper formalities to be able to say I received a fair trial. When I was first arrested I asked for a polygraph test, but my request was denied. Now, after eleven and a half months in jail, the detectives wanted to know if I wanted to take the polygraph test. I knew that ride would get me out of the jail for a few hours, so I agreed. I also knew there was something wrong when the SBI agent went to talk to the officer who was going to administer the polygraph test. When you know in all your knowing that you have told the truth you have nothing to fear. When the test was over the officer asked if I had anything I would like to tell him. He said, "You didn't pass the test. Are you sure you don't want to tell me something?" I told him that I was not going to argue with him, but I know that I told the truth. Man will go to any means necessary to make himself right although he knows in all of his knowing that he is lying. We learned twenty years later there was no record of my polygraph, but it was written on a report that I failed. All I can say about this is that it was a divine intervention from God. On the day my trial started, I was taken from the jail that morning and put in a room at the court house. Out of nowhere, Juanita showed up at that door wanting to know how I was doing. How she knew I'll never know. Juanita, was just another tool God sent to help my stay at the county jail be more bearable and to put my mind at ease.

Two weeks before my trial started the head jailer told me that I was going to get a life sentence and I was going to prison. It was like the deck was stacked against me and there was no way I was winning when I went to trial. My attorney, the district attorney, and all the members of the court knew the outcome of my trial before it started. All we were doing was going through the proper procedures according to the rules of the courts. Isn't it amazing how people with a little bit of authority can take you out of your comfort zone and send you to prison for the rest of your life knowing that their whole theory is based on a lie? I have to say "wow," but I can't leave it at that. Consider for a moment how they use your money, the taxpayers' money, to pay people to make their lie become a truth, to enhance their careers in the judicial system. Someone may ask the question, "Where is your God in the midst of all of this?" I will tell anyone all day long, one must be spiritual in order to see Him.

I grew up in the Lord during those twenty-one years. God was my teacher and He taught me well. The people he allowed in my journey to encourage me and those He allowed me to encourage will carry me for a lifetime. If you begin to look for Him in the circumstances and situations in your life, I promise you, you will begin to see His hand at work in whatever the issue may be. God wants us to know Him, because we can't serve Him if we don't know Him and what He desires of us. Well, my trial came and it happened just as I was told a few weeks earlier, a natural life sentence plus ten years.

When someone is given that type of sentence they don't keep you in the county jail long. I was taken from the courthouse back to the jail by five or six officers. They took me to my cell and ordered me to pack up my belongings while they watched. Then I was carried up front and put in a holding cell with another man named Pete until my judgment and commitment papers came from the courthouse. Once those papers arrived, Pete and I were carried to prison by car. Pete had a second degree murder charge that only carried seven years and being under the Fair Sentencing Act those seven years would be cut in half. Pete knew he would be back home in three years or so. Going into Central Prison, Pete and I bonded somewhat during the orientation stages. We walked to chow together and moved around the area trying to find our way as a team. We heard about the stealing in the dorm so we went to the canteen to purchase locks to make our lockers theft proof. We returned to the dorm to try out our new locks. Pete put both of his lock keys in his locker and duh, yes he did lock it! We asked around to see if anyone knew how to pick a lock, but to no avail. There were no safe crackers in the building. All those criminals and not a lock picker among them! Well, poor Pete had to go back to the canteen and purchase another lock. A Master lock at that time in the prison cost almost six dollars. That's a lot of money out of a weekly prison draw. I learned from Pete and I made a vow to myself to never put my keys in my locker for any reason. Even though I never locked my keys in the locker, I went through many locks during my prison stint and that was no problem. Master offers a lifetime warranty on their locks, so if your lock wears out, you send it to the company with both keys and they will send you a new lock.

I knew I was going to be housed at Central Prison for a while. As soon as Pete completed orientation he would be sent out to another facility. It was a challenge getting used to the food at Central Prison after Ms. Mattie's cooking at county jail. Most of it *looked* like the food I used to eat, but the taste was very far from it. It was either undercooked or overcooked and never seasoned. From time to time God would allow a good cook to come through and the food would be somewhat better. If that cook stayed for a while there would be so much food up and down the tunnel for sale. Cinnamon rolls were a hot commodity, and twenty-five cents would really tighten up your stomach for the night. God gave me a spiritual Jamaican son who really knew his way around in the kitchen. Bobby did good work and sometimes the stewards would let him cook some of those Jamaican dishes. He was allowed to bring food to the dorm every day after his shift ended and we'd eat good for a while. It is amazing how God brings people together. I worked in the big clothes house where I had access to new clothing. I would make sure Bobby and I had new clothes, linen, and towels as well and Bobby fed us at least one good meal a day. Some mornings when they had grits, eggs, sausage, or bacon, Bobby knew that was my kind of breakfast. He knew I liked sunny side up eggs to go with my grits. On those mornings Bobby would have my plate fixed in the hot box waiting for me to come through. On a few occasions the guys sitting at the table with me would say, you must know somebody in the kitchen. I did: Jesus.

Bobby and I studied the scriptures together, prayed and fasted together, and ate together. I was a godly example for Bobby and to see him grow in the Lord was inspiring. When God said it was time for us to part ways, He sent Bobby to Caledonia, and I was sent to Odom Farm, but we kept in touch by writing regularly. Bobby would write me to keep me informed about his baby's mother and the problems they were having. I would always write him back to encourage him because it was hard for him to let go. Being in the prison system with a life sentence, not knowing when you would be getting out, is a hard life. I tried to get him to see that a twenty-one year old lady was not going to put her life on hold for him for twenty years, which is when he'd be eligible for parole. Love is good, but we must still use common sense.

Bobby was sent out of state for a year because the in-state prisons were overcrowded. I had not seen or heard from him in about three years. I had a doctor's appointment at Central Prison one day and on my way out we passed some holding cells. I heard him before I saw him. When I turned the corner, there he was teaching the word of God to a group of men in the cell with him. Talk about joy, yes that really tickled my heart! He told me he was coming back from Oklahoma. Bobby was, and still is today, another tool that God allowed in my journey to help keep my mind stayed on Him. At times, God places people in your journey for a short period and at times He gives us life-long relationships to encourage us and help keep us focused on the goal He desires for us. God allowed Bobby to enter my journey in 1993, and I want to share a letter I received from him on May 16, 2014:

> "Praise the Lord, glory and honor belong to Him. Greetings Bro. Lamb, and how are you on this glorious day? Yes, I have received your newspaper article about your journey in prison. I love you Bro. Lamb. Eddie says hey. He works in the kitchen. Thank you for the scriptures you have sent me, they are very much inspiring, good food for my soul.

> "Anyway, here are the visitation forms and I hope to see you very soon. I haven't gotten a visit in many years now, but hopefully we'll be able to see one another soon. Bro. Lamb, it is Christ that dwells in us, who will complete it, the work, to the end. Remember, the very first day you and I met, you embraced me as a son, and a brother, and you have not changed since that day. Thanks for your love, prayers, gifts, and fellowship. Anyway, I hope to hear from you soon. Continue

writing your autobiography for the Lord our one and only true Savior.

"You are always in my prayers. Please don't forget to sign on the back of the visitation form.

In Christ's Love,

Bro. Bobby"

Knowing Bobby has been an honor and a joy for me just to watch him mature spiritually and physically. We've laughed together and cried together in many joyous conversations over the years.

As time progressed, the food in prison as we had known it begin to vanish. Bone-in pork chops disappeared. Fish with bones also went away. Hamburger steak and fatback meat were no more. The only meats that remained in their natural forms were chicken and bacon. It was a rare occasion when chicken that was served tasted like the chicken I use to eat before my incarceration. It would be safe for me to say that the food we received in the prison system was of poor quality. In the latter part of the nineties we entered into the processed meat era, where we had different types of patties. We had the onion beef patty, the Cajun chicken patty, the chicken riblet, the pork riblet, the veggie patty, and the Salisbury steak patty. These patties were so heavily seasoned with peppers and spices you wouldn't even know what type of meat you were eating. I believe they seasoned the meat that way because the meat was old and they wanted to cover up the old taste or simply give it some kind of taste. A large portion of our fruits came from other countries such as Honduras and Indonesia. These fruits were old by the time they arrived at our facility, therefore, their useful life was almost over. A large percentage of our dry good foods were prepared in Mexico and other Central American countries.

I was sick and tired of being sick and tired of the food and struggling with the decision of whether to go to the dining hall for this meal or that meal. I enrolled in a cooking and baking class. The class was divided into three groups with a group in the kitchen cooking every day. Talk about good food, yes it was so delicious. At times the horticulture instructor would bring fresh vegetables to our instructor for us to cook. Fresh food is always better if it is cooked the day of harvest or shortly after. When you cook vegetables with any kind of smoked meat, oh what a treat! The funding for the food for the cooking class didn't come out of the Department of Corrections' budget, but from the prison college. Oh what an enjoyable time for me, and to taste some real food was out of this world! As my cooking class was coming to an end, I enrolled in the spring horticultural class. It was the right time of year to plant fresh vegetables and to be able to reap the fruits of my labor would be awesome. When the cucumbers and tomatoes began to get ripe, they became my breakfast in the mornings and my lunch as well. I learned it would be very easy for me to become a vegetarian if only I could get the fresh vegetables, fruits, and raw nuts I wanted daily. When I munched on those fresh vegetables, I rarely went into the dining hall during the week.

Being incarcerated for a crime I knew absolutely nothing about, I learned how to be abased and I learned how to abound. Everywhere and in all things I learned what it meant to be in need and to have plenty. The experiences I had and the people I met, I will cherish for the rest of my life. Those twenty-one years in prison made me a more humble and loving man. I wouldn't give anything for that era of my life. In sharing with the men that God allowed in my journey, I used to say, we are a product of our families. We're to represent our families wherever we might find ourselves in life. I'm just an old poor country boy raised in a single-parent home. My mother was a proud little Cherokee lady with a big heart. She taught us to respect and love everyone.

Mom, worked for the Mt. Olive Pickle Company so she could provide for her eight children, me being the baby. Well, you know how babies are; yes, I stayed close to my mom. For many years the pickle company would stop their operation at noon on Good Friday so all the employees who had gardens could plant them on Good Friday. Most Christian folk during that era believed that as Jesus was buried on Good Friday and He is the Good Shepherd, their gardens would make good crops if planted on that day. I would make sure I was in place on Good Friday afternoon to help Mom plant the garden. I would dig the holes for the seed. When I learned to count well enough, Mom would let me drop some seeds. Her tomatoes, bell peppers, and collard greens came in plants. So we made holes with a round peg and when we put the plants in the holes we added some water so the roots would begin to sprout and grow. When we finished Mom's garden, she would give me the excess seeds and plants to plant in my little garden. My garden was only two short rows but it thrived, just as Mom's did. As I found myself in the negative environment of prison, I refused to allow what the justice system had done to me take me out of my character. Therefore, it was important to me to live my life so others could see that a man can walk in a positive manner regardless of being in prison or whatever the situation or circumstance may be.

At Pender Correctional, the recreation department started a garden program in 2006. The memo stated that anyone who desired a row in the garden had to submit a request to the recreation department. Eddie and I submitted requests and were given a row each. The recreation department furnished the seeds, the plants, and the Miracle-Gro to make our plants grow. We planted bell peppers, onions, cantaloupe, honey dew melons, cucumbers, watermelons, and tomatoes. Some of the men even planted squash and they were so pretty.

Eddie and I worked second shift at the sewing plant. We would go over to the garden on Tuesday and Thursday mornings to attend to our rows. We chopped grass, pulled weeds, and watered our rows so our plants would get all the nutrients. When our tomatoes begin to grow. I taught Eddie how to get the nutrient suckers out of plants so the tomatoes would get larger. It is important to keep the grass and weeds out so all the nutrients can feed the vegetables. Mom taught me, if you want plenty of good vegetables you must keep your garden clean and water it often.

Rodger soon entered my journey, and what a bundle of joy he was! Rodger had a smile that would brighten up any room he entered. God had called him to minister the Gospel of Jesus Christ. Rodger had been on death row, yet by God's grace, his death sentence was commuted to life. Rodger's mother was his greatest fan and when she would come to visit with him, his smile would get even brighter. I enjoyed spending time with him talking of the goodness of God. I needed to be around people like Rodger because Satan is always on his job. Talk about a negative environment, yes, I found myself among all types of criminals. There were drug dealers and users, snitches, child molesters, murderers, and thieves.

We shared some of our vegetables with these guys on Mondays and Wednesdays. Our vegetables tasted so much better than the vegetables we were served in the dining hall. My tomatoes were pretty, red, sweet, and so very good. I got a couple of watermelons and a few cucumbers the first year. The cantaloupes and honeydew melons were plentiful. The last year we had the garden, God blessed Eddie and me with thirty-seven cantaloupes and honeydew melons and the tomatoes were very good as well. When we harvested our crops we always shared them with the less fortunate guys. Mom, taught me to show love and share whenever the opportunity presented itself. Because of the drought the following year, the governor stopped all excessive water usage. After that year, the garden program was never reinstated.

I called Pender my base facility because I could work to help take care of myself during that era of my life. I've always been a working man so work is a part of my DNA, even working a job for twenty-six cents an hour. The canteen at Pender had a large variety of products to choose from. I could work wonders with a summer sausage, a pack of chili-beans, a couple packs of Oodles of Noodles soup, and some cheese. I would cut up some of my peppers, onions, and tomatoes. My mixing bowl was a new trash bag. After cooking my sausage, chili-beans, onions, peppers, and tomatoes in the microwave for about ten minutes or so I would pour it in the trash bag on the noodles. I would add mustard, ketchup, and some type of chip to help give my meal a taste that would make you want more of Mr. Lamb's cooking.

A lot of the younger inmates were mesmerized because they had never seen food prepared in a trash bag before. Then, to smell how good my food smelled was really foreign to many of them. And to taste some of my cooking really made their day. On many occasions guys would ask me to cook for them. They would tell me, I have this and that, and if you need anything else let me know. Burritos were my specialty; I made all meat and cheese burritos, jack mackerel burritos, and chicken burritos. Before the Christmas packages would come in, some of the men would ask me to cook for them or help them prepare different foods. Christmas was a joyful time at the Pender facility. The Christian volunteers prepared all kinds of food to feed everyone who wanted to eat. We would have collard greens, potato salad, butter beans, string beans, rice and gravy, corn bread, rolls, fried chicken, stew beef, and barbecue pork. Now, to talk about cakes, cookies, pies, of all flavors and designs; they were all there and oh so delicious. That time of the year did my heart good, to be able to help some of the men prepare their food and you know I got my stomach full as well. I also learned, that I am truly a blessed man, to have been raised in the atmosphere and manner that I was.

As I observed my surroundings during the holidays, there were men who received mail and those who didn't. God put it in my heart to start a Christmas package program to help those that didn't have any support. I wrote a few churches and some people I knew to see if they would purchase a Christmas package for some of these men. The first year the program did well and it grew every year. One year by the grace of God we purchased Christmas packages for thirty-five inmates. It brought much joy to my heart to see the smiles on the faces of these men. You must observe them to know who is who. A young man came to me one year about getting his Christmas package. He told me he had heard about me and what I was doing. He wanted to put his bid in early to make sure he got a package. As I listened to him, he told me that his family would get him a Christmas package. You've heard of having your cake and eating it too, well that was this young man's plan. He wanted me to have the church get him a Christmas package and he was going to have his family send him some money instead. When he finished explaining his plan, I laughed at him and explained how the Christmas package program worked. I let him know the program was for inmates who didn't have anyone to purchase their packages for them.

In all things acknowledge God and He will direct your ways. Be mindful of Him and He will exalt you in due season. God will give us the strength to weather the storms of life if we will only trust Him. In 2002 God called my mom home to be with Him. I can't complain;

Mom was ninety-four years old. God had blessed her with a long, happy, and peaceful life. Being in prison I wasn't allowed to attend my mom's funeral. They gave me a thirty-minute private viewing and none of my family members could be there during the time I was there. I feel that was the coldest thing that had ever happened to me and, to put the topping on the cake, I had to pay North Carolina one hundred dollars for those thirty minutes! If God had not been the head of my life, I would have lost my mind during that time. I pray for the day that my family understands me when I say I wouldn't give anything for those twenty-one years. Most of all I grew up in the Lord. He is my teacher and oh what a marvelous job He has done and continues to do on this ole country boy. I will cherish for the rest of my life the people God allowed to enter my journey. When we begin to look for the Lord in the circumstances and situations in our lives, we will see His hand at work. While I was at the Johnston County facility, God allowed Bro. Howard to enter my journey and, oh, what a glorious fellowship we shared. Bro. Howard was sent out of state during the time when the prisons were overcrowded. I didn't know he had met my spiritual son Bobby.

One day after our evening worship service was over, Bro. Howard and I lingered on the yard talking about good Christian brothers we had met over the years. Howard told me of this Jamaican brother that was with him out in Oklahoma. He said that brother was full of God's word and was teaching the word every day on the yard. As Howard was trying to remember the brother's name, he said, "I think it was Bobby."

I asked, "Bobby Burk?" and Howard nodded his head. Oh what a joyful time that was for me! As we wondered about Bobby and where he was, guess what God did? The very next week we were having our evening prayer circle and they called out on the PA system, "Bobby Burk report to Operations."

Howard and I talked about another good Christian brother, Bro. Thaddeus, and in a week or so, God brought him to visit us. I enjoyed the both of them for the three weeks they were there with us. I enjoyed the awesomeness of God and to see His word come alive was something to behold. He said if we do His will He will give us the desires of our hearts. One might say for this guy it is all about

God and He never had a bad day. Satan is always present seeking whom he may devour. God said if you serve me I will fight your battles, I will go before you and make your way straight. Therefore, we must choose this day whom we're going to serve.

Pete wrote me a few times after he was released from prison in 1997. But then the communication stopped. I inquired about Pete with several people from his home town without getting a reasonable response. I often wondered what became of him. I also wondered about another fella we called "Pork Chop" and asked some of the older inmates about him. I learned that he had accumulated a lot of infractions and he was back in close custody. Rodger figured they would never let Pork Chop leave the maximum security facility. He'll probably die in prison.

In 2012, I was taken to Johnston County for parole evaluation. The day that I arrived they called me to medical as part of their normal routine. As I sat there waiting to be seen, guess who walked through the door? Rodger. This was the first time I had seen him since 1994. Rodger still had that gigantic smile, and although it had been beaten and battered over the years, that smile still spoke volumes. I was only at Johnston County for four days, but Rodger and I walked all the tracks laughing and talking in harmony and sweet fellowship. Some folks will say Rodger and my reuniting was a coincidence, but I know that God controls every situation in this universe. God said it was time for me to learn of some of the thoughts I had pondered for years and He gave Rodger and me some time to catch up on the paths He had allowed us to travel.

I was now under minimum custody and had been admitted to a mutual agreement parole program beginning on May 1, 2013. I knew I would be transferred to Wake Advancement Facility. I knew Jesse was there too, so my message for him was, "I've come to visit with you for a little while before I go home." When I first saw him, he was all smiles grinning from ear to ear. As we walked the track, catching up with what was going on with each other, it was just like old times. I was waiting on the decision from the judge for my exoneration. Jesse and I had some great times eating ice cream with the many flavors to choose from. It truly amazed me how God works in the lives of His people. The three-year garden program was fulfilling to me as well, because I had the chance to share some of the skills my mom taught me, as well as share my vegetables. I could see how the greatest Creator of it all could take a small seed and make something astonishing from it. In closing I'll leave you with this, wherever you might find yourself in life, always look for the one who made you, the world, and everything that is in the world. I bid you God's speed!!

* * *

For Larry, it seems being in prison was a blessing. His fierce belief in God grew stronger with every prison experience. This unconditional belief was his panacea, his cure-all, his answer to whatever adversity befell him in there. His intense belief continues to prepare him, now, for all that may come his way. Larry's mother was also a driving force for him as she was for all her children. She would always say, "Whatever you do, do your best!" In retrospect Larry wishes he had listened to his mother more often. Had he lived more like she taught, he might not have found himself in prison, or so he believes. Even though life may have been a little harder because he ignored his mother's wisdom, Larry's experiences have carried him a long way and for that he feels blessed.

Larry began serving his sentence in 1993. Levon "Bo" Jones, one of the other two men convicted for the same crime and sentenced to death, was exonerated in 2008 after Lorden recanted her 1993 trial testimony. The district attorney dropped the charges against Jones, but it was another five years before Larry would be exonerated of the exact same crime based on the exact same recanted testimony of Lorden. The North Carolina Center on Actual Innocence took on Larry's case and in 2009 filed a motion to retry Larry in light of Lorden's recanted testimony. Initially, the prosecution agreed to the motion to retry, but after learning that Sam Gales, a prosecution witness thought dead, was still alive, the prosecution withdrew their support. In the 1993 trial, Gales had implicated Larry in Grady's murder but later said he could have been off by one year on the date that he thought Larry had come by his house talking about Grady. Finally, in 2013, a hearing was held to determine whether Larry would be retried. The presiding judge vacated Larry's conviction on August 8, 2013 noting that the court was "... more than reasonably satisfied that the testimony given by Lovely Lorden at Lamb's trial was false and that there is more than a reasonable possibility that, had false testimony not been admitted a different result would have been reached at the trial of Larry Lamb."

* * *

20 Years Lost Yet Not Forsaken

By Patricia Pemberton

My grandfather was incarcerated when I was a young girl around the age of two. When I was younger riding along with my grandfather, if he didn't stop or get me something to snack on, I'd ask him to loan me ninety-nine cents. Mom knew Hardee's had a special on Cool Kids Combo Meals for ninety-nine cents, and that's why I needed money. As we rode along, I was aware of my surroundings even at the age of two. If we were passing a Pizza Hut, I could tell him, "Pizza, pizza, Granddaddy!" He thought I could read, but in reality I remembered that we had been there and that we had eaten pizza. My brother and I would spend time with our grandfather and one time he got us a puppy. He said I was scared and my brother was not. As soon as he took my brother towards the puppy I'd cry out, "No Granddaddy, don't hurt my brother!" This assured him that I would be protective of my brother. I have many similar memories of the time I spent with Granddad before he was arrested for a crime he did not commit.

I also had many experiences without him but he shared in them from afar. I could write an entire novel, but for the sake of time I will share only a few of those experiences. While grandfather was away in prison my parents separated. I felt that I was in a happy place and as a young girl my dream was for my parents to stay together. As time passed, my desire to have a complete family grew stronger, but their marriage ended in a divorce. That was a sad time for me. My grandfather wrote me letters and sent cards to encourage me and give me hope. Hearing from him helped pick me up in devastating times. When I was around thirteen years old, before my parents split, my father was teaching me how to drive and I ended up driving my mother's Chevy Lumina into a ditch! At that instant, I knew I was in big trouble but God showed me favor by sending a man on a tractor to pull me out. My parents went to visit my grandfather and before long, he sent me a letter telling me that he knew all about it. He reminded me that I was a Christian and I had no business driving without a license. He was concerned about my future, he wrote, "You don't want to lose your license before you get them." In spite of Granddad's incarceration, we shared so many memories. It was just like he was there with me. He knew everything!

During the many years Granddad was in prison, I learned what faith, love, and endurance really are. I remember a letter I received from my grandfather telling me how to observe the example God set before me. He was referring to my mom. My mother had plans to go to college after graduating high school. Her plans were put on hold when she got pregnant with me. My mother struggled and worked countless hours. She was a single parent working a full-time job and a part-time job. She did all that while going to school full time and running a household by herself with three crumb snatchers under foot. My grandfather shared with me that he didn't want me to struggle like Mom did. She had to struggle to fulfill the plans that she had for her life. I once wrote my grandfather to tell him that I was being teased for not following the crowd by talking back to my teachers; for not succumbing to peer pressure and being sexually active. My grandfather commended me for that and referred me to the Word of God where it says that fornicators will not enter the Kingdom of Heaven.

I remember the day my mother began talking to me about my grandfather, I was asking her where my name came from. I'm named after my grandparents on my father's side. My name is Lamara and that came from my grandfather's name Larry. I remember receiving my first letter from him and it was addressed to "Stuffin." My grandfather said I got that nickname because of the way I loved to eat when I was as a child. The name stuck. As I got to know this wise gentleman who was my grandfather, I was amazed at how full his life seemed. It was whole and you could feel the peace of God over his life even through the pages. It seemed to radiate from his words. He had a relationship with the Father. I remember praying for my grandfather's return and crying. I would hold his letters in my hands next to my heart and plead that God set him free. I felt that I needed him to physically be there with me. I never felt that he was given a fair trial and I knew that it was unfair. I also knew that I served a just God and that he would answer the petition of my heart.

My faith was strong and I believed with all my heart Granddad would be set free. I longed for him to share the many events in my life that he missed being away; things like my first honor roll in school. I was reading above grade level since the second grade. In elementary school, we had grandparents' day. In middle school, there were granddaughter and grandfather dances. These activities would have created enjoyable memories for my grandfather and me; memories that I could have shared with my own children. It was not his fault that he couldn't be there and he wanted above all to be there for me. Award ceremonies, proms, military balls, eighth grade graduation, and high school graduation; so many lost opportunities. I knew he'd attend, he had the heart to; he just wasn't able to be there. As I grew in God, He revealed in me the gift of dance. I was a youth leader in my church and the dance leader. I ministered several times and I knew Granddad would be proud of me.

Sure enough, God allowed my grandfather to keep up with my life even when we lost touch. He had a friend named Helen who saw me in church or when I was out and about. She sent him reports of how I was doing. He also had a friend named Lee that came to my place of employment on an assignment from my grandfather. The night Lee came I was not working and I had actually left on a leave. My manager and the people on the job gave me a rave review. They told Lee I was a great asset to the company and during my time away they would miss me. Lee reported these commendations back to my grandfather. That's putting your faith to work. My grandfather didn't allow his condition to limit him. In the midst of his incarceration God allowed him to know that I was doing well in school and continually seeking him and spending time with him and others in fellowship. This assured my grandfather that I was doing just fine.

I remember going through puberty as an adolescent and my grandfather helped me through it from behind bars. I wrote him to announce I had become a woman. He wrote me back immediately and politely corrected me. He told me that my female cycle didn't make me a woman and that I had a while before I became a woman. By his standards, he said, a girl became a woman at the age of eighteen, but, by me being his granddaughter, I would become a lady in my early twenties! Some might think that was funny, but I knew that great wisdom lay in Granddad's words. I knew he was telling me not be too grown for my age and not to be anxious about becoming a woman because it would come in time.

Other things that my grandfather was able to do from behind bars were nothing short of magical. I remember receiving birthday cards every year with money in them, drawings on holiday cards for no particular reason; he'd just be thinking about me and shower me with love in various ways. Missing my father, those types of gestures helped mold my expectations of a father figure. Granddad helped fill in the gap that was left by my father's absence. I'd have to say that love kept me uplifted during some of the most difficult times in my life. I had then and still have an assurance that he loves me. He was accountable for his responsibility as my grandfather. He didn't let the circumstances in his life impact mine. He didn't allow his situation behind bars to limit his obligations to his "Stuffin," and he never neglected me as a grandparent, not one time. The type of love he had for me carried me during my hardest times in life. When no one seemed to care, I knew for a fact he did.

My grandfather was found guilty for a crime he was completely innocent of but he endured. He overcame the ridicule, the sentencing, the slander, the shame, and stood his ground as an innocent man. He didn't waiver. He was strong, and above all held his integrity. To think of it, my grandfather never wrote me a letter whining, complaining, badgering the judicial system, or bashing those that bore false witness against him to make his conviction a reality. He took no time to glory in that, rather, he'd use his words to encourage me; telling me how much he loved me and expressing how much he missed me. He was more interested in being there for me and helping others along the way. I was his baby then, and as a matter of fact, I still am.

My grandfather never exhibited any signs of weakness. Because of him, I know that whatever life may throw my way, I am more than able to conquer through Christ Jesus. I used to think of how much better my life would've been if he had been here with me. Now I say, "My life is so much better because of him."

I know it may seem like our family suffered a twenty-one year loss by not having this amazing man as part of our lives in person, but the lessons of faith, love, and endurance are countless and will, for each of us, last a lifetime. My grandfather wouldn't want me or the family to think of his wrongful incarceration as an opportunity for vanity but for giving all thanks and glory to God. My grandfather says, "I grew up in the Lord. God was my teacher, He taught me very well." God taught him to love everyone. In those twenty-one years God taught him to be a better man for the rest of his life. If I could describe my grandfather's story in one scripture it would come from Hebrews the twelfth chapter and the second verse where it reads "Looking unto Jesus the author and finisher of our faith; who for the joy that was set before him endured the cross, despising the shame, and is set down at the right hand of the throne of God." Yes, it seemed as if we lost, but we have everything to gain.

* * *

Larry's life could have been very different had he made other choices early in life. Larry was a smart boy and he knew it. He was a good student with the best grades and passed all his tests. He was also hard-headed. He figured that being as smart as he thought he was there was no reason for him to stay in school so he dropped out when he turned sixteen. He found out later that his mother had been saving money to send him to college. It was too late to change his decision, or so he thought at the time. He also could not just take his mother's money, so Larry suggested to his mom that they use the money to build her a house.

Larry's mother and father divorced when Larry was young. She had worked hard all of her life and had always lived in a rented house. Larry began working at the pickle factory where his mother worked. With the money Larry was able to save and the money his mother had saved for his college education, they built her a house. It was a nice little three bedroom house, Larry recalls. He was proud and happy that his mother finally could have her own house—completely paid for, all hers.

When he decided to quit school Larry did not do so on a whim. He had a plan to see the world. He was a curious young man and he wanted to do a lot of things with his life. While they were building his mother's house, Larry told her that when it was finished and she had her housewarming, he would start traveling. At eighteen, with his mother's house completed, Larry left home. His travels took him places that most folks from his area would never see. When he joined the military, Larry's travels took him beyond the United States to Indonesia, Vietnam, Hong Kong, Philippines, and Japan. He would come home to visit his mother whenever he could, but Larry loved to travel and experience new places. Larry was drafted into the army in 1969. He did two years of active duty in Vietnam and four years of inactive duty. When his six years in the army were done, he moved back to North Carolina to live with his mother.

When he came home from Vietnam, Larry's family met him at the airport. They all spoke at once catching him up on everything that had been going on in the neighborhood while he had been away. His mother made a special point to warn him about the folks he should steer away from like a cute little girl who was now living in the neighborhood. "Larry, there is a pretty little girl in the community. She don't mean you no good," his mother warned. Larry heard what she said, but he was not really listening. Larry's mother spent a lot of time teaching her children about respect, about the kinds of people to associate with, about the things and people that were good for them and those not good for them. Larry paid attention to the things she taught him, but sometimes he conveniently forgot those things, especially when it came to women.

Larry had always had a soft spot for pretty young ladies. He liked them and most often they liked him. He saw the pretty little girl his mother warned him about the day after he returned home. "I see this young lady, fine little pecan-tan girl, big wide hips, and stuff," he remembers fondly. "Oh, yeah, I like that," he remembers thinking to himself. What else was he going to do but pursue her? Larry had just returned home from war. He was going to enjoy himself with his pecan-tan girl. Before long, things became serious and Larry found himself headed down the aisle. He would remember his mother's warnings later on in his marriage. He often thought had he paid attention to his mother's warnings he may have never found himself in prison. Getting involved with his pecan-tan girl was fraught with many troubling and unhappy days.

Larry was married for ten years, but the marriage started going sour much earlier. It was a "wrestling match" for Larry as he put it; she liked to "step out" without him. He had always said that if he ever got married and had children he wanted to be with his children and see them grow up and be a part of their lives because he did not have that relationship with his own father. Being with his children was Larry's driving force. He spent a lot of time wrestling with whether he should walk away or stay. When they had their first child Larry wanted to stay; he needed to stay. By the time ten years had passed, Larry was done wrestling. It was time for him to walk away. Larry's wife thought about it for a minute and decided she was done being married, too. They had four children between them—two she brought to the marriage and two they had together. Larry's stepchildren were older and soon would not need his care.

Back in those days it was difficult for a man to win custody of the children, but Larry wanted to keep his children with him. "It was hard," Larry remembers, speaking of their divorce. The children's teachers attested to Larry's dedication as a parent, citing the attendance, grades, and behavior of his children. In the divorce, Larry was awarded custody and child support. He wanted the children to know their mother and arranged visitation times that she often missed. She also never paid the child support the court mandated. As difficult as it may have been for Larry to become a single parent, it was a blessing for him. He confessed that even through all the hardships of the divorce and custody battling, caring for his kids has been a blessing. He believes he is a better man because of it. "I had to work to provide for them. I had to come home and clean the house and cook and wash and help them with their homework and take them to any extra-curricular activities they had after school and get them to choir rehearsal at church. They slowed me down. They helped me more than I helped them." Larry also gives credit to his mother and sisters. While he may not have always been listening, on some occasions he did pay attention. He learned a lot from them too.

When he married he moved to his wife's home town. This was where he was arrested for the crime he did not commit. If he had listened to his mother he would not have gotten married; he never would have moved there. Yet Larry feels blessed for all that he has experienced in his life. His decision to drop out of school may have seemed like a mistake, but his confidence in himself afforded many job opportunities of which he was able to take advantage. His military, experience, he believes helped him deal with his wife; having learned to work through difficult situations with discipline and calm. That same discipline and calm also helped him navigate through prison. Having grown up in a house with his mother and six sisters, he also learned how to keep a house, how to cook, how to create and maintain a garden, and how to care for himself—all of which eventually helped him care for his children.

Larry was released on August 13, 2013 at the age of sixty-four, after being incarcerated for twenty years. His mother passed away while Larry was in prison. She never got to see her son released and exonerated, but she always had faith that her son would be released. Larry's family and a host of friends and supporters greeted him at the prison on the day of his release to congratulate him and bring him home.

Today Larry lives with his son in Massachusetts. There are a lot more opportunities and support programs in Massachusetts for people who have been incarcerated, such as the After Incarcerated Support System—AISS which provides a host of services for men and women who have recently been released. According to Larry, "If you need housing, then they are there. You can get your GED. They have a GED class coming out of there, and they have different programs coming out like anger management or thinking for a change. They have support for you if you want to go to college. Just about anything you need. If you need your driving license they help you get that. They say it's the only program like that in the country."

AISS conducts mentorship meetings regularly. Larry happened to attend one evening and they asked Larry if he might be interested in mentoring after hearing Larry share some of his life's story. He agreed and worked toward and received his certification to become a volunteer mentor. Now he goes into prisons, jails, pre-release programs and even on some occasions high schools, and speaks about his life and provides mentoring to those who want or are in need of that service. As for caring for himself financially and unlike younger exonerees, Larry was fortunate enough to have worked for many years before his incarceration and is able to collect social security income.

Larry is fiercely independent at his young age of sixty-four having only recently re-entered into society as a free man. He does not ever want to be a burden and manages to get around without a car by himself. He intends to have a sweet life his next forty years. Yes, he said it and he truly believes he has at least another forty years to live. He works hard to ensure that he does and longevity runs in his family. Most of his relatives lived long into the later years of their lives without incident. His mother lived to be ninety-four and some siblings are moving well into their seventies and eighties. Larry is intending to do the same.

Larry awaits a governor's pardon so that he can receive reparative compensation for his wrongful conviction. His lawyers are hopeful that a governor's pardon may come in November 2014. Then he will spend time pursuing a civil suit.

Larry's prison experience brought him much closer to God. He met men and women in prison who uplifted him spiritually, protected him, gave him a peaceful, reverent and orderly community in which to live; one that typically does not exist in prison. Larry believes that his faith opened up atypical opportunities for him. He worked in the kitchen, where he had access to good food, and in the big clothes house, where he had access to new clothing, linen and towels, which he shared with his close brothers inside. He was able to use the gardening skills his mother taught him in the prison garden with bountiful results. Having these good fortunes were blessings for Larry, but Larry believes his biggest and most important blessing was how many people he would mentor in the system. Men inside and outside of the prisons still speak with Larry today and are grateful for his friendship and spiritual counsel. This experience for him was two-way—to help and to be helped. When asked about his prison stay Larry says without embarrassment or apology that they were the best twenty years of his life.

His sons, however, are troubled by this. They feel that Larry was away from them for twenty years. The idea that these were blessed days for him is incomprehensible to his sons. How could their father feel that twenty years away from them were blessed? Larry says he understands what they are feeling and hopes one day they will come to understand what he means when he makes such a proclamation. Those years taught Larry a lot about himself and helped him to a deeper relationship with God. "It'll just take some time," he says, hopefully.

Larry's prized assets were those people and situations inside prison that deepened his faith. Everyone and every experience that he came across while in jail and in prison, Larry says, was designed by God and helped him to forget about his wrongful conviction as an inconceivable, unimaginable, and terrible event in his life. These people and experiences continuously strengthened his faith and constantly reminded him of the infinite possibilities when God is in control. They helped him realize that every day is a blessing, every experience is a blessing and that his life, no matter what, is a blessing.

Larry continues his efforts to bring people closer to God when he goes into prisons to provide support.

Since food has been such an important part of Larry's life, both inside and outside of prison, we wondered if there was something special he wanted to eat when he was released. "Fish!" he exclaimed laughing. "I wanted some fish!" Larry and his family found themselves at the Golden Corral all you can eat buffet. "I just pigged out!"

Larry Lamb lives with his son in Massachusetts where he is a mentor to young men at risk of entering the prison system and to parolees. Patricia Pemberton is Larry's granddaughter.

CHAPTER 12
Virginia "Ginny" LeFever

As the oldest of four children, Ginny was responsible for her younger siblings, a sister and two brothers. She often had to balance her parent-like duties with being a big sister and this made for a somewhat distant relationship between Ginny and her siblings. Ginny also was a serious student. When she graduated high school the only other person in the entire family who had accomplished this was her father. Ginny was the first in her family to attend college and get a degree, but this happened later in her life. Her sister graduated high school, but both of her brothers dropped out of school. When he was nineteen years old, Ginny's younger brother killed himself. Ginny was twenty-two years old at the time and her family could not overcome the death of their son and brother. They were already somewhat estranged from each other and just could not deal with the pain and stigma of his suicide. "I'm not sure you really overcome it," Ginny would say about the disintegration of her family. "At some point you learn to live with it or fail to." These words would prove to foreshadow Ginny's future.

Ginny was born on June 27, 1951. In 1968, she married her high school sweetheart, James Holmes, and left home while finishing high school. They had two children—a girl, Heather, and a boy, Jamey. Ginny described her high school sweetheart as a "great date, lousy husband." Jamey was born five weeks early in December, 1976, but by then the marriage was history. Jamey suffered brain damage as a result of oxygen deficiency during labor and delivery and had myriad medical problems. He was hospitalized for the first three months of his life. Ginny was still dealing with her brother's suicide and now she had a sick child and had been abandoned by her husband. She filed for divorce. Not soon after her divorce was granted, Ginny met William LeFever. They found in each other a kindred spirit and began to date exclusively. In those early years they enjoyed being together, talking for hours on end about everything. They married hastily in 1997 after knowing each other for only a few months.

When Jamey was almost two years old, and Heather by now ten, Jamey began attending an all day program for severely handicapped children. Ginny found it hard to be separated from her son, and decided that she would use the time while he was away to attend nursing school. She believed that studying nursing would educate her on how to best care for a child with special needs. Nursing school was easy for Ginny. She formed good relationships with her fellow students, many of which persist to this day. After two years of nursing school, Ginny delivered Corey, her third child and Bill's first, in January. In May, she graduated from nursing school and at about the same time Jamey went to live at Heinzerling Memorial Foundation, a facility that provides care and treatment to non-ambulatory individuals with multiple developmental disabilities. Jamey stayed there for three years, but Ginny could see no improvement. He was still not toilet trained; he continued to have seizures; he suffered from corticol blindness; he could not speak or feed himself. Ginny thought it best that Jamey return home. Jamey would eventually succumb to his health complications, dying at the young age of nine.

Jamey's short life, Bill and Ginny would discover, was due to poor medical attention. They prevailed in the settlement of a medical malpractice suit in connection with Jamey's hospitalization and medical care not long after his death.

Ginny was twenty-six years old when she married Bill. She completed her nursing degree in 1980 and became a registered nurse. Ginny and Bill's second daughter, Sarah, was born nineteen months after Corey. Bill and Ginny would have two more children before their relationship really began to fall apart. Sadly, their third child, Rachael, died from a rare genetic disorder called Werdnig-Hoffmnan Syndrome only fifteen weeks after her birth. Their last child, Alex, was born shortly after Rachael's death.

Early in their marriage, Bill was very supportive of Ginny's studies and helped her cope with the tragedy of her brother's suicide, but that support would soon disappear.

The deaths of Rachael in 1983 and Jamey in 1985 devastated Ginny and Bill. He retreated into drugs and alcohol while she lost herself in work. Even if she had wanted to follow Bill into a drug-induced stupor, Ginny knew she had to keep working so the family would stay afloat. "I just had to work with, I don't know, barely putting one foot in front of the other," Ginny says about this period of her life. She wanted Bill to get help with his addiction and, not long after Jamey's death, Bill was admitted to an in-patient treatment facility. Unfortunately, he started drinking again only two days after returning home. A psychologist at the facility diagnosed Bill as seriously depressed and indicated that someone suffering from such serious depression, when combined with drug abuse and dependency was at risk of committing suicide.

Over the next few years, Bill's drug and alcohol dependency worsened and his behavior became increasingly erratic. He began hanging with a younger crowd and was almost always stoned. He added pills to his drinking and pot smoking. Eventually Bill began to yell and scream at Ginny and the children. Soon his yelling became physical and he began to abuse Ginny. She recalls one night when he knocked her to the floor of their bedroom and began to choke her. That was the last straw for Ginny. She did not want herself or her children subjected to this and on July 27, 1988, she filed for divorce. Heather was already away at college so Ginny and the three children still at home moved out of the house, at one point living in a battered women's shelter. September was back-to-school time for the children and Ginny moved with them back into the house after Bill confirmed with the divorce court judge that he was no longer living there. Bill tried to convince Ginny not to go through with the divorce by leaving her notes declaring his love for her and the children, and how he would not be able to go on without her. Ginny continued with the divorce proceedings and worried that Bill might try to kill himself or harm himself in some way.

The final hearing on their divorce was scheduled for September 27, 1988. In the meantime, the court allowed Bill to have time with the children while the family awaited the final divorce hearing. On one occasion when her car would not start, Ginny asked Bill to drive her to work. Again, Bill tried to convince Ginny not to divorce him. On September 20, 1988 things came to a head when Bill came to the house to pick up some of his stuff. The day before, he had read an article about his company being acquired and he was worried that he would not have a job once the employees had been relocated to the new location. Bill was hanging out at the house while Ginny and the children watched a movie and played a board game. Bill fell asleep and when it was time for her and the children to go to bed Ginny tried to wake Bill up to go home but she could not awaken him. At around 10:30 p.m. she left him asleep in the family room and went to bed.

Nine year old Corey woke up in the middle of the night after hearing loud noises and banging coming from outside. He found his dad acting crazy, hugging the trash can and talking about a dead cat named Ghost. It was around 12:15 a.m. when Corey ran to get his mother. They found Bill in a downstairs bathroom and the room was a mess. Bill had tracked in dirt from outside, the shower and toilet were overflowing, the mirror was cracked, and the door had been yanked off of its hinges. The next morning, September 21, 1988, Ginny noticed an empty bottle of Elavil, an antidepressant that had been prescribed to her after Rachael died. She suspected Bill of taking the roughly twenty 100 mg pills she had left in the bottle. Ginny thought Bill had overdosed, but she was scared he would beat her if she called paramedics. Bill continued to act erratically and eventually Ginny called one of his drug buddies who told her to call 9-1-1 and he would say he made the call. She called paramedics at 4:45 p.m. and Bill was admitted to the emergency room at Licking Memorial Hospital.

Over the next several hours Bill alternated between being calm and being so violent that he had to be restrained so blood samples could be taken from him. Bill's condition worsened while he was in the hospital. At one point he was suffering from such profuse diarrhea that a tube was inserted into his rectum. His body temperature also increased during this time. Bill was injected with physostigmine to control his diarrhea and for a while he became calmer and more lucid. During one of these lucid periods, Bill admitted to taking the antidepressants. When the nurse asked about his bruises, Bill said Ginny would "beat the shit out of him" when he was passed out. At around 11:05 a.m. on September 22, 1988 Bill had a heart attack and stopped breathing. His medical team performed cardio-pulmonary resuscitation and took other measures in an attempt to revive him. Bill never came to and was pronounced dead at 11:37 a.m. on September 22, 1988.

During the course of his treatment at the hospital, Bill's blood had been drawn twice. Each blood sample was tested for toxins and the tests results showed that the levels of amitriptyline, the key ingredient in Elavil, in Bill's blood had declined from the first blood sample to the second blood sample. After Bill died, two tissue samples were taken, one of which showed a higher level of amitriptyline. James Ferguson, the county's chief toxicologist, attributed the increase to the toxin leeching from Bill's muscle—which only would have happened if the amitriptyline had been injected with a needle instead of ingested orally. Ferguson testified that the toxin dissipated slowly because it had been injected into a muscle and collected in a pocket just underneath the muscle. A higher toxicity level also could be the result of an improperly collected sample. Most cases of death by amitriptyline poisoning were classified as suicides, not homicides. In his final report, Ferguson stated that the toxin levels in samples taken from Bill's blood had been increasing.

Police investigators found evidence of rat poison and other toxins in the LeFever trash. No evidence of these new poisons was in Ferguson's toxicology report until after police detectives showed him what they had collected from the LeFever trash. On November 30, 1988, the Licking County Grand Jury indicted Ginny on one count of aggravated murder in connection with Bill's death. Ginny's trial began on February 4, 1990. Ginny waived her right to a jury trial, so the bench trial commenced. Eighteen days later, the judge found Ginny guilty of aggravated murder and sentenced her to life in prison.

Two other forensic witnesses for the prosecution relied on Ferguson's report to reach the conclusion that Bill had been poisoned. At trial the prosecution and defense presented other evidence and called other witnesses. One nurse testified that Bill told her he had taken the pills and was trying to kill himself. Another nurse testified that Bill told her Ginny tried to force feed him the pills. Still, it was Ferguson's testimony that provided the thread that held the prosecution's case together. It would be Ginny herself who would pull at that thread years later and unravel the prosecution's case.

One Day at a Time

By Ginny LeFever

It seems ironic to me that this topic confronts me at the zenith of one of the toughest challenges I have faced as a free woman. I thought the biggest hurdle was getting out, and while it certainly was, there are still many obstacles I must face. I have heard addicts say that if they had to be clean and sober for the rest of their lives, recovery would be impossible. However, if they reframed that concept so that all they had to do was remain sober today, and have no plans to use tomorrow, they were able to do "one day at a time." I applied much the same concept to my incarceration.

I continue to struggle with whom to trust, especially when it comes to legal decisions. I would like to be able to write that Jesus or Buddha or tea leaves have guided me, and I am certain in this collection of stories there will be many who will attest that is exactly how they survived and thrived during their toughest challenges. I will not be among them.

Hope can be fleeting; hope can be mercurial. But in the calm stillness that lies at the core of each of us, there is a place where we know what we know. I found during my long years of incarceration that it was difficult to tune out the noise of the chaos that surrounded me. The same chaos swirled within me as well.

My own fears were often even louder, especially as I tried to wrap my brain around a life sentence for a crime I knew I had not committed. I am not even sure when I found hope again. I allowed myself to be medicated for depression for a time. I clung to every possible person, place, or thing that came my way in person, through the mail, or in print or television, constantly searching for that spark of hope.

When my younger children stopped visiting within the first couple of years of prison, I ate myself to a dangerous weight. I woke one morning after my usual fitful night of almost no sleep, looked myself in the shiny metal that passed for a mirror above the sink in my two-woman cell, and had a heart-to-heart pep talk with myself. It went something like, "Self, you are fat! You cannot walk, stand, sit, lie, or even roll over in bed, and the kids still aren't coming to see you. Are you really ready to die?"

That very afternoon, I waddled myself out to the track and managed to get all the way around the zero-point-one-mile perimeter. Next day it was a little farther, and by the end of summer when there was not sufficient daylight and the track was essentially closed for the winter, I was over three miles per day, and had lost nearly forty pounds. That pep talk had rekindled my hope and the conviction deep within me that I was not going to die in prison, that I was going home. I didn't know how, and I didn't know when, but in the very marrow of my bones and the deepest recesses of my soul, I knew I was leaving.

The actual way out was long and tortuous. I saw the parole board three times, and each time was turned down. The first time was devastating, because I was given an additional ten years. By then I had served thirteen and a half. Changes in Ohio law and various court decisions called me back in front of the parole board two more times. I went reluctantly, knowing nothing would change. I was not disappointed—the parole board just affirmed the ten extra years they gave me at my first hearing. It didn't matter because I knew in my heart and mind the parole board was never my way home. They didn't change anything for me because I didn't allow them that power.

Today after over three and a half years back in the free world, the challenges have shifted but are by no means gone. People and opportunities come and go in my life. When it comes to anyone or anything, nearly all I really trust and believe in is my own gut, my core or my essence. My faith in organized religion died long ago.

I do believe there is something beyond the existence we all see, taste, touch, and experience each and every day. I believe some spark of that same essence resides within each of us, if we are able to stop the noise long enough to hear it. That belief is what sustained me throughout my long years in prison, and it is what sustains me today. I get through these days, remembering almost always to have some short-term goal for each day, and to find something to laugh about. I often say that the worst day out is better than the best day in.

Ginny discovered Ferguson had lied about his credentials as a toxicologist and the circumstances that led her to that discovery were pure serendipity or just plain dumb luck. She was grasping at straws, trying anything to get a court to listen to her claim of innocence. Like many innocent inmates, Ginny spent a lot of time in the prison law library. She found a thin ray of hope in the Ohio Revised Code, Section 313.19, which states that a court may direct the coroner to change his decision regarding the cause, manner, and mode of death previously provided in a death certificate. Ginny decided to file a motion requesting the court make such a direction under this provision and proceeded to find out as much as she could about Ferguson.

As an Ohio native and graduate of The Ohio State University, Ginny always watched the Ohio State-Michigan game. During the 2008 game, OSU football legend Chris Spielman launched the OSU Cruise for Cancer to benefit the Stefanie Spielman Fund for Breast Cancer Research. Stefanie, Chris's wife, was being treated for breast cancer and the couple had organized a cruise where passengers could meet and socialize with some of the star OSU football players. Stefanie and Chris made an announcement during the telecast and at the end of the announcement, Stefanie said, "If you want further information, contact the Buckeyes Alumni Association," at which point an email address appeared on the screen. Ginny, being in prison, had no experience with email, but she wrote down the information and called a friend. Ferguson was an OSU graduate; maybe she would be able to find out something useful about him.

"What about this," Ginny asked her friend over the phone. "Can you send an email for me? He claims to have graduated in 1972," Ginny explained.

"Sure," her friend replied. "It's the weekend so it might take four or five days, but sure, no problem. I'd be happy to do this for you. Call me Wednesday."

When Ginny called her friend on Wednesday she answered the phone before the end of the first ring. A student who worked in the OSU archives had returned her call. The records back to the 1970s were not computerized, so he had to look through boxes of index cards and files to find Ferguson's records. He discovered that Ferguson did not graduate in 1972 and had not graduated in the 1970s at all. The student archivist could not find any records to indicate that Ferguson was even enrolled in OSU during the 1970s. Apparently Ferguson attended OSU in the 1960s but did not receive a bachelor of science degree in biochemistry until 1988. His resume claimed he graduated in 1972. He also did not appear to have been studying for his PhD in forensic sciences, which he indicated was the case in a letter dated October 2, 1987 to the Franklin County Coroner requesting a salary increase: "I am actively pursuing my Doctor of Philosophy degree in the Forensic Sciences. I anticipate graduation in June of 1988." This was an outrageous statement since Ferguson had just completed his undergraduate studies and had not yet received his B.S. degree.

"Gotcha," Ginny whispered confidently when her friend told her the news about Ferguson. Ginny shared the information with her defense team, which subpoenaed his school records. When the judge saw the subpoena he was so appalled he ordered Ferguson's transcripts from OSU. Apparently Ferguson had not completed half of the core requirements for graduation in 1972. In February 2009, Ginny's defense team filed a motion requesting a new trial. On November 22, 2010, Judge Mark Wiest granted Ginny's motion for a new trial and ordered her immediate release from prison. Judge Wiest had been the finder of fact at Ginny's trial and had referred to Ferguson as "The key witness to the State's case..." In his order granting a new trial Judge Wiest noted that "Ferguson's testimony was directly linked to the Licking County Coroner, Dr. Raker, and the Forensic Pathologist from the Franklin County Coroner's office, Dr. Fardal. They relied heavily on testing done by Ferguson to reach their conclusions. Ferguson was the linchpin holding the State's case together. Without his testimony, the State's case would have fallen apart." Judge Wiest had been convinced of Ginny's guilt back in 1990 and he was uncertain whether he had changed his mind about her guilt or innocence, but he did recognize that Ferguson's false credentials made the prosecution's case patently unfair. Ferguson violated the public trust but the only punishment he received was thirty days in jail plus probation and a small fine. Judge Wiest ordered Ginny's release on November 22, 2010. The prosecutor dismissed the charges against her in April 2011.

The tenuous nature of her freedom does not escape Ginny. "It's just lucky that I had been watching that Buckeye game. If I hadn't, I'd still be there. If I just hadn't and that light bulb hadn't gone off I'd still be there. Nobody would have found this out. He'd have gotten away with it forever. He would have gone to his grave with the secret."

After her conviction had been vacated, Ginny began the process to be declared actually innocent. Unfortunately for her, the court did not consider the other evidence she presented in her motion for a new trial. The court decided that Ferguson having false credentials as sufficiently egregious that he could vacate Ginny's conviction without considering the rest of her evidence. As a result, she has had a difficult time proving her innocence and no court has yet addressed the many deficiencies in the forensic evidence, not just the fact of Ferguson's fake credentials.

In a deposition, Ferguson admitted the theory he espoused at trial about the toxin collecting in a pocket beneath the muscle was his own theory and that there was no scientific theory to support his conclusion. An untested theory of homicide from someone with Ferguson's lack of credentials should be dismissed as fantasy at best. Ferguson's testimony was riddled with other perjury as well. He claimed that Bill was in a coma when he was admitted into the hospital, but the hospital records indicate Bill was awake when he was admitted. Ferguson testified that Bill did not have diarrhea and so anything found in his lower colon must have been inserted rectally and not orally. The hospital's records directly refute Ferguson on this point. Furthermore, Dr. Robert Raker, the Licking County Coroner, wondered why any substance that might have been inserted into Bill's rectum did not come out in the diarrhea or the rectal tube. Ferguson also did not hire qualified lab technicians and had not implemented quality assurance protocols at the lab even though Dr. Patrick Fardal, a pathologist with the Franklin County Coroner's Office, understood that Ferguson's tests were subjected to a second opinion analysis.

The two county coroners appeared to have serious reservations about the cause of Bill's death and whether homicide was indicated. Dr. Fardal conducted the autopsy on Bill and his notes indicated he determined there was no conclusive evidence of what caused Bill's death. Dr. Raker's handwritten notes indicate that he understood the chronological order of the blood samples taken from Bill and that the toxicity levels were decreasing, not increasing—yet Dr. Raker testified toxicity levels were increasing in support of Ferguson's bogus "pocket theory." Dr. Raker's notes had been withheld from the defense until long after the conviction, which could be a Brady violation. Knowing what they must now know about Ferguson's lack of academic credentials and lack of lab verification procedures, it is doubtful that either Dr. Raker or Dr. Fardal would rely on Ferguson's report.

Ferguson's lie and the perjured testimony connected to it did more damage than just wrongfully convicting Ginny, it also destroyed a family. When Ginny was arrested, she asked a friend to pick up her children for the weekend. Ginny thought she would be home some time during that weekend, but she did not come home until over twenty years later. Meanwhile, three of her children were put into the foster care system and moved through five different families until the parents in that fifth family petitioned to become their permanent guardians. The break-up of her family hit Ginny hard.

"I had a house full of kids," Ginny remembers. "I took care of sick people. I drove the Brownies when they went on their little field trips and took the kids to T-ball class. Sarah was dancing. We attended mass on a regular basis at the local church. I wasn't anybody. I was just some person from Ohio just getting through her day."

Ginny's youngest son, Alex, saw their family life in pretty much the same way. "[My childhood] was a typical childhood," he recalls. "You go out and play. You run errands. It was a typical normal childhood for a very middle class child. We lived in a little subdivision there in Newark and had a nice house and a car." Alex remembers family activities like going to the park. He remembers his dad visiting the children even as his parents were going through a divorce. He does not remember much about the circumstances of his father's death or his mother's arrest and trial. "The police showed up at the door and asked for Mom," he recalled. "I don't remember the whole incident, my dad and all that was going on at the house when he passed away...when the police officers showed up at the house I didn't really know what was going on."

A simple twist of fate can change your life irreparably. Ginny's divorce would have been final the day she was arrested but instead she would spend the next twenty years in prison and her children would become wards of the state. "My kids were essentially orphaned and all alone in the world," Ginny says sadly. At four years old, Alex was too young to attend the trial. Corey and Sarah were older and they did attend the trial. That could be part of the reason why they continue to have an estranged relationship with their mother.

"I was just in such shock. I just walked around shell shocked for a while after they put me in Marysville. I really thought I had died and gone to hell except that I was not dead. "Buried alive" is the best description I can give you. I felt like I was buried alive. I was." Ginny's children lived in their own sort of hell. The younger ones developed substance abuse problems. Alex also had numerous run-ins with the law.

* * *

We Have Tomorrow

As Told By Alex LeFever

Growing up as a teenager I got involved with drugs and drinking and other rebellious behavior. I always used my past as an excuse to do what I did back then. My brother and sister were involved in the whole drug scene too, but not, I think, to the extent that I was. They hadn't been arrested as often as I had. My sister's got her own issues going on right now, but my brother turned out fantastic. He got married and has a good job living out on the West Coast. I think moving out west helped him get right. Sarah isn't doing as well, but we all got to get there our own separate ways.

Corey and Sarah don't believe Mom is innocent. They don't even talk to her. Corey, at least, is supportive of me talking with

Mom and trying to build a relationship with her. He won't talk to Mom and asked me not to give her his phone number.

"If that's what you want," I said. "That's entirely on you guys. I'm not here to step in and say you need to talk to Mom."

Sarah's the same way except she's not that supportive of me building a relationship with Mom. Once Corey moved west, Sarah became more dependent on me. We partied together for a while until I decided that enough was enough. I found forgiveness and faith in something other than running around drinking and drugging all the time. That's the wedge that pushed us apart. Sarah and I were best buddies in the party scene and then I stopped. I think she felt I was abandoning her. We don't talk any more, but it's not like we don't care about each other. It's just strained. I ran into her at the store a couple of weeks ago. Her daughter, my niece, ran up to me. Sarah and I talked for a moment and then went our separate ways.

Corey and Sarah are still angry with Mom, but I think they're really angry at life, at the bad things that have happened to them in this life. My relationship with them is strained because I've been at Mom's side since her release. Corey and Sarah, they chose the other side. They were opposed to her release. I was only four years old when Mom went on trial so they don't think I remember what happened. I don't know whether I remember it from myself or from the newspaper articles. The parents in our last foster home made a sort of scrapbook with news clippings. Whenever I tried to look at it they said "Wait until you're older. We can discuss this when you're older and you can understand a little bit better."

When it comes to Mom, I think the main difference between Corey and Sarah and me is that I just decided not to worry about her guilt or innocence. "I'm done carrying this around," I thought. "Guilty or innocent, I'm done hating somebody that I really don't know especially when I don't know whether she's guilty or innocent."

Prayer got me to the mental place where I'm at today. I asked God to take away the heaviness of trying to decide Mom's innocence. I didn't want it to destroy my life. A month later Mom was being released. I'm not saying the two were connected. I'm just glad I set it all aside before she got out so we could begin to rebuild our relationship. On Christmas Eve, after her release, Mom asked me

"Well, what do we do to fix this?" I told her there was nothing we could do to fix it other than just moving forward.

"The past is the past," I said. "From this day forward we have a tomorrow." Not having my parents there when I was growing up taught me how important it is that I be there for my children. I just want to be there and provide more than money and things. I want to spend time with them.

My foster parents used to take us up to Marysville when Mom was housed in the prison there. Mom tried to be upbeat around us. She didn't want us to worry so she'd just say "I'm going to get out. This is a mistake. They're just trying to figure this out. I'll get out and everything will be okay again." She was trying to give us hope that things would change.

By my eighteenth birthday I was ready to be out on my own. As it turned out, I had little reason to stay with my foster family. On the day that I turned eighteen, I saw their truth—they were in it for the money. "Seeing as how you've turned eighteen, we've got to take you to the attorney to get this money."

They had been collecting my social security payments for all those years and told me I owed them this, that, and the other thing. "Well," I snapped, "I'll tell you what. I'll be gone tomorrow." I had everything I needed to take with me and the next morning I was out of there. I moved in with Sarah temporarily. I wasn't there long and a couple of years later I was married. I'm still married.

My wife and I dated for a couple of years. I was still in party mode at that point. She put up with all my shenanigans. I was living with Sarah for a while. I paid the rent and utilities and still had enough for drugs and drinks. At one point I moved into my buddy's basement and that place was a dump. It flooded whenever it rained and it was always damp. My wife, then girlfriend, announced one day that she was going to join the Navy. We decided to get married so I could move out to California with her; the ship was stationed in San Diego. We lived there until we had our first child, then we moved back to Ohio. It was while we were out west that I quit doing drugs. If I hadn't I'd probably be dead by now.

I was still drinking but my wife had quit. She started going back to church. Every Sunday she'd say, "We're going. Do you want to come with us?" I just wasn't ready for all that. Up to that point nothing in my life made me believe in God. I kept drinking and church kept her in the marriage. It got her through my verbal abuse and my anger with my life. I was never physically abusive; I'd just yell and shout. Still, every Sunday she'd invite me to go to church with her and our kids. "Nah, I'm good," I'd say. "I'll stay home. I've got stuff to do."

The drinking was making me physically sick. One day I just had enough. Something was telling me that enough was enough. That was the end of it. I quit drinking and on Sunday I went to church with my family. Eventually I got baptized. I know it sounds unbelievable, but that's what happened. As much drinking as I had been doing, I should've had DTs or something, some sort of withdrawal, but there was nothing. I didn't get sick. I didn't have the shakes. I believe it was some sort of divine intervention. What else could it have been? I quit drinking cold turkey after years and years of constant drinking and drugs since I was really young. A while after I had quit, an old buddy from the partying days invited us down to the local bar. I had just one beer and I don't know when I ever felt so sick and so anxious. I wasn't intoxicated but I didn't feel well. I knew at that moment, *that* beer had been my last drink. Now I'm a licensed drug and alcohol counselor.

Quitting drugs and drinking wasn't the only divine intervention. During that period I was able to survive because my boss never gave up on me. He owns a pizza parlor and gave me enough work to pay my bills. Through all the drug and alcohol issues I had he never fired me. I always had a job. He even supported me when I decided to go to college. I graduate in twelve weeks and he's already asked me if I'd like to help him open up another restaurant and manage it. I'm thinking about it but my degree is in criminal justice and I want to go into juvenile probation. I know how things in the adult world can screw up a kid. If someone had been there for me, to intervene when I was going through some things as a teenager, my life might not have been as bad as it was back then.

I think about my life as a child before Dad's passing. My parents loved me. We had a good life. My experience in foster care wasn't as bad as some of the stories I've heard about, but it wasn't really nurturing. My foster parents, especially the last family I lived with, did their best but we didn't have an emotional bond. When things were bad for me I could not just curl up in their lap so they could make me feel safe. I think about that and how alone I felt back then and I don't want my children to ever feel that. I want them to know they can come to me when they're having a bad day. I don't want them to end up in juvie or in a group home like I did. Sometimes I talk about these things with my mom, but not too often. I might mention something that happened when I was locked up and that will remind her of something that happened to her. I think talking with me about what happened to her is helping her re-acclimate to being on the outside. Sometimes she's fine and other times it's like she wants to shut down and not be around other people. I guess it's the institutional mindset. I think she suffers from post-traumatic stress disorder. She's in a support group and I think the group helps her. Like I said when Mom was released, it hasn't been Sunday dinners at grandma's house, but at least we're talking.

* * *

Although she is no longer in prison, Ginny is not assured of her freedom. Since her case was dismissed without prejudice she is still at risk of being re-indicted. The prosecutor has made it clear he would like to recharge Ginny and re-try her. In fact, he has appointed a special prosecutor to assess whether the State can re-try her and win. Ginny hasn't let this stop her. Before she was released, the prosecution offered her deals on lesser charges with time served, but Ginny refused to take them. She continues to live her life, pursuing a graduate degree in nursing. She speaks out on wrongful conviction, participating in events at law schools and with civic organizations. She decided to stay in Ohio partly because it's her home, but also because she doesn't want her life disrupted again if the prosecutor decides to try her again.

Ginny tried to compartmentalize the various disparate parts of her life. She did not want to talk about what happened to her; the record had been sealed. Ginny just wanted to get back to her life. What she found, however, was that she could not do it; she could not stay silent. "If we don't open our mouths," she explained, "they continue to get away with it." The "they" are ill-intentioned prosecutors and law enforcement and "it" is wrongful conviction. Ginny has decided to put her story out there so others can learn from her situation.

After spending more than twenty years in prison Ginny only wanted to do two things. First, she wanted to let her daughter, Heather, know that she had been released from prison. As soon as she was outside, she borrowed a mobile phone from one of her attorneys. It was an iPhone and became the first phone that Ginny purchased. "It's the only phone I know how to operate," she says, smiling. The second thing Ginny wanted was something she'd dreamt about—a western omelet from Bob Evans. Her first meal was dinner at a really nice Italian restaurant; and she says she can have breakfast tomorrow.

Ginny LeFever lives in Ohio and continues to pursue a certification of her actual innocence. She speaks out against wrongful conviction at law schools and civic organizations across the country. Alex LeFever, her son, also lives in Ohio and is a sponsor to former addicts and alcoholics.

CHAPTER 13
A Case In Progress

[The following story was written by a man currently fighting to prove he is innocent of a murder conviction.]

* * *

Dirty Meatloaf
By Anonymous

I'm forty-six years old and currently serving a life sentence without parole for a crime I did not commit. This is my twentieth year of incarceration. I've been fortunate enough to be transferred to a Level-4 prison in the Department of Corrections (DOC) and the only prison in the DOC that has kitchens in the housing units with single burner stove tops, convection ovens, grills, pots, and pans. Cooking in our cells is not allowed. We also have a commissary that sells a variety of items including ground beef, chicken breast, flour, pancake mix, garlic cloves, onions, pepper, olive oil, Crisco oil, beef hot dogs, pancake syrup, ice cream, and bananas. With these items, and some of what is served on the regular chow line (cole slaw, pasta sauce, veggies, potatoes and the like) I've been able to make and prepare different recipes.

My mom, who is on a fixed income, is my only regular, financial support. She tries to send me something once a month and I divide the money between phone credit and my commissary account for clothing and food. I remember when I first got here; guys were selling plates of food for a book of stamps, which has a resale value of four dollars. They made things like fried chicken with rice, mac and cheese, calzones, pizzas, burgers with onion rings, and chicken sandwiches. When I realized I had to try to supplement my income, I thought, "I can cook. I like to cook, so why not sell plates?" I knew I wanted to do something the other guys weren't doing, and whatever I did had to be easy to transport inconspicuously in the yard. Prison authorities frown upon inmates having food in the yard. As the saying goes, however, "where there's a will, there's a way!" I began first by figuring out the cost effectiveness of my plan to make and sell food. It meant that I would have to use some of what was served on the regular chow line each week and spend the least amount of my own money, while still making plates that could compete on taste with the other plates on the yard.

You're probably wondering what kind of food I can realistically make in a prison, with limited supplies. Well, first of all some recipes call for ingredients we don't have available through the commissary, things like eggs, baking powder, and baking soda. We have to make substitutions, although sometimes we may be able to get our hands on these items from the guys who work in the main prison kitchen. If I can't get eggs or baking powder for baking, I use mayonnaise and pancake mix.

I love to cook; I find it therapeutic. I find that when I'm cooking, my mind goes into creativity mode and my focus is on what I'm preparing, what seasonings to use, how much, what flavors will those seasonings bring out, along with the presentation of the dish after it's done. While those things are going on I'm in another place. Often I find myself thinking about being at home cooking with proper ingredients without the prison restrictions. I also wonder what my mother would think of what I'm making, which in turn gives me hope of one day cooking for her. When we talk, I tell her about the food I cook and she always says, "Mmmm, I wish I could taste that."

My response is always, "In time, ma." Then I imagine her reaction when she tastes my egg rolls with special dipping sauce or my dirty meatloaf. My mind goes to so many places—my ideal kitchen, the utensils and equipment that I would use like food processors, mixers, knives, and other things. For the time that I'm cooking, I'm definitely not here. Then, of course, there's the enjoyment of the food after I'm done cooking. Mmmm, mmmm, good.

Onion rings, egg rolls, meatloaf, chicken parm, spaghetti and meatballs, mac and cheese, scalloped potatoes, spinach and cheese pies, pizza, calzones, and cottage pie are just some of the dishes I've prepared in our kitchen. But, my specialty item is my egg roll.

I remembered egg rolls from a Chinese restaurant in the neighborhood I lived in before prison. I figured with commissary prices at that time I could spend twenty dollars and pretty much double my money. So, I set out to make egg rolls that tasted as good as the ones on the outside. My recipe was simple:

Cole slaw, served on the chow line

1 pound of ground beef

2-3 turkey sausages w/ honey and brown sugar

1 kippered steak

1 bottle Crisco

10 tortilla packs of 6

1 package Thai rice noodles with seasoning packet

Again, I had to have something different as a selling point, so I decided to make a special dipping sauce using:

1 20-oz. bottle of Pepsi

1 cup sugar

¼ cup hot sauce

¼ cup soy sauce

¼ cup ketchup

1 spoon of coffee

The dipping sauce mixture is cooked down until it reduces to a thick syrupy sauce, sweet and spicy. If I need to make a buffalo sauce, I use hot sauce and butter from the chow line. Sometimes I buy honey or honey mustard from the commissary to make different sauces. I develop my sauces through trial and error; some hit, some miss.

To make prison egg rolls, I start by rinsing the chow line cole slaw in cold water to get rid of the mayonnaise and other ingredients (hot water opens the pores of the cabbage which causes it to take in the mayonnaise taste). I buy all of the other ingredients in the commissary. Then, I cook the ground beef in the largest pot available with a little of the Asian seasoning from packaged Thai rice noodles, adding soy sauce, and the diced turkey sausage and kippered steak. The size of the pot may vary depending on what is available in the unit's kitchen at the time.

After the meat mixture cooks, I take it out of the pot, leaving the seasoned grease from the ground beef to which I add the cabbage from the cole slaw and allow it to cook down with added seasoning. I cook it down, but make sure it still has a slight crunch. Then, I add all the meat, mix it up and let it sit covered while I steam the tortillas so they're easy to fold and roll. To steam the tortilla, I use a wok and a pizza pan. The pizza pan sits in the wok perfectly. I fill the wok with water to the halfway mark and then lay the pizza pan in the wok and put on the wok cover. After the water starts to boil, I place a tortilla on the pizza pan. This allows the steam soften the tortilla. By the time I finish rolling one egg roll, the next tortilla is ready.

I use 1/3 cup of the meat and cabbage mixture in the middle of the tortilla and then I fold, roll, and seal it with a little solution of water and flour. I can roll fifty to sixty egg rolls in one batch. Then I fry them in oil until they get crisp and golden. I tried baking a few, but they taste much better when they're fried. I put the dipping sauce into pouches that I had previously fashioned from small trash bags and package four egg rolls with one pouch of sauce. I sell that meal for one book of stamps. Every batch of egg rolls makes me a profit of as much as two-hundred dollars off of an investment of about twenty-five dollars, most of which I send home to my mom. I keep the egg rolls and pouches in a cardboard portfolio that I can take on the yard and advertise. I tell the guys, "I got them egg rolls with a special dipping sauce!" Once they hear that, I can be sold out within the hour, and every week guys are asking about those egg rolls!

Of course, too much of anything loses its value, so I had to figure out other dishes to make. I set out to create smothered meat-loaf sandwiches with homemade (if you want to call anything here "homemade") bread and mac and cheese. When a mistake happened in the recipe I discovered "dirty meatloaf." Since most people are unsure about anything made in a prison and called "dirty," let me tell you what happened.

The first time I made the meatloaf meal I served it with gravy and two side dishes—rice and mac and cheese. When I decided to do a sandwich I figured I'd slice the meatloaf and put the slices in the pot of gravy so that those flavors would fuse. Then, I could place the meatloaf on the bread and it would pretty much be drenched in the gravy and taste delicious! The problem was that when I went to remove the slices of meatloaf they broke up into chunks and what I envisioned for the sandwich quickly became a disaster. Still, all was not lost! When I put the meatloaf on the bread it became messy and sloppy so I coined the term, "Dirty Meatloaf" which everyone loved! The thing about making up a name for something is no one can tell you how to make it, or what to put in it. In here, everyone seems to have an opinion, but there's something about a messy sandwich that just tastes better. It's like comfort food, like the sloppy joes of our childhood.

Step 1

Step 2

There are many guys in here from different nationalities and cultures that enjoy cooking. From time to time we'll give each other tips, but what I really like to do sometimes is just sit in the kitchen area and watch other guys cook. I pick up different styles and cooking techniques. I even learn how to make new dishes—of course I put my own twist on them. I also get a lot of my information and ideas from a cookbook called, *The Joy of Cooking*. In the pages of *Joy* I can find information on everything from nutrition to cooking methods and techniques. It's an encyclopedia of cooking and I'm glad I have it.

One of the things I'm looking forward to the most when I'm finally exonerated is going home and cooking for my mother and friends. I have a vivid imagination, so I often find myself designing my ideal kitchen. I love the thought of watching their faces and their expressions after tasting my cooking. If someone doesn't like something for whatever reason I want to know why. What was missing? What do they think I should've or could've done to make it taste better? I will tinker with a recipe until I improve it.

We have a culinary program here, but the list of people wanting to take the class is long, and the fact that I'm a lifer hurts my chances of getting in the class. They only allow a couple of lifers into each class and the wait is even longer for us. In the meantime, I will be patient and continue teaching myself, learning from cooking shows, books, magazines, and other cooks in here. I have faith that my legal team will prove my innocence and I'll be exonerated. When I am, I'll cook dinner for my mom just so I can watch her face when she tastes my egg rolls and dirty meatloaf.

Will I ever be a master chef? Time will tell and one thing I have on my hands right now is time.

If you wnt it you can get it,

The author of this story is still serving time and is pursuing his claim of innocence. Because he might be bending the prison's rules by cooking contraband food, we are not identifying him and have removed all references that might identify him. We decided to include his story and his recipes because they are examples of the ingenuity that is locked inside our prisons. Since this author is not yet an exoneree, he will not be receiving a share of the royalty payments as an exoneree at this time. We hope the author prevails in his writ of habeas corpus so that he may share in future royalty payments as an exoneree.

PRUNO,

RAMEN,

and a side of

HOPE

Their Photos

Arthur Carmona and his mother, Ronnie Sandoval, on the day of his release.

Arthur Carmona at Preston California Youth Authority with his mother, Ronnie Sandoval.

A young Arthur Carmona with his sister Veronica.

Ronnie Sandoval enjoying some time with her friend, Della Reyes.

FERNANDO BERMUDEZ

Fernando Bermudez in Paris, from Innocent Inmate to Inspiration (photo by Crystal Bermudez).

Fernando and Crystal Bermudez taking a break from Fernando's speaking engagement in Paris (photo by Crystal Bermudez).

Carissa and Fernando Jr. enjoy some playtime with their father, Fernando Bermudez (photo by Crystal Bermudez).

Carissa Bermudez (photo by Crystal Bermudez).

(from left) Linda Starr, Obie Anthony, and Paige Kaneb await the judge's ruling at Obie's hearing. (Photo courtesy of Northern California Innocence Project.)

Obie Anthony enjoys a break during a speaking engagement. (Photo courtesy of Northern California Innocence Project.)

Obie and Denise Anthony share a dance at their wedding.

Gloria Killian shares her story.

Gloria Killian at the NCIP 2014 JFA Dinner. (Photo courtesy of Northern California Innocence Project.)

Maurice celebrates, on the day of his release, with his family, legal team, and friend. (L-R) Paige Kaneb (lawyer), Deborah Caldwell (sister), Maurice Caldwell, Linda Starr (lawyer), and Rick Walker (fellow exoneree and friend). (Photo courtesy of Northern California Innocence Project.)

Above Left: Maurice Caldwell with his girlfriend Pamela Haynes and their family. Above Center: Maurice Caldwell enjoys what would be his last visit with his mom, Maxine, visiting room at Folsom Prison. Above Right: Maurice Caldwell leaves prison a free man. Left: Deborah Caldwell awaits her brother's release from prison. (Photo courtesy of Northern California Innocence Project.)

SABRINA BUTLER PORTER

Clockwise from above: Sabrina Butler Porter at home with two of her children, Joe, Jr. and Danny; Sabrina Butler in prison; Little Walter Dean Butler (deceased).

GINNY LeFEVER

Ginny LeFever graduating from nursing school with her son, Corey, in her arms (1980).

TABITHA POLLACK HERSHBERGER

Clockwise from above: Tabitha enjoys some family time with her sister Sue Ostrowski and her nephew, Joe; Tabitha Pokkack, 1999; Tabitha Pollack's children, Preston and Jami Sue (deceased).

ANTOINE GOFF

Above: Antoine Goff visits with his brother Sam Seymore, and niece Samara, in prison. Left: Antoine Goff at the NCIP 2014 JFA Dinner. (Photo courtesy of Northern California Innocence Project.)

Clockwise from above: Larry Lamb in prison (2003); Larry Lamb in his Marine uniform shortly before his deployment to Vietnam; Larry Lamb at 8 years old; Larry Lamb's mother (deceased); Larry Lamb's granddaughter, Lamara Patricia Pemberton.

California Exonerees at NCIP 2014 Justice for All Dinner (JFA). Pictured left to right: Ronald Ross, Obie Anthony, Armando Ortiz, Gloria Killian, Johnny Williams, Francisco Carrillo, Ronnie Sandoval, Maurice Caldwell. (Photo courtesy of Northern California Innocence Project.)

Co-founder of NCIP, Professor Cookie Ridolfi (second from right) with NCIP attorney Paige Kaneb (second from left) and three California exonerees (from left) Maurice Caldwell, Franky Carrillo, and Antoine Goff. (Photo courtesy of Northern California Innocence Project.)

Afterwords

Courtney B. Lance

In 2012, I was invited to participate in this project by my good and long-time friend Nikki Pope. I was surprised at the invitation because I practically knew nothing about exonerations or wrongful convictions save for, as a Chicagoan, what I knew about John Burge's violently abusive and tortuous methods to obtain "tailored" confessions from innocent men. This may not even count. I was curious, however. What would I have to offer a project focused on wrongful convictions? Nikki and I have worked together on other projects and because we work well together perhaps I was a likely choice but there had to be more than just that. I came to find out that certainly there was. I am a chef and Nikki had the idea of putting together a prison cookbook based on the engaging conversations she had with exonerees and their very interesting stories on creatively preparing meals outside of the chow hall and on the down low. Because of my love for food, Nikki knew I would be interested.

We talked around the idea quite a bit and then finally in some detail as she shared the many dishes in which ramen noodles played a leading role and the recipe for Pruno, a curious contraband hooch concocted from available special ingredients, mixed and "aged" in a big plastic garbage bag. The thought was to create a prison food cookbook of these unusual but hopefully tasty dishes and cocktails. But the part of our conversation that resonated the most for me was about the wrongful convictions. I was shocked hearing about prosecutors' behavior and witnesses led to misidentify suspects, and the length of time some of these men and women had been imprisoned for crimes they didn't commit. What was I hearing? I just couldn't believe the injustices that were taking place. Add insult to injury, these exonerated men and women were no longer guilty and therefore were entitled to none of the benefits afforded ex-felons. I was so angry hearing all of this and I didn't know where to put my anger except into the efforts of this project. I was on board.

Nikki recommended that, in doing this project a portion of whatever we made would be provided to the participants, since there were no guaranteed support services. And perhaps we could enjoy working the project, rather than be angry, knowing that the end result would be for a worthy cause. Nikki thought it best to engage a publicist to help promote this great idea. We hired Snap Productions' Ginger Campbell. We also appealed to The Innocence Network to put the word out that we were looking for recipe submissions from exonerees to publish in our book. Nikki suggested that we begin interviews and that I come to California.

In 2013, I found my way to California. We were to meet two exonerees, Rick Walker and Maurice Caldwell and from those interviews understand how inmates were able to fashion interesting and money-making dishes from what was available in prison commissaries and any other food that somehow became available.

Our conversations with Rick and Maurice were informative. Rick shared rather amazing stories and examples of some of the familiar dishes. We spoke with Maurice for a very long time and got some of the same. But we were still left wanting just a little more. Throughout our conversations I couldn't help but wonder "How in God's name were they able, as innocent men, to endure so many years in prison?" And I think while I was really trying to stay on point and talk food I believe my questions kept leading to "How did you manage this? How did you endure those many years in prison having not committed a crime?" We talked with Maurice for more than three hours that afternoon. I was full.

On the way home and into the evening, Nikki and I talked about our interviews with Rick and Maurice. We were both moved by how these innocent men managed to endure imprisonment. I think it was on this evening that we decided to redirect our focus from food to hope. Our publicist, Ginger Campbell, with whom we had regularly discussed our ideas, exhaled in a sigh of relief. For me, it was that sigh that strongly suggested we were on the right track. The focus on food was a good idea we all thought, but many others had thought so as well. We figured we didn't really know who would be interested in our book, begging the question who would be our audience? Who would purchase our cookbook containing prison recipes created by men and women who were wrongfully convicted? Difficult to answer and not nearly as clear and simple as who would be interested in a book about hope amidst such horrendous conditions and seemingly hopeless circumstances; everyone, of course. Who isn't interested in stories of hope? We reconstructed our plan, redirected our purpose and requested stories of hope from the exonerees.

The idea evolved into not only collecting stories of hope from those wrongfully convicted but also collecting stories from those family members or friends who lived on the outside of the cell and through the ordeal by supporting and keeping hopes high for their incarcerated loved ones. We learned from these stories how family members and friends were always working to help free their loved ones, hoping their work was impactful, worrying that they were not doing enough, and waiting and waiting and waiting, frustrated that decisions or resolutions weren't coming fast enough.

I had the honor of interviewing each and every one of these men and women. My notions about prisoners and prison life have been shattered. I've also become acutely aware of how wrongful conviction can impact family and friends. Families are split up or some family members self-medicate to get through the days, wringing their hands for not being able to do more than the most they've already done. And where to get the money to pay the attorneys? Those who were considered good friends and who were expected to be there no matter what disappeared. But these families tenaciously continued to support their imprisoned loved ones as best they could, mortgaging homes, trying to find better attorneys, and accepting those excessively expensive collect calls each week or even every day, even though they could not afford them. And those folks never thought to have been great friends appeared out of the blue supporting these incarcerated men and women at every opportunity.

In hearing their stories of hope and endurance I was affected. The obvious—I learned so much more about wrongful convictions, and prison life. The not so obvious—I fell in love with these men and women. They stirred my emotions; they roused my spirit through their humility and gratitude. Not necessarily what one would expect from folks who've received the cards that should never have been dealt. Some exonerees were disappointed and sad but where were their anger, their rage; where was the bitterness that I was expecting?

I am angered by the injustice; defense attorneys that were ill prepared, inexperienced and often took being poorly paid as an excuse to perform inadequately. Or the prosecutors that conveniently withheld evidence, or denied evidence or delayed proceedings. I am disappointed with our officials who are charged with administering justice and missioned to protect and serve, but who have failed us. Who is being held accountable for this lack? I hurt for these men and women who have missed large chunks of their lives behind bars; stripped from their families, having lost valuable and important experiences that would inform their own development and prohibited from participating in their family milestones from birth to death. I am frustrated and concerned that these men and women who have been forever altered by this experience were released into a world that had vastly changed receiving no support services; no counseling, no jobs, no money, nothing to help them re-enter an unfamiliar world. Each story in this book has some of all of that.

The strength of the exonerees' human spirit is completely exposed here, and I am in awe of their ability to forgive, and to be grateful not only for their release but in some cases for their prison experience. That's huge.

I, too, have been forever altered. I am no longer naïve to our unhealthy justice system. And I feel compelled to speak for the wrongfully convicted at every opportunity. These men and women need their voices heard. I'm hoping to help that happen. This book is my first step. The opportunity to know these men and women, for them to trust us with their stories, and to be inspired by and advocate for them has been one of the greatest experiences of my life and for that I am extremely grateful. I thank them all for that. I also hope that by reading these stories you, too, are inspired. The wrongfully convicted need a voice. We all can give them that. We can make that happen and I trust we will.

Thank you for reading this book and giving it a voice.

A friend asked, "What do you want readers to take away from this book?" The question caught me off guard because I hadn't considered what I wanted readers to think or do after reading *Pruno*. I suppose I just hoped to give these courageous women and men an opportunity to have their say. For the longest time no one really listened to them. At a public speaking workshop for a small group of California exonerees, organized by the Northern California Innocence Project (NCIP) and Aldo Billingslea and Kimberly Hill, two Santa Clara University professors, the exonerees were learning to focus their storytelling into a twenty-minute talk. Maurice Caldwell kept going over the allotted twenty minutes. When Aldo told Maurice he would have to shorten his story, Maurice replied, "For twenty years I had to keep my mouth shut. I have something to say and now I'm gonna say it." All around the circle of participants' heads nodded and you could hear murmurs of assent. So that's one thing I want from this book—to give Maurice and all the others a forum for having their say.

Although these innocent people are no longer in prison, many of their lives are still held hostage by their wrongful convictions. The time gap in their lives cannot be explained away, making it difficult to get a job. The lack of skills marketable outside of prison limits them to low-paying, low-skilled work. Very few have the opportunity to go to school or improve their economic situation. This is why we have agreed to share half of our proceeds from the sale of this book with the women and men whose stories you have been reading. The more books we sell, the more money they earn. You may think this doesn't mean much; you surely will if you've read stories of multi-million dollar payouts to exonerees. Yes, there have been some large compensation awards, but they are rare. Most exonerees receive no compensation. Some states have a statutory payment scheme, but the threshold for eligibility is often impossible and certainly difficult to meet—even after exoneration. Thankfully, you bought this book so I want you to feel good about helping provide at least some income to these men and women.

Another thing I want is for readers to experience just a little of what these innocent men and women experienced; to see what we saw—that no matter how difficult we think our lives are, our sufferings are nothing when laid beside the injustice of being wrongfully convicted and imprisoned. I hope that these stories show readers a way to find the same inner strength to survive the challenges in their lives and rise above the injustices they experience.

Even though the justice system wrongfully convicted the men and women in these stories, there is hope that the system can be improved because this same system also exonerated them. In many cases the exoneration was an incredibly lengthy process, but in the end the innocent person was freed. What I want most from readers is to demand that our justice system actually be just and fair. Lawyers must be held to and live up to a higher standard. Prosecutors who withhold evidence must be punished, not with a reprimand, but with jail time and disbarment if found guilty. Prosecutors should not have absolute immunity for intentional acts of misconduct. Defense lawyers who show up in court drunk or sleep through a trial (yes, it even happens in death penalty trials) should be disbarred. Judges who fail to apply rules properly or who let lawyers sleep in court or show up drunk without sanctions or suspensions should be removed from the bench. When a convicted person claims he is innocent and DNA evidence will show it, test the evidence. A defense attorney should not have to go to court to first prove that the evidence exists and then go back to court to force the police and prosecutors to test the DNA. What could happen? Testing could show the person is guilty. It could show the person is innocent. It could be inconclusive. Isn't it better to know? What I want readers to realize is that we, all of us together, can demand a fair and just system. We can make it happen. We can choose not to elect or re-elect prosecutors who break the rules. Where judges are elected, we can vote bad judges out of office. Where judges are appointed, we can hold politicians accountable for removing bad judges. We need to educate ourselves about our justice system and those we rely on to mete out justice on our behalf. Reading this book may be the first step, but it should not be the last. We must educate ourselves and then take action. If we don't our justice system will continue to fail men and women like those whose stories you read in this book. One day, it may fail you, too.

So, here is what I want readers to take away from this book:

- Demand that the justice system work better.
- Share in the good feeling from helping exonerees reclaim their lives.
- Understand that these men and women are us and that any one of us could become a victim of our broken justice system.

Thank you so much for buying and reading this book. Please spread the word so we can help more people. Twenty percent of the proceeds also go to organizations that help exonerees after their release and help them in their fight to freedom.

Glossary and Information

Abased and Abound—From the Bible, Philippians 4:12, *to be abased* is to be humbled or brought low and *to abound* is to have great quantities or excess.

Absolute Immunity—Government officials, including prosecutors, are completely immune from criminal prosecution and lawsuits as long as they are acting within the scope of their official duties, even if those actions are malicious or in bad faith. Public officials may not be sued for official acts regardless of motive.

Accountability—(as defined by the Illinois Supreme Court) Accountability is not a crime in and of itself, but rather a mechanism through which a criminal conviction may result. To be deemed legally responsible, a defendant would have to promote or facilitate the commission of the offense and would have to knowingly solicit, aid, abet, agree to aid, or attempt to aid the other person in the planning or commission of the offense.

Admonishment—Under the rules of the American Bar Association an admonishment is a private reprimand which declares the lawyer's conduct improper, but does not limit the lawyer's right to practice law. The California State Bar Association defines admonition as a written, non-disciplinary reprimand.

Aggravated Murder—In the State of Ohio, aggravated murder is a first-degree felony involving the unlawful and purposeful killing of another person or unlawfully terminating a pregnancy under certain circumstances: (i) murder is premeditated, (ii) murder occurs during the commission of felony, (iii) victim is less than thirteen years old, (iv) perpetrator commits murder while in prison for committing another felony or while escaped from prison, (v) victim is a law enforcement officer engaged in official duties or perpetrator intentionally targeted a law enforcement officer.

Assistant District Attorney—An assistant district attorney is part of the prosecution team and represents the State in a criminal trial.

Bench Trial—A trial by judge instead of a trial by jury.

California Conservation Corps (3Cs)—3Cs is a state agency that employs young people between the ages of eighteen and twenty-five to work outdoors improving the state's natural resources and assisting with emergency response to disasters like forest fires, floods, mud slides, earthquakes, and pest infestations.

California Department of Corrections (CDC)—The State agency responsible for running the jails, prisons and juvenile detention centers.

Circumstantial Evidence—Evidence that relies on an inference to connect it to a material fact in crime. *Example: A witness testifies that she heard a gunshot and moments later saw the defendant standing over the victim with a gun in his hand. This evidence is circumstantial; the defendant may have been a bystander who picked up the gun after it had been fired by someone else.*

Close Custody—Inmates are classified according to custody level. Close custody, also called close confinement, requires an inmate to have close supervision and observation and under security control at all times while inside an armed perimeter and to be under direct armed supervision when outside of the perimeter.

Dismiss With Prejudice—In a criminal procedure, dismissal with prejudice bars the government from prosecuting the defendant again at a later time on the same charge. It is a final judgment.

Dismiss Without Prejudice—In a criminal procedure, dismissal without prejudice leaves the government free to prosecute the defendant again on the same charge.

Eyewitness Identification Best Practice for Photo Array—Best practices for photo identification in New York State seek to make the procedure as neutral as possible for the witness. The goal of the best practices is to help persons conducting eyewitness identifications avoid influencing the witness in any way. Ideally, the person conducting the photo identification, the administrator, should not be involved in the investigation of the crime and should not know anything about actual or potential suspects. The administrator conducting the photo line-up should give no opinions about the witness's ability to make identification. In fact, the officer should avoid even indicating whether a suspect has been arrested, unless the witness specifically asks if someone is in custody.

New York State differentiates an investigation with a known suspect from an investigation without a known suspect. When there is no suspect, the administrator may show multiple photographs and should try to have a computer program select the photographs shown based on witness descriptions of the perpetrator. The administrator should keep track of which photos were shown and the source of each photo. When there is a known suspect, computer selected photos should be used when possible. In addition to the known suspect, the computer also should include photos of persons who have similar characteristics to the known suspect and the photos should be of a similar quality, size, and color. The other photos are called "fillers" and none of the fillers should be known to the witness. There should be at least five fillers, for a minimum of six photos in the array—also called a six-pack. If there are multiple suspects, each suspect should be included in an array with five fillers, never with other suspects.

Any instructions to the witness should be given *before* the identification procedure begins and not while the witness is in the process of viewing the photo array. Ideally, such instructions should be in writing so there is a record of exactly what instructions were given with a place for the witness to sign to confirm that these were the instructions given. The administrator should be out of the witness's line of sight to avoid any possible influence from the administrator's expressions or body language. The administrator also should not make any comment about the procedure until it is completed and has been documented. Questions asked after the witness views the photographs should not influence the witness and should include only the following: (1) do you recognize anyone, (2) if so, what number photograph do you recognize, and (3) from where do you recognize this person. If the witness's answers are vague or unclear, the administrator should ask the witness what she or he meant by the unclear answer.

If there are multiple witnesses, each witness should be told not to speak to the other witnesses. The administrator can ensure this by putting each witness in her or his own room, apart from other witnesses. If there are not sufficient rooms, an officer can sit with the witnesses to ensure they do not speak about the identification procedure or the case. Each witness also should see the same six-pack as the other witnesses.

Eyewitness Identification Best Practice for Line-up—Best practices for identification through a line-up procedure are similar to those for a photo procedure, but some are unique to an in-person line-up. The line-up participants may be standing or sitting, but they should be of a similar height and build. If there is a suspect participating in the line-up, the suspect should be allowed to pick her or his position in the line-up. If the line-up follows a photo array procedure, the suspect should be in a different number position in the line-up than she or he was in for the photo array and the fillers should be different persons than the fillers from the photo array. Defense attorneys are not allowed to speak in the viewing room when the witness is present. If one line-up participant is asked to do something, such as speak or put on an item of clothing, all line-up participants must do the same thing. If possible, the identity of the witness must remain confidential. The location should be secure so the witness, suspects, and law enforcement personnel are safe. If possible, all law enforcement personnel who come into contact with the witness in connection with the line-up should have no knowledge of the investigation.

Environmental Neglect—(as defined by the Illinois Department of Children and Family Services) The child's person, clothing, or living conditions are unsanitary to the point the child's health may be impaired. This may include infestations of rodents, spiders, insects, snakes, etc., human or animal feces, rotten or spoiled food or rotten or spoiled garbage that the child can reach.

Exculpatory Evidence—In a criminal trial, exculpatory evidence is favorable to the defendant; it exonerates the defendant or tends to show that the defendant is not guilty.

Expungement—An expungement is a process to clean up a person's criminal record by setting aside a conviction or the sealing the record so that the conviction no longer shows on the person's record. The expungement itself will continue to appear on the record, however.

Exoneration—A person has been exonerated if he or she was convicted of a crime and later was officially cleared of that crime based on the presentation of new evidence of actual innocence.

Fajitagate—Name given to an incident that occurred in the early morning hours of November 20, 2002 involving three off-duty San Francisco police officers who beat up two young men after the victims refused to give their steak fajitas to the police officers, who had been drinking. The police officers were not arrested. Subsequently the incident was covered up by the San Francisco Police Department (SFPD), which led to an investigation of the SFPD by then San Francisco District Attorney Terrence Hallinan.

Felony Murder—A felony murder occurs when a victim is killed during the commission of a felony. A co-conspirator or participant in the crime can be charged with felony-murder even if he or she was not present during, involved in, or even aware of the victim's death.

Field Identification—A form of eyewitness identification that occurs close to the crime scene, typically because the situation requires the witness see the suspect immediately. Also called a "showup," this procedure can be highly suggestive and, if proper procedures are not followed, can lead easily to a wrongful conviction.

Filler Photo—A filler in a six-pack or live lineup is a person of similar height, build, and complexion as the suspect with other identified features such as facial hair, hair color, tattoo and the like. For the eyewitness identification to be admissible in court, the fillers should not be too dissimilar in appearance from the suspect. Most states require at least four fillers be included in a lineup. Fillers are also known as "dummies" and "known innocents."

Fish/Fresh Fish on the Line—Someone who is in prison for the first time, newly incarcerated.

Gaslight—A type of psychological or emotional abuse in which one partner tries to undermine the other partner's perception of reality by denying certain events ever occurred, to the point where the abused partner constantly second-guesses herself or himself. The term takes its name from the stage play and film *Gas Light* in which a husband attempts to drive his wife crazy by constantly dimming the gas lamps in their home and then denying that the lights had dimmed.

Gladiator School—Prison slang for juvenile detention centers in California. So called because of the torture and abuse inflicted upon the young men housed in the detention centers. Young men who spend time in these detention centers have said the center prepares you for prison life not for returning to society.

Hats Up—Prison slang for a fight that is about to begin.

Hogtied—The hogtie is a method of tying a person's limbs together, leaving the person unable to move. It was originally applied to pigs and hogs in preparation for slaughter.

Intake—The procedure through which all new inmates are brought into a prison system. Through this process inmates are correctly identified with the use of photographs and fingerprints, housing is assigned, job assignments are made, clothing and bed linens are distributed, and any medical needs are assessed.

Jailhouse Lawyer—A jailhouse lawyer is a prison inmate with some knowledge of law who gives legal advice and assistance to fellow inmates.

Kite—A contraband letter or note delivered to an inmate on the sly by another inmate or prison worker.

Latent Fingerprints—Latent fingerprints that are not visible to the naked eye buy may be revealed when magnesium powder is gently brushed over the surface where there may be a latent fingerprint. Once revealed, the fingerprint can be photographed or lifted from the surface using tape.

Level-4 Prison—In California, a Level-4 prison is a maximum security prison reserved for the most violent offenders and inmates who cause problems while in prison.

Life Sentence—Someone sentenced to life in prison may be eligible for parole in ten or more years depending on state law, but the inmate also could remain in prison for the rest of his or her natural life. Someone sentenced to Life Without the Possibility of Parole most likely will die in prison. Multiple life sentences may be served concurrently or consecutively, at the judge's discretion. An inmate serving concurrent multiple life sentences will become eligible for parole in the minimum number of years allowed in that state regardless of the number of concurrent life sentences. In most states, if the multiple life sentences are served consecutively as soon as the minimum number of years allowed under the first life sentence is reached, the clock begins to tick on the next life sentence. Some states have a maximum number of years that must be served under multiple consecutive life sentences before an inmate is eligible for parole. *Example: Assume the minimum number of years to become eligible for parole is ten years and the inmate is serving five life sentences. If the life sentences are concurrent, the inmate would be eligible for parole after ten years. If the life sentences are consecutive, after the first ten years the second life sentence would begin and so on until the tenth year of the fifth life sentence—the inmate would not be eligible for parole for fifty years (10 x 5 = 50).*

Live Lineup—In a live lineup, the suspect appears in a line with five people with physical characteristics resembling the suspect.

Mijo—A contraction of the Spanish words "mi" and "hijo" used affectionately when talking to any boy, not just a son or relative.

On the Merits—A decision on the merits is based on the fundamental issues involved in the case and not on a technical or procedural matter, such as a late filing or a failure to read a suspect her rights.

Preliminary Hearing—After a prosecutor files criminal charges and in lieu of seeking a grand jury indictment, a preliminary hearing is held to determine whether there is enough evidence to go to trial, including a finding by the judge that there is probable cause that a crime occurred.

Pruno—A prison classic, homemade alcohol using fruit, fruit juice, or fruit peelings and bread to create a fermented alcoholic beverage.

Recantation—The retraction of previous testimony when the witness no longer believes the previous statement is accurate or true.

Rigor Mortis—Rigor mortis is the stiffening of the body after death and normally starts around two hours after death. The body's smaller muscles are affected first and the body is completely stiff within eight to twelve hours of death. The body remains stiff for up to eighteen hours, after which the process of rigor mortis begins to reverse.

Segregation—The housing of inmates from the general population in special units. Disciplinary segregation is for a specified period of time and is given to an inmate who commits a serious rule violation. Administrative segregation is non-punitive detention for inmates in special circumstances who (i) require protective custody, (ii) are traveling to another institution and cannot be placed in the general population, and (iii) are awaiting a disciplinary hearing.

Sequential Lineup—In a sequential lineup, an eyewitness sees each suspect or the suspect's photograph one at a time and only once. A sequential lineup is less likely to result in a mistaken identification. The alternative is a simultaneous lineup where an eyewitness sees all suspects or photographs at the same time.

Set Aside a Conviction—When a conviction is set aside the jury verdict is overturned and the conviction is no longer a matter of public record. This does not mean the criminal record is erased only that it is not publicly available.

Simultaneous Lineup—In a simultaneous lineup, an eyewitness sees all suspects or the suspects' photographs at the same time. A witness viewing a simultaneous lineup is more likely to choose the person or photo that most resembles the person the eyewitness saw, resulting in a mistaken identification. The alternative is a sequential lineup where an eyewitness looks at each photograph one at a time and only once.

Six-Pack Photo Lineup—A six-pack photo lineup includes a head and shoulders photo of the suspect and five fillers. All six photos on the same page is a simultaneous six-pack lineup. Separate photos shown to the witness one at a time is a sequential six-pack lineup.

Stipulate to the Facts—In a stipulation, opposing parties agree to certain facts and those facts then do not need to be argued at trial. An oral stipulation in open court is binding. A stipulation made in the judge's chambers must be in writing to be binding.

Writ of Habeas Corpus—A writ of habeas corpus requires the State to justify the detention of a prisoner. In support of the petition, the prisoner presents an argument that his detention is in violation of his constitutional rights.

A Note on Sources

The exoneree stories in this book are based on the recollections of the exonerees and their friends and family members, court documents and records, and newspaper articles contemporaneous with the crimes and the exonerations. The written sources for each chapter are listed below. The authors also interviewed each exoneree and their friends and family members for background material, some of which appears as re-imagined conversations throughout the book. Excerpts from trial transcripts were not changed.

Chapter 1

1. *United States v. Garsson*, 291 F 646, 649 (SDNY 1923)

2. National Registry of Exonerations (www.law.umich.edu/special/exoneration/Pages/about.aspx)

3. *Trial By Fire*, David Grann, The New Yorker, September 7, 2009

4. *Ordinary Justice: How America Holds Court*, Amy Bach, Holt Paperbacks, 2009

5. *Killing Time: An 18-Year Odyssey From Death Row To Freedom*, John Hollway and Ronald M. Gauthier, Skyhorse Publishing, 2010

6. *Picking Cotton: Our Memoir of Injustice and Redemption*, Jennifer Thompson-Cannino and Ronald Cotton with Erin Torneo, St. Martins Press, 2010

7. *Connick v. Thompson*, 131 S.Ct. 1350 (2011)

8. *Fresh Doubts Over A Texas Execution*, Maurice Possley, The Washington Post, August 3, 2014

Chapter 2

1. International Network for Innocent Arson Defendants, George Souliotes

2. *A Conviction Up In Smoke?* Maura Dolan, Los Angeles Times, May 31, 2010

3. *George Souliotes v. Anthony Hedgpeth*, Case No. 1:06-cv-00667 AWI MJS HC, Findings and Recommendation Regarding Statute of Limitation Issues, US District Court, Eastern District of California, April 26, 2012

4. *New Science Frees Modesto Man in Arson Murder Case*, Bob Egelko, San Francisco Chronicle, July 2, 2013

5. *Former Modesto Landlord is Free After 16 Years in Prison*, Rosalio Ahumada, Modesto Bee, July 3, 2013

Chapter 3

1. National Registry of Exonerations: Obie Anthony

2. *"Murder on 49th Street,"* Miles Corwin, Los Angeles Times, March 26, 1995 (excerpt from Mr. Corwin's book "The Killing Season")

3. *Charges Dismissed In Case Of Man Convicted 14 Years Ago Of Murder During Botched Robbery*, Hector Becerra, New York Times, July 4, 2009

4. *In Re: Obie Steven Anthony III, Petitioner, on Habeas Corpus*, Case No.: BA097736, Findings of Fact and Conclusions of Law on Petition for Writ of Habeas Corpus, CA Superior Ct., September 30, 2011*Innocent Man Freed After 17 Years In Prison For Nothing*, Charlene Muhammad, Los Angeles Sentinel, October 28, 2011

5. *Friends Wrongfully Imprisoned For Nearly Two Decades— Until The Innocence Project Won Their Freedom*, Christiana Kyriacou, LA Weekly, October 18, 2012

Chapter 4

1. National Registry of Exonerations: Fernando Bermudez

2. *Innocent: The Story of Fernando Bermudez*, Paul von Zielbauer, The New York Times, April 13, 2007

3. *On 11th Try, Man convicted in '91 Killing Gets Hearing*, Paul von Zielbauer, The New York Times, August 14, 2009

4. *People v. Bermudez*, 2009 NY Slip Op 52302, Supreme Court of New York County, November 9, 2009 (unpublished)

5. *Fernando Bermudez Wrongfully Jailed For 18 Years, Finally Gets Justice*, Jennifer Peltz, Huffington Post, November 12, 2009

6. *18 Years later, Judge Tosses Case Against NY Man*, Innocence Blog, Innocence Project, November 12, 2009

7. *Man Jailed for '91 Murder Is Cleared by Judge*, John Eligon, The New York Times, November 13, 2009

8. *Freeing Fernando; Conviction in '91 Killing Overturned*, Claude Solnik, The Villager, Vol. 79, No. 25, November 25—December 1, 2009

9. *Wrongfully Convicted Man Sues New York for $30 Million*, Julie Strauss, ABC News, February 23, 2011

10. *Exoneree on Lecture Tour in Japan*, Kana Sasakura, Life After Exoneration—North America, November 5, 2013

11. *An Exoneree's Veritas Against Wrongful Convictions*, Kana Sasakura, Life After Exoneration—North America, April 24, 2014

12. *Breaking Chains in France*, Kana Sasakura, Life After Exoneration—North America, March 15, 2014

Chapter 5

1. National Registry of Exonerations, Sabrina Butler

2. *Sabrina Butler v. State of Mississippi*, No. 90-DP-0449, August 26, 1992

3. *Exonerated: The Sabrina Butler Story*, Sabrina Butler-Porter, Young Lions Publishing LLC, 2011

4. Senate Bill 2904 passed in the 2013 session (awarded $50,000)

5. House Bill 1511 passed in the 2012 session (awarded $50,000 and an additional $32,900 to attorney William Starks II)

Chapter 6

1. National Registry of Exonerations: Maurice Caldwell

2. *In Re Maurice Caldwell, On Habeas Corpus*, Case No. 5917, filed on February 18, 2009 with the Superior Court of the State of California

3. *Innocent Man Exonerated After Twenty Years In Prison*, Jeffrey Hammerschmidt, Hammerschmidt Broughton Law Corporation Blog, April 15, 2011

4. *After A Wrongful Conviction Shouldn't There Be An Investigation?* Nancy Petro, The Wrongful Conviction Blog, February 25, 2012

5. *Conviction Overturned for Northern California Innocence Project Client Maurice Caldwell*, Northern California Innocence Project at Santa Clara University School of Law, May 15, 2012

6. *In The Matter Of The Claim Of Maurice Caldwell Against The State Of California*, Before the California Victims Compensation and Government Claims Board, March 31, 2013

7. *No Support Given To Local Exoneree*, Wayne Freedman, ABC-TV, May 3, 2013

8. *Maurice Caldwell's Son Is Born*, Northern California Innocence Project at Santa Clara University School of Law, September 13, 2013

9. *The Man Who Returned: Trying To Build A Life After 20 Years Of Wrongful Imprisonment*, James Robinson, SF Weekly, October 16, 2013

10. The authors and editors also interviewed Maurice Caldwell for additional information.

Chapter 7

1. National Registry of Exonerations: Arthur Carmona

2. *In re Arthur Paul Carmona, Habeas Petition*, Case No. G026615, Orange County Superior Court of California

3. *In re Arthur Paul Carmona—Stipulation*, Case No. G026615, Orange County Superior Court of California, August 21, 2000

4. *Pro Bono Report*, Sidley Austin Brown & Wood, Winter-Spring 2001

5. *Hell, Yeah, I'm Angry*, Nick Schou, OC Weekly, March 23, 2006

6. *Doing Time For No Crime*, Arthur Carmona, Los Angeles Times, July 13, 2007

7. *The Kid Is Dead: Arthur Carmona, 1982-2008*, Nick Schou, OC Weekly, February 21, 2008

8. *Governor Signs Arthur Carmona-Inspired Wrongful Convictions Bill*, Nick Schou, OC Weekly, October 12, 2009

Chapter 8

1. National Registry of Exonerations: Antoine Goff

2. *People v. Green*, 31 Cal. App. 4th 1001, January 20, 1995

3. *3 Off-Duty S.F. Cops Probed in Beating Assistant Chief's Son, Still on Probation, Involved in Incident*, Jaxon Van Derbeken, San Francisco Chronicle, November 21, 2002

4. *Clearly, a Cover-up*, Savannah Blackwell, San Francisco Bay Guardian, March 26, 2003

5. The details of post-conviction evidence are taken from *Order Granting Amended Petition for Writ of Habeas Corpus and Denying Motion for Evidentiary Hearing as Moot*, Tennison v. Henry, No. 98-3842 CW, August 26, 2003

6. *Tennison v. Henry*, 2003 WL 25851307 (N.D. Cal.), August 26, 2003

7. *In the Matter of the Claim of: Antoine Maurice Goff and John J. Tennison*, Claim Nos. G541855 and G542416, December 23, 2004

8. *Tennison v. California Victim Compensation and Government Claims Board*, No. A112313, June 28, 2007

9. *$7.5 Million Payout Endorsed in San Francisco Police Case*, Marisa Lagods, San Francisco Chronicle, July 28, 2009

10. *Tennison & Goff v. City and County of San Francisco, et al*, No. 06-15426, 9th Circuit, Filed December 8, 2008 and Amended June 23, 2009

Chapter 9

1. *State of Illinois v. Tabitha Pollock*, Supreme Court of Illinois, October 18, 2002

2. *People v. English*, No. 3-96-0767, 2001

3. *Judge Denies Certificate of Innocence*, Lisa Hammer, Quad-Cities Online, September 8, 2012 (http://qconline.com/archives/qco/display.php?id=607486&query=tabitha%20pollock)

Chapter 10

1. National Registry of Exonerations: Gloria Killian

2. *Gloria Killian*, Bluhm Legal Clinic—Center on Wrongful Conviction

3. *Gloria Killian v. Susan Poole, Warden*, 9th Circuit, March 13, 2002

4. *Conviction for Murder Reversed*, Henry Weinstein, Los Angeles Times, March 14, 2002

5. *Wrongfully Accused?* Rebecca Leung, CBS News—48 Hours, August 26, 2003

6. *In the Matter of Christopher Thomas Cleland*, State Bar of California Hearing Department, Decision and Order Imposing Admonition, November 4, 2008

7. *One Woman's Triumph Over Wrongful Conviction*, Innocence Project—Innocence Blog, April 6, 2012

8. *The Conversation: How the Innocent End Up in Prison*, Foon Rhee, Sacramento Bee, June 13, 2012

9. *Innocence Lost...And Found*, Andre Colman and Kevin Uhrich, SAFE Californi.org, July 5, 2012

10. *Full Circle: A True Story of Murder, Lies and Vindication*, Gloria Killian and Sandra Kobrin, New Horizon Press, 2012

11. *After Innocence: Exoneration in America—Gloria Killian*, Phoebe Judge—Producer, WUNC—North Carolina Public Radio, June 10, 2013

12. *Astronaut's Mom Helps Overturn Murder Conviction*, Thom Patterson, CNN, March 14, 2014

13. *How Astronaut Sally Ride's Mom Spent $100,000 on Investigation that Freed a Female Murder Convict After 17 Years*, Louise Boyle, Mail Online, March 14, 2014

Chapter 11

14. National Registry of Exonerations: Larry Lamb

15. *Innocent North Carolina Man Exonerated After 14 Year On Death Row*, ACLU, May 2, 2008

16. *Levon Jones Exonerated in North Carolina*, Mandy Locke, NewsObserver.com, May 2, 2008

17. *Innocence Center Turns Attention to Next Case*, Sloane Heffernan, WRAL.com, February 22, 2010

18. *State of North Carolina v. Larry Lamb*, Order, File No.: 92 CRS 4527, 4528, 4529, Superior Court of North Carolina, August 8, 2013

19. *After 20 Years of Proclaiming His Innocence, Larry Lamb's Convictions Have Been Vacated*, North Carolina Center on Actual Innocence (press release), August 9, 2013

20. *Man Wrongly Convicted of Murder Walks Free From Wake Prison*, Kevin Holmes, WRAL.com, original posting August 13, 2013 (updated on August 14, 2013)

21. *Man Wrongly Convicted of Murder Released From Jail*, Mitch Weiss, Associated Press, original posting August 13, 2013 (updated August 27, 2013)

22. *Ex-Prosecutor Stands by Murder Conviction of Exonerated Man*, Bryan Mims, WRAL.com, original posting August 15, 2013 (updated August 16, 2013)

23. *In Justice System, Back to Business as Usual*, Julie Linehan, NewsObserver.com, September 3, 2013

Chapter 12

1. National Registry of Exonerations: Virginia LeFever

2. *State of Ohio v. Virginia LeFever—Defendant Virginia LeFever's Motion for New Trial*, Case No. 1988 CR 17117, Judge Wiest, Court of Common Pleas Licking County, Ohio, February 17, 2009

3. *State of Ohio v. Virginia LeFever—Judgment Entry*, Case No. 1988 CR 17117, Judge Wiest, November 22, 2010

4. *What Jurors Should Know About Expert Witnesses*, James Balagia, Avvo Experts, posted 2010

5. *Woman Says Mother's Release From Prison 'Blow to Her Heart'*, WBNS-10TV, November 24, 2010 (original posting), December 15, 2010 (updated posting)

6. *Woman Sues After Her Prison Release*, Alex Stuckey, The Columbus Dispatch, October 10, 2011

7. *Free After 20 Years, Woman Sues Ohio*, Kevin Koeninger, Courthouse News Service, January 27, 2012

8. *Virginia LeFever v. State of Ohio*, 2013 WL 567562 (Ohio App. 10 Dist.), October 17, 2013

9. *Virginia LeFever v. State of Ohio—Decision*, Case No. 12AP-1034, Supreme Court of Ohio, October 17, 2013

10. *Virginia LeFever v. State of Ohio—Memorandum in Support of Jurisdiction of Appellant Virginia LeFever*, Case No. 12AP001034, Supreme Court of Ohio, January 24, 2014

11. *Freed Woman: Trial Tore Family Apart*, Josh Jarman, The Columbus Dispatch, November 24, 2014

Acknowledgments

Courtney B. Lance

To have confidence enough in a person to allow them to share in heartfelt and important work is immeasurable. Thank you to my co-author and life-long friend, Nikki Pope for having that confidence in me. It's been a joy. Because of your confidence I have received wisdom of a lifetime. To the men and women—the story tellers: Thank you for your trust, your candor, and your sacrifice. I am forever changed because of you. Know that you are loved and appreciated. To all those who have had a hand in helping us get this book written and published—Ginger Campbell, Nancy Mullane, Post Hill Publishing, NCIP, Ted Bell, and Everett Spier—my goodness how fortunate we are to have received your advice, wisdom, expertise, and counsel. Thank you so very much! To all my friends, too many to name here, who have forgiven that I have been MIA for quite some time, but who continue to be there for me; listening, and counseling. You are my rocks and my inspiration, have talked me off the ledge and supported me all the way. Thank you for sticking it out, you have my heart. To my family—I breathe because of you. Thank you Darwin Walton for warning me that writing is a jealous lover. How right you are dear Darwin. I am committed and I am faithful. And Isabel Allende, who said to me "just write," and so I did. To my nephew Theo, whose artistic talent and quest to not be basic has made an indelible impression on me. You have no idea how much you mean to me, Theo. To my loving and devoted husband Sotiri who has held me so close to his heart and supported me in this endeavor with grace and humility. You have been so generous in allowing me all the space that I have needed. I will love you forever. And lastly, my parents Joyce and Squire Lance who have since left this world. They have given me so much; such a rich life I have because of them. All that I am is from them. I like who I am and that's because I loved who they were. Their talent flows through me. Their care for and commitment to the underserved carries me. Their authenticity informs my life with every step I take. I miss them dearly, love them more and look forward to the day when I can be with them again.

First, thank you for buying this book. Your purchase is helping the men and women whose stories you have been reading and the organizations that help them. I am especially grateful to these men and women and their family members and friends for opening their hearts and sharing their stories with us and allowing us to share them with you. Two people were essential to the success of this project—Ginger Campbell and Courtney Lance. I appreciate Ginger's guidance and support. As our publicist and communications specialist, if not for Ginger, we might not have a publisher and this might have been a prison food cookbook! Courtney, my co-author and friend since childhood, kept it real and made sure each chapter was true to the voice of the exoneree featured. Michelle Gustafson helped me ditch the legalese in the first chapter we wrote and write the facts of the cases for a non-lawyer audience. My boundless thanks to Cookie Ridolfi for writing the Foreword to our book and for inviting me to join the NCIP Advisory Board back in 2005. If not for Cookie, I probably would not have met the men and women who are the motivation behind this book and this book might not exist. There are so many more people, like Nancy Mullane, who encouraged us to write this book, and lawyers who helped us review and untangle the factual information. I am truly thankful for my friends and family members who supported me throughout this project and who understood when I didn't show up for events and meals or left them early to work on this book. You know who you are and you have my thanks. Heartfelt thanks to Michael Wilson and the folks at Post Hill Publishing for taking a chance on two first-time authors. They made our dream of helping exonerees and raising awareness about wrongful conviction come true. And finally to my parents, Lena and Roland Pope, who instilled in me an insatiable appetite for knowledge. Their love and example sustained me while we worked on the book. I'm so glad Mom is alive to share this accomplishment with me. I wish Dad were here, too. I know he'd be proud.

About the Authors

Courtney B. Lance is an audit professional with the real estate firm Draper and Kramer in Chicago and is the founder of The Third Place, a nonprofit organization whose mission is to empower people to honor and appreciate the power of the creative spirit through visual, performing, gastronomy, and conceptual arts. She has been a columnist for a neighborhood periodical published for the Englewood community and currently authors *A Life Well Fed*, a blog exploring and sharing her creative life. She also is a director of Louis' Groceries, a nonprofit organization that helps the residents of underserved communities in Chicago adopt healthy eating habits. She was formally introduced to wrongful convictions in 2012, when her long-time friend Nikki Pope approached her with this book idea. She believes the voices of the wrongfully convicted need to be heard so we all may understand how they remained hopeful during the many years in spent prison for crimes they did not commit. Their voices need to be heard for readers to witness the strength of the human spirit. *Pruno, Ramen and a Side of Hope* is her first book.

Nikki D. Pope is an attorney at the law firm of Cooley LLP in Northern California where she specializes in securities law and corporate governance. She became a member of the advisory board of the Northern California Innocence Project in 2005. She is a member of the California Bar Association and the Bar of the Supreme Court of the United States. She also is a director of Moving Train, Inc., an organization that provides fiscal sponsorship for documentary filmmakers. She is very interested in prison reform and, as a member of her firm's pro bono practice group, provides free legal services to organizations that work with California prisoners—Insight Prison Project, The Last Mile, and the Prison University Project, all programs based at San Quentin State Prison. *Pruno, Ramen and a Side of Hope* is her first book.